The Ghost of

Scootertrash Past

by

Mark Tiger Edmonds

Livingston Press
at
The University of West Alabama

ISBN 1-931982-04-X

Library of Congress # 2002116384

This book is printed on paper that meets
or exceeds the Library of Congress's
minimal standards for acid-free paper.

Printed in the United States by:
United Graphics

FIRST EDITION
2 4 5 6 3 1

Typesetting: Heather Leigh Loper
Typesetting title page: Gina Montarsi
Proofreading: Shannon Pendergrass,
David Smith, Josh Dewberry,
Danny Hyche,
Leslie Tucker, Stefanie Richardson
Cover Design: Joe Taylor
Cover photo: Ray "Shooter" Hale

Tiger Edmonds may be reached at
MarkTigerEdmonds@hotmail.com
Livingston Press is part of
The University of West Alabama and
as such welcomes tax-deductible contributions
to support literature

visit our website: www.livingstonpress.uwa.edu

The Ghost of Scootertrash Past

Contents

Pre-Ramble   1
1. Reintroduction   3
2. Better Border Crossings, Wounded Angels,
    The Code,...   6
3. Domestic Authorities, Women in Uniform,
    More About the Code   14
4. Bridges, Tunnels, Disney Music, and 20w50 Oil   25
5. Wind, Mathematics, and Minority Groups   34
6. Old Broke Down Rides, and Nashville in the Fall   45
7. Zen and the Art of Motorcylce Riding   51
8. More Wind, Niche Markets, and Reconstructed Rides 58
9. Old Unreconstructed Riders, and Old Roads   67
10. The Perfect Job, Multiple Breakdowns, and Women   73
11. Festivals, More Niche Markets, and More Women   85
12. Wisdom and Advice, And Overloaded Teenage
    Ninja Bikers   91
13. Fallen Riders, Two-Lane Roads, and Young Women   97
14. The Killer Federal Foliage Incident, ...   102
15. The Horror of I-75, and a Tennessee Tank of Fuel   111
16 Superslabs, Incompetence, and Convenience   123
17. More Zen Stuff, Literary Criticism, and Dirt Roads   128
18. Dirt Roads and Signs   138
19. Camping, or Not, Promised Rants, and Laments   143
20. Bad Drivers, Rivers, A Christmas Story, ...   154
21. Highway History Lessons, Food, and Photographs   166
22. More Lamentations, Youthful Memories,
    and Ostriches   179
23. Lessons Along the Way, Odd Jobs, and Directions   190
24. Dreams, Schemes, Hopes, Fancy Fantasies,
    and Endings   201

This one is for Captain Zero and Tom Abrams and Doug Simms and Prof. W. Joe Taylor and Nancy Pacey and Mother Thomas and Dr. Bill Condom and my dad and my Favored Niece and a few others who always read my stuff and tell me the truth about it. Literate friends have always enriched my life.

For my cousin, Lee Ann, my prettiest living relative, who threatened to kick the stuffings out of me if I didn't find a way to mention her in a book.

And for Juanita Nichols, without whom I would have never written anything. She feeds my dogs and cats and horse for me while I'm out on the road.

Pre-Ramble

When I showed an early draft manuscript of *Longrider* to a friend, the guy got about as far as the part about the dot-headed motherfucker who was trying to rob me at his motel. Yup, that was where he stopped reading and went into knee-jerk political correction. He began, "Tiger, you dumb bastard..." Then he called me a bigot and told me I should remove all the profanity and all references to cigarettes, alcohol, and drugs from the book. And that stupid son of a bitch thinks I'm the bigot.

Similarly, I had a couple people take umbrage with two stories in that book about encounters I had with black children. Permit me to emphatically state—That was a comment on contemporary YOUTH, not a statement of any racial significance. You dumb bastards.

If you think political correctness is more important than the First Amendment or the sanctity of personal opinions, and you want sterilized history and lies about who didn't inhale and who was a Vietnam war hero in the national guard, go get yourself a newspaper or a contemporary high school textbook. Without apologies to loud, angry lesbians, I will talk interchangeably about pretty girls and women and mean no disrespect at all. And I will condemn Iranian motels and McFood without intending general castigation of near or middle Easterners or clowns either one. Same deal with cities and idiots.

This here one is going to start out with high praise and references not to Local Indigenous Pre-Columbian Aboriginal North Americans, but to Indians. And I will allude to dogs as dogs, not as canine companion Americans. Similarly, I will make reference to a dot-headed thief if that's the case. And if the bastard turns out to be a Presbyterian in a porkpie hat, I will point that out.

Over the years and along the way, I've talked to a whole lot of other old rounders. Most of them in the rain. We all got our own sad stories. Longriders talk about roads. Besides speaking of roads and telling one another our old highway tales, we usually get around to discussing why we ride.

Theories range from: We do it for the stories we can tell, to we do it because when you fall, you fall alone. We are sworn to independence, dedicated to the passin' through. And in between those perspectives, some of us claim we were born to it; others contend it's the only thing we're any good at.

Most of us agree with my Grandfather, the shaman, that we couldn't have done it any different if we'd tried.

1 - REINTRODUCTION

The plains Indians of western North America used to say that today was a good day to die. They would announce this to the rising sun each morning. They would reassure themselves this way as they rode into battle. I have read that the Cossack cavalry had a comparable custom. And the Mongol hordes of Ghengis Khan apparently had a similar credo and practice.

Likewise, and while I don't know this to be a fact, I suspect the Crusader cavalry, and quite probably the mounted Muslims they were trying to kill, must have considered and embraced this sort of philosophy. And I have been told that Attila the Hun and his nomad people had a like outlook on things.

It is neither accident nor coincidence that these peoples were all mounted horsemen, that they were all just passing through. My Grandfather, the equestrian, upon completing the only motorcycle ride I was ever able to take him on, grinned at me and commented, "Well, hell, Boy, it ain't nothing' but a short, fast, noisy horse, is it?"

Motorcycles really are like that, like horses. No, I don't mean you set or ride them the same, but the basic activity is real similar. At least if you do it right it is. There is no place, no where else in my life that makes me feel as whole, as real, as right, as in the saddle in motion on the highway. Few things I would rather look at than the distance through the handlebars.

I have been told, often by former wives and their ilk, that part of it is a control thing. I don't think so. It's much more an orientation thing. And I truly do think most of it is genetic. Some of us really do belong to be nomads, allowed to run wild and free. I've also heard tell it's a locomotor phallic thing. But I ain't real sure I even know what the hell that means, much less have any serious understanding of it.

And I've heard it said that it's for the risk and the danger, and the fact that you could kill yourself, or be killed by others, real easy real often. No, that ain't it either. It's much more about life than it is about death. And it's because it makes life so very good that today truly is a good day to die.

I've even had folks tell me it has to do with the glamor and romance of it. That's the dumbest thing I ever heard about except for New Coke, Auto World, pantyhose, and buying stuff with a computer and a credit card. There is just about as much glamor involved in being scootertrash as there is in changing your oil in the rain or healing up from a bad dose of roadrash. None of us chose to be longriders. But a few of us embraced our destiny.

Some of it has to do with the ancient mysteries of motion, with the passin' through. And a little has to do with running from your devils and demons. Part of it is about the rhythms of the road. Most of it has to do with freedom, and some of it is about the distance. An element in it has something do with a need to get out there and spend a portion of your money on some high test gasoline. A share of it is tangled up in just passin' through. Part of it is in wondering—What's Next? And an important component of it is about watchin' the sun go down from a different place.

Might be a piece of it has to do with an inability to set still for very long. Much of it has to do with private therapy and personal mental health. Some of it is in knowing that there ain't but maybe a few hundred other people can say they been the places you been to, seen and done the things that you've seen and done.

Part of it really is for the stories we can tell. A lot of it is about solitude, about peace and harmony. There is some primal part of it that is about finding out what is down that road, around that next curve, across that river, on the other side of the borderline, over beyond that lake, beyond them mountains yonder, on the far side of the horizon, in the distance.

Most ancient cultures, not just those on horseback, believed that there was a rhythm, a cadence to life, a beat to the very earth itself. They believed that it was the obligation of the people to find this pulse, this beat, and to adapt and live in harmony with it. There are still a few contemporary peoples with similar beliefs, but we are seldom paid attention to. But that's OK, because I've done found and hit my stride. Some of us, we really weren't made to lead or follow, neither one.

I've been to a lot of places, seen a whole lot of sights, and I've done a lot of things along the way between all that. But in motion on a cycle down the road is the only place I've ever found the rhythm. Some times it's so sweet and clean and free that you truly understand that it is a good day for anything, including dying. Hell, maybe especially dying.

You get to see things on a bike that you are completely unaware of in a vehicle. And you get to hear and taste and smell and feel them, too. If you do it wrong, you get to feel and taste some things you'd rather not. But, if you do it right, you get to be part of it all.

I always begin a long ride by asking for a highway blessing. I appeal to the three elements in the trilogy. In honor of the sky; for the sake of the road. And in the name of the boxer twin engine.

2 - BETTER BORDER CROSSINGS, WOUNDED ANGELS, THE CODE, BROKEN REDEMPTION SONG, AND DECISIONS

There was a border crossing into Canada one time, must have been in the late 1970s or early '80s, that almost made up for some of the other hassles and prejudice and bad treatment at the hands of the over-zealous under-trained in uniform. Almost. I was with another guy on that trip. It was a gray and overcast day, and we hit the borderline in a light rain around mid-day. The other guy was riding lead, so they got to him first.

The Canadian uniformed authority told us to park our bikes. This was a typical, if unfair, request. They seldom make the drivers of vehicles park and join them in the building. What made this one unusual was that the border guard was considerate enough to tell us to park under an overhang there so our bikes would be out of the rain. And, even better, the parking places were right in front of the building where we could see our motorcycles while we answered inane questions. Normally they insist you leave your ride out in the rain someplace far away where you can't see it, can't watch everything you own soak up another forty pounds of water. Sometimes and places, they make it hard for you to pass through.

My pardner parked and dismounted first, and as he was walking into the building with the border cop, I heard him giggle, and say, "Wait'll you hear what the other guy does."

As I had no idea what they were talking about, it made me nervous and uneasy. I mean I do a lot of things, and I began reviewing which amongst them might be considered illegal in Canada. Then I heard another snatch of conversation and figured out they were discussing what each of us did for a living. The wind picked up, and it got darker.

The guy I was with worked as a corrections officer of sorts. He worked at a kiddie jail of some kind. You know the kind. The young felons are called clients or residents or something other than degenerate criminals. Sometimes they refer to them as at-risk youth instead of sociopathic killer kids. Always seemed like to me that anyone within pistol range was who was at risk. And instead of punishment for their crimes, the residents get to watch color cable TV and go on outings and field trips, horseback rides and such. Anyway, the guy had some kind of badge that he had shown the Canadian border guard.

When I joined them in the building, my friend was nearly beside himself with mirth. He chuckled and pointed at me and said, "Go ahead, Tiger, go ahead. Tell the man what you do for a living." The Canadian border authority already had a skeptical look on his face.

When I told him I taught English at a little college down in Florida, skepticism turned to incredulity. He demanded proof. So I handed him my little picture I.D. I don't think he believed me, because before he was done he had examined every single piece of identification in my wallet and on my person. Then he scrutinized the old dog tag on my key ring. He even inspected hunting and fishing licenses and my library card. Then he did the same with my companion's papers. I glanced out the windows, where the sky was lower and the rain had intensified.

Apparently it was a slow day at the Canadian border there in the rain, because about a half dozen of his colleagues sort of drifted over to our inquisitor's desk to observe, and, in some cases, to assist in our interrogation. They had us empty out our pockets, then they fondled the contents. My pocket watch got passed around enough to wear the finish off it. And some fool got a ruler out and began measuring my jack knife. As he did that in Canadian millimeters, I have no idea of the outcome of his findings. But I did get to keep my knife.

Good damn thing, too. That's a fine knife, and it was a gift from a fine woman. Girl was named Lizabeth, and I have had the knife for nearly thirty years. When she bought it for me, she told the clerk at the store that she needed a knife I could kill rattlesnakes and make peanut butter sandwiches with. While I've never actually done either one of them things with it, I have skinned a couple snakes and cut up some food with it. Hell, I've used it as a hammer and screwdriver and a weapon. I bet I've cut the twine on a thousand bales of hay with that knife. And I have cut several gas lines and other hoses to size, and used it on numerous roadside repairs, generally employed it as a utility tool for way too long to leave it at the border or anywhere else. It's a Puma.

One of the border guards suggested they should check our money. It was early on in our ride, so both of us were carrying a few hundred dollars in American cash money, back when that was a lot of money. That confirmed their Canadian suspicion that we were somehow up to no good. I bet they counted that money five or six times while we explained to them that it had been our intention to spend a great deal of it in Canada, but that they were currently dissuading us of that plan.

I got up from the interrogation desk and walked to the window to watch it get darker and rain harder. There was some thunder from the Canadian side of the border. Traffic was waved through in the hard drizzle. And I recalled the words of my Grandfather, the geographer, who pointed out that most of the population of Canada live within fifty miles of the American border. I lit a cigarette, and every uniformed human being in the building yelled at me like I had set fire to a nuclear skunk. So I opened the window.

That escalated things from suspicion and incredulity to pissed off. I honestly think some of them thought, at least for a minute, that it was an escape attempt on my part. A couple of them headed to telephones and computers to check us out with headquarters, or the Mounties, or the Queen, or the mothership, or someone with potential information on our criminal nature and history.

One of them actually checked into my buddy's credit card balance. They were bothered by the fact that I had no such card or account. I was bothered by how easy they got access to his financial status, and I was glad that I didn't have a credit card.

Another one of the Canadian border cops tried to engage me in a conversation about this alleged college where I allegedly worked, allegedly teaching English. Apparently Canadian scholars look different from me. I doubt that it would have been so much a problem if I had taught something other than English. Most Canadians don't really think Americans even speak English, eh?

Eventually our money and papers were returned, and I thought we were done with it and could go back to a wet ride in the cold rain. Nope. Several of them walked us back out to our bikes. We were both instructed to remove and open our saddlebags. So we did.

The first things they discovered in my saddlebags were a little compact Scrabble game and a paperback dictionary. I have no idea what they were expecting, but that wasn't it. They all stared long and hard, and then they straightened up and sort of backed away and looked at one another. It got so weird that for a minute I was afraid Scrabble might be illegal in Canada.

The first things they got to in my pardner's bag was the little souvenir-of-someplace thimble he had picked up for his old lady and the teddy bear he had gotten for his kid. Then they got to his current issues of *Time* and *Newsweek* about the same time they discovered a copy of Bickerton's *Roots of Language*, it had just come out, in my saddlebag.

We were excused. Last time I saw that many men in uniform shaking their heads stupidly and bumping into one another, I was in the army, and they were in charge of me. We rode off into the cold Canadian rain.

I've had lots worse border crossings, lots of them. Sometimes the passin' through don't come easy. And, as many a harassed rider has said—It Ain't Fair. No, it ain't. Ain't even close. A woman I was once with years ago during one of these international near-incidents discussed it with me. She began her topic, as these points are often begun, with, "Tiger, you dumb bastard..." Then she pointed out that if I had a haircut, and if I drove a Buick, and if I wore a suit and tie, and if I had a better attitude, then the border commandos wouldn't fuck with me.

And I explained it to her just like my Grampaw, the philosopher, explained it all to me when I was a little child—if a jukebox was shoved up a buzzard's ass, then there'd be music in the air.

Had a thing happen in Oxford, Mississippi once upon a time a long time ago. Ain't many people can say that to begin with, but this turned out to be a good thing. I disremember exactly when this was, or where I was going to or coming from. But it was high summer and hotter than hell. And I do recall that I had a woman with me. I had found a convenience store in Oxford, got gas, left her with the bike, and went on in.

While I was in there, I realized I was the only white guy around. Looked out the window and figured out I was the only white man for several city blocks in all directions. OK with me. Black folks have always been just as good at selling me stuff as white people. And usually they are friendlier about it. And I been the only white guy lots of times.

But I figured my woman might be some uneasy out there by herself in the parking lot, so I sort of hurried my shopping and got back outside. Well, I am sure there was no reason for worry to begin with, but even if there had been, a local guy named Zack had me covered. He was standing by the bike talking to the girl when I got back. She was smiling, and so was he. She introduced us.

Zack was probably about my age, but he looked lots older. His eyes had that telltale yellow and red cast to them. He squinted in the outdoor light, even though we weren't in the sunshine. His hands trembled a little, he shuffled from foot to foot, mostly to maintain balance. Zack was a drunk. Holdin' back and chokin' back the shakes with every breath.

But he used to ride, and he wanted to talk to us about that some. So we did. I felt obliged. And sometimes you pass through together awhile. Here was a former highway brother who had recalled The Code and gone out of his way to put my old lady at ease in this situation. The least I could do was spend a minute with him. I can't remember what it was he used to ride. Seems like it was English. Nor do I remember what all we discussed there in the shade in Oxford. But I do recall that we talked about how he had quit riding so he could drink, and about how I had quit drinking so I could ride. And I remember distinctly his comment on that. He said, "You gots to decide."

Over the years since then I have thought often of getting that tattooed on my arm or on a good friend so I can review it often. Comes as close to pure truth as anything ever said to me by anyone except my sainted Grandfather, the logician, who explained to me when I was very small, "You ain't got to decide but two things, Boy. You got to decide what's important. And you got to decide what it's worth. And then you're all done deciding, and you can get up off your ass and get to it."

And last summer, out there by myself in the wilderness, I got to reflecting on old Zack, who I bet is dead by now, and upon his wisdom. Yeah, you got to decide. And on a motorcycle, you got to decide about every two seconds. And a lot of the decisions really are of a life and death nature.

Turns out that riding, much more so than driving, involves constant, often critical, decisions. I don't believe I ever got around to thinking about it this way before. But, because of the nature of riding, I was able to reflect on it at some length and get it to where I could get my mind all the way around it. Yeah, you got to decide.

You have to decide about which part of your lane to ride on. Find the best surface. You got to decide if that is a pothole or a shadow or a grease spot. You have to figure out if it is safe and prudent to go some over the legal local speed limit. You need to determine whether you need to wear your leather, and is it cold enough for gloves. You have to decide if there is enough sand in that curve to slow down for. And how much.

You got to know what the shoulder is like in case you have to head that way to save yourself. You have to figure out what it means when a pretty girl smiles and waves at you around here. You need to know if that fence that is way too close to the road is made of barbed wire or bull wire. You have to figure out how fast that truck up ahead of you is going before you wind up underneath it.

You got to determine if the idiot at the stop sign with the tinted windows has seen you or if he is going to pull out and try to kill you. You got to figure out if the elderly, senile, heavily medicated little woman peering through her steering wheel and her Coke bottle bifocals at you has really seen you, or if it's a damn trick, and she is going to pull out and try to kill you. You need to know if those little dogs are going to frolic out into the road in front of you. You need to know the same thing about those big cows. And the unattended children.

You have to answer the question about what does it mean around here when a local cop smiles and waves at you. You have to figure out if that truck is spilling and slopping slag coal sludge or nuclear waste as it goes around the curve in front of you. You have to figure out if it is worth it to try to get through the big city at rush hour, or should you just find a place to set and wait until the thrash is over before trying.

Then there are other less vital decisions, like can you leave your ride and all your gear unattended in the parking lot while you tour the local attraction. Or is this the best cheap motel you are going to find in this town, or should you ride on through and see what's on the other end, or in the next town. You have to decide if gas is going to be cheaper in the next state, or county, and have you got enough in the tank to get there. You have to instantly interpret local roadside signs.

And you need to figure out the weather ahead of time. You need to know if it is going to rain, and when, and how hard, and for how long, and which way is it all going. You need to figure out what that amount of rain will do to the road surface that you are riding on. You have to determine if the rain is going to increase or turn to sleet or snow. Then you need to figure out where to hide from the weather when you turn out to be wrong in your predictions. Should you bail off the road and seek refuge under the overhang there at the convenience store, or is there better shelter down the road some. You have to figure out if that hamburger just tastes real bad or if it is going to seriously poison you.

Sometimes you have to decide which is the lesser of the several evils you are presented with. One time I saw the rock truck in front of me spill some of its load. A particular rock, about the size of a baseball, bounced once and headed right at me. And I had to decide. My options were to try to snap the bike out of the way of the trajectory of the rock, no mean feat at high speed, or to just take the rock in the fairing or even in the windshield. On this particular occasion, I erred, and the rock got my damn headlight.

Sometimes you have to decide whether it's better to put the bike down rather than run into whatever got in front of you. You have to decide that one real fast. Other times you need to determine whether to stand on your brakes or to gun the bike and run through or around the potential mess. Yeah, you got to decide. What you do in a car can result in a dented fender; what you do on a scooter is more consequential. The passin' through ain't always easy.

For example, back there somewhere I mentioned barbed wire fences. Once upon a time I was called upon to rescue a friend who had put his ride off a hard curve and into a barbed wire fence. When he called me, he told me to bring some wire cutters. Good idea. Turned out the man who owned the pasture that the fence enclosed wasn't home, and his wife, who had let my buddy use her phone, didn't know where their wire cutters were. She did find us a roll of barbed wire and some staples to fix the mess he'd made of her fence. As I recall this, she also managed to somehow find us some gloves, too. Three of them, all lefts.

The guy had somehow managed to get off the bike when he first got involved with the fence. He wasn't in especially good personal shape, but compared to his ride, he was in pristine condition. He finally confessed that he was going around sixty when he left the road. He was riding one of those big Suzuki 1000s. And it was enshrouded in six wraps of barbed wire from headlight to tail light. He had decided that he could do that curve at sixty. Turned out to be a forty-mile-an-hour curve.

His ride had torn two fenceposts right out of the ground. The bike's seat was shredded, as was the front tire. The tank had hit one of the fenceposts and was bashed in all along one side. The headlight, the tail light, and both front turn signals were torn off the bike, no doubt as it had swapped ends between fenceposts. We never did find one of the turn signals. The rest of the cycle was scratched and scraped all the way to the metal. The handlebars were twisted into the shape of the Greek letter epsilon. The front wheel was an oval.

It took about two hours to cut his bike loose from the barbed wire and get it loaded on my truck. It took another couple hours to get the fenceposts back in the ground and string new wire for the nice lady and dozen or so Santa Gertrudis cattle who supervised the entire operation.

It took about two weeks before that boy could walk good again. It took a couple months to get the parts and put his bike back together. It took him about an hour to sell it after we had it running again. And he hasn't been back in the saddle since.

There used to be a story bikers told each other about how a rider was fleeing the police one dark night, several cop cars in pursuit. And they radioed one of their brother officers, who was several miles up the road. And, as the story goes, he pulled his cruiser sideways across the road in a blind curve, turned his lights out, got out of the car, and sat on the side of the road waiting for the biker. The tale used to end that the rider hit the cop car broadside going about ninety, flew off his bike, and cleaned the entire mess of lights and sirens and so forth off the top of the cruiser as he died.

To quote my Grandfather, the spiritual advisor, "We all got to come to it somehow."

3 - DOMESTIC AUTHORITIES, WOMEN IN UNIFORM, MORE ABOUT THE CODE

That might be one of them stories like the guy with a hook for a hand escaping from the insane asylum. But then again it might could be true. I've seen cops do worse.

Saw such a thing one time when I stopped at a cafe up along the Canadian borderline in Montana. This was way back in the real early seventies, when too many bad Hells Angels movies had made the general public, and especially those who were armed and in uniform, particularly paranoid, suspicious and fearful of bikers, even one at a time. The parking lot and the cafe were both empty.

I parked right in front, so I could see my scooter through the window while I ate. The waitress, Shirley Ann Sheila Gail, was real nice to me, as most waitresses are prone to be. But the character who did the cooking badly got on the phone and alerted the local authorities as to my whereabouts.

Evidently the various jurisdictions were sharing a radio frequency, and it was apparently a slow day for law enforcement up along the northern borderline. Before it was over, I had every constabulary agency except Alcohol Tobacco and Firearms and the Texas Rangers represented there. Two different local municipal police, three assorted county sheriffs, state cops, border guards, federal forest officers. The local fish and game cops even showed up. Might have been a couple stray, overzealous volunteer firemen involved. And there was one boy there didn't even have on a uniform. Undercover I figured. I never did figure out what bailiwick he represented.

They parked so close to my scooter that I had to mount it over the rear fender when I finally left. All of them checked my bike out. Many of them wrote my license number down. A couple appeared to be checking out the mileage on my odometer. One guy was fascinated by the little bell hanging on the inside of my fairing. They all minded their manners. No one touched anything. I worried and watched them through the window as I planned my escape. They all remained at a respectful distance while they surveyed my ride.

Eventually they all came into the place. And not a damn one of them, and there must have been eight or nine guys in assorted paramilitary uniforms, said a single word to me. Honest. They all frowned and stared. Some of them wrote notes in their little notebooks. They discussed me over their walkie-talkies and radios. They discussed me among themselves. They discussed me with Arnold Irving Homer Felix, the paranoid fry cook who had called them. But none spoke directly to me.

I'd been in situations sort of like this before. Only it usually involves a whole bunch of local guys wearing John Deere caps or cowboy hats. This time there was a variety of military headwear, and as usual, there I was with a helmet.

I wanted to go to the jukebox and see if Bob Seger's "Turn the Page" was on it. But I didn't. I wanted to engage them in bizarre conversations, maybe about the merits of martial headwear, but I didn't do that either. I wanted to go to the bathroom, but not bad enough to head that way. When the uniforms all sort of surrounded me in the cafe, I damn near confessed to every major crime of the last half century. But I didn't do that either.

What I did do was rapidly finish my coffee, pay my tab, leave a substantial tip for the waitress, and then I quickly and quietly got gone, passin' through. I had the distinct impression that if I had opened my mouth to do anything but breathe, I would have been in trouble. Hell, I was already in trouble. I would have been in what my Grampaw, the linguist, used to refer to as A Bitch of a Fix.

Had an Alabama state trooper come upon me from behind of a sudden a few summers back. I was out in the wilderness on a two lane, poking along, admiring the wildwood flowers and all, when suddenly I had lights and a siren up my ass.

As I was innocent of everything but maybe inattention, I quickly dropped it a gear and bailed off onto the roadside to let him by. He damn near ran over me pulling off the road behind me. A cloud of dust covered my bike. Turns out I was the target.

I saw him burst from his cruiser in my mirrors. I could tell it was going to be a somewhat lengthy roadside interaction, so I reached down and shut the petcock off on my gas tank. Yeah, that was stupid. He had his gun out faster than Marshall Dillon. And I put both my hands up on the top of my windshield as I have been trained to do. Kept watching him in my mirrors.

When he got up to the back of the bike, he took his attention away from aiming his pistol at the base of my helmet to my license plate. Then he got up beside my bike and looked me over closely, frowned and put his gun away. I dropped my hands and looked at him. He was young, and he was embarrassed. He sort of kicked his shiny cop shoe in the dirt and muttered something about how this year's Florida license plates looked just like last year's Alabama plates.

Nope, I didn't think so. I could tell that he had mistaken me for someone else. And it was real personal. I suspect it somehow involved his little sister. And I believe he perceived that I had figured that out. He apologized and looked foolish. Another classic case of universal mistaken misidentification. But, it isn't often anymore that you encounter a trooper with a sense of humor or even enough sense to be embarrassed, much less to apologize.

So I told him it was an easy mistake; after all, we do all look alike. He got over some of his embarrassment, laughed and agreed with me. Then I took a moment there at the roadside in the Alabama mid-day sun to explain to him that the only way you could really tell us apart was by looking at our bikes.

A mile or so down the road, there were Canada geese on the Warrior River and bluebirds in the air. Later that evening, there was home-made bar-b-que and an evening with some old friends. They laughed about my brief roadside incarceration, but they listened close to the part about looking at our bikes. They paid attention to the portion about the passin' through.

One of the problems with writing this is that I have told these old stories many times over the years, mostly around campfires and in bars and scootershops. And many of them wound up in that first volume. And now I am having some trouble recalling which ones. Good thing I got to this when I did.

That part about leaving your cycle and everything you own in the parking lot reminded me of the prettiest woman I ever saw in a uniform. She works at the Booker T. Washington National Memorial in Virginia, or at least she used to years ago. This isn't a casual observation. Over the years and along the way, between WACS and cops and waitresses and park rangers and girlsuits and emergency room nurses, I've seen an awful lot of good looking women in uniform. But this woman wins that competition without even getting to the bathing suit or talent portions of the contest.

I was in Virginia, running north through some back roads, real early in the morning through the fog. I was heading on up to Washington, D.C. to visit an old friend, when I saw the little sign for the Booker T. Washington National Memorial. Bothered me that I didn't know about it to begin with, so I went ahead on and followed a couple more signs and eventually pulled into an empty parking lot in the morning mists there in the Virginia mountains east of the Blue Ridge. I thought the place was closed at first, but then I realized the lights were on in the visitor center, and there was a guy pushing a lawnmower out back where there was a recreated cabin and so forth of Booker T. Washington's birthplace.

So I parked the scooter and went on in. The prettiest woman I ever saw in uniform looked up from some paperwork on her desk and smiled at me. I understood right away that it was a work-related smile. Last time a woman this pretty really smiled at me was in the early seventies sometime. And in retrospect, I got a hunch that one was probably laughing at me.

Anyway, this girl had a khaki uniform, and her Smokey The Bear hat was on her desk in front of her. She stood up so that I would know she was just exactly the right size. And she had eyes the color of some of those alpine lakes out in the Northern Cascade Mountains. Blonde hair that should have been in a shampoo commercial was hanging down her back. About the prettiest smile you can imagine. Dimples. Eleven freckles across the bridge of her cute little nose. I counted. When she smiled and said, "Good morning," it became one.

As she walked around the counter, I wished it was a half mile long. I could have watched that woman walk all day long. Found myself sort of humming along as she walked around that counter. I forgot about passin' through.

She welcomed me, and asked me to please sign the guest book, and showed me the diorama thing with Booker T. Washington's biography portrayed on it. And she gave me a brief, but thorough, synopsis of Booker T. Washington's life and times. Then she handed me a couple brochures and pamphlets, one of which had a map of the recreated homestead. And she showed me the postcards with photographs of the recreated slave quarters on them. And I stood there and grinned like an idiot, my usual behavior around beautiful women.

As a disciple of my Grandfather, the charm school headmaster, I do firmly believe that some women can do more damage with their dimples than they could with a gun.

The point of all this really isn't that the prettiest woman I ever saw in uniform was working at the Booker T. Washington National Memorial. No, the point is that the folks who work the parks and the monuments and memorials and other places that deal with tourists are some of nicest and most competent people around. This girl is a good example. She didn't have to be nice to me. Most people aren't. It wasn't even her job to be nice to me. She could have perceived her job as keeping the scootertrash riffraff out of the National Memorial. She could have seen her job as being disgusted by a burned out old boy in denim and leather passin' through her world. But this girl was real nice to me.

And I think I finally figured this one out. It's like that phenomenon I used to encounter in my youth where I kept on running into really sweet old women who were just especially nice to me, went out of their way to help me, sometimes feed me. I finally came to on that one. I reminded them of their grandson. The one who went wrong.

Anyway, this more recent thing with youthful female park rangers and the workers at various other tourist draws and waitresses and such is sort of like that. I think that I remind them of their weird old burned out illegitimate grandfather.

These people encounter bikers all the time. And most of them have figured out that most riders are decent folks. Now I don't mean to imply that motorcycle riders are all fine people, great humanitarians and the like. There is a proportion of idiots and pricks and obnoxious bastards on bikes, too. But I honestly think it's a lower ratio than with most groups. And most of the people in uniforms and Smokey The Bear hats have long ago gotten over any left over from the Hells Angels movies paranoia. They know that guys on motorcycles are mostly good people. Women on cycles, too.

Awhile back several friends sent me a clipping from *Playboy Magazine*. Apparently they read the articles. "In a nationwide survey by Progressive Insurance, percentages of male motorcyclists who are emotionally moved by poetry: 62%; percentage of non-motorcyclists so moved, 23." So there; we're a sensitive lot, too.

Truthfully, I didn't figure this thing out all by myself. I've talked to a number of public employees in uniform at parks and memorials and such over the years. Most of them agree that riders are a better class of people than most tourists. I've had these folks tell me bikers are more polite, more decent, and much easier to deal with than the general public at large. Riders seldom have noisy, nasty, pre-socialized children with them, just for openers. We just aren't the kind of people who take our kids to the Mart-Mart Store to whip them. We seldom throw trash on the roadside. A couple of the public servants in uniform have even spoken to me about The Code.

Had a neat thing happen at work a couple years ago to sort of illustrate and verify all this. It was the first day of the semester, and students were frantically scurrying about and bumping into one another trying to find and get to their new classes. I was leaned up into a corner smoking a cigarette when I saw this pretty little girl looking intently my way. I didn't even turn around to see who she was looking at.

That's one of the advantages to leaning up into a corner. The other is that they can't sneak up behind you. Woman I used to be married to once commented on my ability to cop a lean with my back to the wall even when there ain't no wall.

It turned out the pretty little girl was looking at me. No, I didn't know her. Never saw her before in my life. She walked up to me, looked me right in my good eye, and asked me if I rode a cycle. I told her yes, and she smiled and sighed a huge sigh of relief. Then she introduced herself, and I told her my name.

She was a brand new freshman, and she was lost and scared and confused and overwhelmed and frustrated. And her grandfather, who ran a biker bar in Daytona, had told her that if she got in a jam and needed help, to find herself an old rider, and she would be safe and taken care of. Told her that it was part of The Code. He was right. I guess grandfathers often are. She said she had been looking for someone with boots and a leather all morning.

So I found her a class schedule and drew her a map of where the assorted buildings were. Showed her how to find various offices. Explained as how it was a ways to a town with a Mart-Mart Store and even farther to a city with a plaza mall. Told her a couple local places to eat, a couple not to.

The epilogue to this is pretty funny. She wound up, quite by chance, in one of my classes later that day. She didn't know I was faculty. She figured I was a real old burned out student, or that I worked on the grounds crew or the maintenance staff. That happens a lot. All she knew was that I was an old biker and that I would take care of her.

Freaked her out some when I walked in the classroom and began writing on the board. She wasn't sure if she was supposed to call me Dr. Tiger, or what. But she turned out to be a damn good student and a pretty fair writer, and she came to me when she needed help until she graduated. The Code. It involves, among other things, ladies in distress.

Turns out the Mennonites or Amish or one of them kind of groups know about The Code too. One time I hauled into a rest area on an interstate in Illinois. There were about twenty real well maintained late model pickup trucks parked in a wad. I guess that makes them Mennonites. If they'd been Amish, they'd have had fine looking horses and wagons. I think. Anyway, I walked into the bathroom only to find long lines at all the urinals, stalls, and sinks. Mostly Mennonite guys with beards and black hats and dark clothing, but there were a few regular civilians too.

I got in a line, and before my turn came around, one of the Mennonites who had gotten up to the urinal ahead of me turned and looked around the group. And then he handed the infant child that he was holding in his arms to me. He checked my leather and helmet and looked at me right in my eye and only said, "Please," as he did it. I have no idea how obscure religious orders know about The Code, but it would seem they do. It also involves being good to old folks, dogs, and real small children.

Most people would be somewhere between of scared stupid and somewhat trepidatious about handing their infant child or their near grown granddaughter to anyone who looks like me. But then most people don't know about The Code.

Once, years ago, in a conversation with a friend who didn't ride, I was asked to explain The Code. I told him that it had to do, as my Grandfather, the metaphysician, had explained it to me, mostly with realizing that—It don't matter none about the dead, but you can never leave your wounded behind.

Back to that mounted horseman thing again. I suspect some of the last vestiges of chivalry are dying with old bikers. I know a whole lot of other things are. I came to a belated understanding the other day. In this, the era of credit cards, debit cards, ATM cards, discount cards, telephone ordering, computer buying, and cyber-money, it turns out is much easier to spend money than it is to make it. Hell, you can spend it before you've made it. Something wrong with all that credit. I blame Ronald Reagan, the actor.

Some other parts of that code thing are, similarly, the same as my Grandfather, the economist, taught me when I was a boy. Pay what you owe. Pay with cash money. Don't make a lot of noise. If you borrow a man's knife, return it sharper than you got it. If you borrow his gun, clean it thoroughly and replace his ammunition. If you can't stand tall, at least stand up.

More non-biker women seem to know about The Code than men, I think. At least women are much more likely to seek and accept help from bikers than men are. Maybe they have a better understanding of the passin' through. They seem to somehow sense that riders will take care of them if they need taking care of. Maybe they even understand that riders will leave them alone if that's what they need. Women are also more likely to treat scootertrash with some civility and respect. Waitresses, and again I have done personal research on this, know that most riders are going to behave themselves and tip pretty good. Some of that is because we appreciate being fed more than most people, but chivalry is a big part of The Code, too.

One of those food service ladies I talked to told me that people on motorcycles just have better manners than most folks. That could be part of The Code too. This same woman also mentioned that it was people with good behavior who reacted the fastest and hardest when someone else displayed bad manners, exhibited trashy behavior, or fucked with them in any way.

And that, for sure, is part of The Code. There are some things that longriders won't do to other people, and we expect the same in return. Don't often get it, but we expect it. That might be part of the reason that most bikers and all longriders are independent loners. You get awful damn tired of realizing that other people have such different standards. My Grandfather, the grandfather, used to explain to me that he hadn't raised them other children, so he wasn't responsible for their bad conduct.

Most longriders make it a point to never try to make another man's life harder. I think because we know how hard life can be without random variable assistance.

A day or two after I encountered the prettiest woman I have ever seen in a uniform there at the Booker T. Washington National Memorial, I rolled into Washington, D.C. Under normal conditions I would much rather have a bad rash and eat beets than ride into or even through a big city. But I have an old friend in D.C., a former student of mine, who had invited me there.

It isn't just the traffic in such places that terrifies me. I get real anxious around tall buildings and big crowds too. The noise and multitude frighten me. Metropolitan areas always stink worse than any feedlot or paper mill I ever rode by. And I have trouble breathing in cities. When you try to take a breath, it's like that air has done been used three or four times already. After that, I resent the hell out of being asked to pay twelve dollars for a tank of gas and more than that for a basic breakfast. And urban inhabitants tend to talk too loud for me, and they move about, both afoot and in vehicles, with great haste, and often, seemingly, with anger and aggression, for no apparent reason. Well, maybe they have a reason to be angry. I know it would piss me off if I had to live in such a place. But that hurrying thing they do continues to baffle me. I mean unless they're leaving, I just don't see much point to it.

The Washington, D.C. traffic began piling up and trying to kill me out around Manassas someplace. By the time I got to the western edge of the Beltway, I was terrorized. But I continued bravely on east toward Washington. And then I missed my exit into Arlington and wound up on a bridge across the Potomac River.

That was when I went from moderately terrified to overwhelmed. The damn pedestrians ganged up on me along with the thick vehicular traffic, and they almost made me pull over and cry. Then I somehow found myself in the parking lot of the Kennedy Center. No, I have no idea how. But I had to move a few sawhorses in order to make my escape. Eventually, I think it took four tries, I found the way back across the bridge and ultimately to my friend's place there.

Joel Lee Sherman is a Southern Gentleman, and in that fine tradition of hospitality, he had arranged a place for me to leave my bike in a secure underground parking facility. My friend Captain Zero out in San Francisco has done the same for me over the years, and I will always be grateful to them. I am pretty sure that when you die and go to Hell, you are given a motorcycle to ride around in heavy big city traffic. Maybe even worse, I bet they make you park it out on the streets of Hell at night so you can worry about it instead of sleeping.

The downside of being given a place to put your ride in the secure parking and storage place is that you are now pretty much abandoned and forsaken and afoot and left to the evil perverse whims of public transportation. I have never been especially comfortable in a crowd of any kind, but when the crowd is jammed into a little box hurtling through a hole in the ground, or through the air, I become downright uneasy. For the most part, I don't much enjoy being moved around like cargo. And I make it a point not to climb on or into anything that I can't ride or drive myself. I even avoid elevators and escalators on the unfortunate and rare occasions that I am confronted with them. I refuse to get on roller coasters, or anything that goes up in the air or under the water.

And I spent the next few days in Washington riding countless elevators, escalators, buses, trains, subways, and one taxi cab driven by a guy who couldn't even say "Where to?" in English. In fact, it seemed like to me that English has become a second language there in our nation's capital. Wasn't like Brownsville or Miami where all you got to do is figure out some Spanish. The denizens of Washington seemed to speak damn near everything but English. And they did it at great volume.

But it was worth it. My friend, Joel, is young and tall and very good looking. Handsome in fact. His friend, Matt, is similarly endowed. And they took me into Washington on a tour. Well, both of them boys put on their urban yuppie fashion stuff. Trench coats, blue blazers with shiny buttons, dress shirt, necktie, nice pants, loafers with tassles on 'em.

And then they put me between them because they each of them had an umbrella, and Hurricane Bertha was making its way up the coast, and it was raining on and off in D.C. And these are both good boys, and they were trying to keep the old dude dry.

On my best day I ain't much to look at. Last woman was out to my house told me the place looked right out of *Lonesome Dove* and that I looked like I had been left outdoors too long. And on this occasion in our nation's capital, I looked even worse than usual. Not only by comparison with my hosts, but also because I'd been out on the road for a few weeks. Looked like I'd been left outdoors too long.

The tourists, and some of the indigenous locals, and more than a few cops, paid more attention to us than they did to the damn Lincoln Memorial. I mean we got more looks and stares than the two guys in dresses and high heels who were arguing with another guy in a clown suit in front of the White House. I was pretty sure they were all three of them elected officials, but the boys persuaded me otherwise.

I have, over the years and along the way, gotten used to being looked at in scorn and derision and disgust, often with merriment and amusement, sometimes even sadness and regret. But these tourists were just confused.

I heard some of the comments as we walked by. Tourists talk even louder than native urbanites, I think because they are just passin' through. They could not figure out if I was someone famous and important and the two big, well-dressed young men with me were my bodyguards, or if I was someone infamous who was being moved to another facility, and the two big guys were just my regular guards. Some of them talked like they figured it must be some kind of old geek rehab program.

The Oriental tourists, of which there were many, had the funniest reactions. They would huddle in a group and chatter in their native language as various among them popped their heads up to look at us. Then they would break the huddle, all stare and point at me, and while one of them took several pictures, they would all smile and say, "Weerie Nerson." And I didn't even have my hair in braids.

Ain't the first time. Years ago a friend of mine who was in Amsterdam, over there in Holland, Europe ran across old Willie Nelson and thought it was me. Then, as she ran over to say hi, she realized that it couldn't be me, not unless they had built a bridge to Europe while she wasn't paying attention. But she was already at the guy's table there in the apparently badly lighted hash bar.

She reported that Willie is a real Texas Gentleman and a real good man. Apparently he understands The Code, as he was real nice to this girl. She told me he should have been a biker.

4 - BRIDGES, TUNNELS, AND 20w50 OIL
IN THE HINTERLANDS

Bridges ain't all that much fun on a bike either. Most of them have some kind of grate surface that reduces the amount of tire you have on the ground down to where it damn near don't matter. Reduces your control of your bike just about that much too. A guy I used to know who raced cars once told me that at any given time each tire on the car has surface on the road equivalent to just about the size of the palm of your hand. Think about that a minute. And then reduce that some for narrower motorcycle tires. Then divide by two.

There are a few bridges around where I live. Most of the real local ones are made of wood, which gets really slimy when wet. And I've had my ride slip some sideways on way too many damp wooden bridges. Like riding on pudding.

Tampa is about an hour to the south of me. Whole damn town is full of bridges, all kinds and sizes. And the only constant seems to be that people drive even worse than usual when they are on a bridge. One of my greatest personal fears is encountering someone yappering on his cell telephone while driving inattentively on a narrow bridge. Occasionally one of the guys fishing from the bridge will make a back cast that threatens to snag you off your scooter.

I damn near got orbited off the Golden Gate Bridge one time. There is some of the nastiest wind in the world comes through that gap. The wind, it seems to sort of hold and build out there on the ocean until it is strong enough to hurt you on a bike, and then it comes at you all at once. I mean I switched lanes several times without meaning to and damn near swapped ends a time or two on that particular crossing. And a giant huge old-fashioned Danish sailing vessel called the *Christian Raddich* popped into view from the fog below me, all its sails and flags afurl and billowing in that evil wind. I thought sure as hell it was a ghost ship come to carry me home when I got blown off the damn bridge.

I've been over that Golden Gate Bridge, both ways, a dozen or more times, and I don't ever recall being real comfortable. And when you are running north, out of The City, the next place you get to is The Waldo Grade. Nasty winds through there too.

The other bridge out there in San Francisco, the Bay Bridge, the one that we saw come apart on the TV in that last earthquake, is another kind of nasty. Isn't really that much wind back that far inland, so they make up for that with bizarre traffic. The inbound lane of the bridge is more of a tunnel hanging in the air than a bridge, so that makes it even worse.

The Mackinac Bridge up in Michigan has some truly ugly winds blow around, over, and through it, too. And one time, years ago, it took about four hours to cross it. Seems that they were having a holiday marathon walk or a foot race of some kind, and they actually decided to close the whole damn bridge to regular traffic while several thousand idiots walked or ran, or whatever it was, across it. Honest. And they didn't charge a single one of those fool pedestrians a damn dime to make that mess. But they sure nailed me a tidy sum to cross over, after having held me up for several long hours. Honest. But then, they had me. My alternative was to ride around either Lake Michigan or Lake Huron. Instead, I sat in the lee of a real cold wind, the same one that blows through the bridge, for four hours.

They do that south of Tampa, too. I think it is called the Sunshine Skyway Bridge. It spans the south end of Tampa Bay, with the Gulf on the one side and Tampa Bay on the other. Bad shit happens all around that bridge. Years back a boat slammed into it and broke it, and a whole bunch of people fell off in their cars. Lots of suicides there, too. Awhile back some clown bailed off that bridge with his Rottweiller in his arms. The dog was rescued. But the alternative is to ride around Tampa Bay.

Sometimes they try to trick you and call it a "causeway" instead of a bridge. There is one of those in Tampa, too. What it is a long, narrow pile of dirt through the shallow water with a road on top of it. Ran into one of them up in the Canadian Maritimes once. The Canso Causeway. Typically, it was down at sea level. The wind was as bad as the Golden Gate. Cold Canadian water lapped up onto the road the whole way across it.

Oddly, perhaps, Louisiana has some great bridges. That one that runs out of New Orleans over Lake Ponchartrain is an exceptional bridge. I doubt it gets you more than ten feet above the water, and I also doubt the water is ten feet deep. But there is seldom killer wind or traffic, and it's free, or at least it used to be. And you can see a lot of things, and from a long way off, from a bridge when you're not busy fighting the wind to keep your ride down on the road and in your lane or fighting with local commuter traffic just trying to stay alive as you pass through.

The reason for the wind on some bridges is of course the huge expanse of water the wind travels over without anything in its way to break it any. Sort of like the eastern Wyoming effect. And bridges are usually, strategically, situated on a narrows of some kind, and that funnels the wind.

The other really wonderful bridge in Louisiana is actually several bridges on I-10 out across the Atchafalaya Swamp. There are massive cypress trees blocking any long vistas other than down the road, but you still get some pretty views down little creeks and bayous. Minimal wind, too.

The trouble with this series of bridges across Louisiana on I-10 is that there are few, if any, places to pull over and admire the water and the forest. I've spent a month or two of real fine hours setting beside rivers and shorelines, in rest areas and scenic pull overs and picnic areas and boat ramps. Very contemplative, big moving water.

The best bridges are the ones down in the Florida Keys. And this is because there is seldom a bad wind trying to turn you and your ride into an attractive and expensive boat anchor. And there are some magnificent things to see, mostly a few hundred shades of blue water. And there are lots of places to pull over down there. The traffic down U.S. One can get downright gridlocked anymore, but that run across The Seven Mile Bridge is damn near worth it.

I've not been down that way in ten years or more. Last time was kind of a mixed trip. Two couples of us rode down on two bikes. My last most previous ride down there had been at Christmas, 1980. And I swore I would never do it again. And that time in 1980, we didn't even get all the way to Key West. Got as far as the Mile 23 marker, and I just couldn't deal with the traffic and development anymore and turned it around. This more recent trip was in May, and in all fairness, the roads weren't really all that bad clogged with tourists. But the motel prices were outrageous.

We rode down to around Big Pine Key, and it was still early afternoon, but I began scouting for a place to stay. Lady at a place on Big Pine looked at me right in my eye, smiled, and told me a room for two couples would cost a hundred and forty-five dollars. Per night. Keep in mind this was more than fifteen years ago. I was perplexed and puzzled. I frowned and thanked her, and we rode on south toward Key West. The next two places I checked were so excessive it was embarrassing. At least it should have been.

I asked the guy at the second place what the hell was I doing wrong. He chuckled and told me I was going south. Even though he didn't know me, he said, "Tiger, you dumb bastard ... the farther south, the closer to Key West: the more expensive." That didn't used to be the case. But it had been a long time since I had passed through here.

So we rode back north, up to between Marathon and Islamorada I think, where I convinced the gay couple who owned the motel, Bernie Bruce and Larry Lance, that, as they didn't have a big waiting list or a bunch of reservations, during this, the off season, sixty bucks cash money for a room for four was better than nothing. Even though it used to not be the case, I suspect they thought we were colorful. And they let us have the deal. Think we stayed there with them three or four days.

And, to be fair, all the innkeepers I dealt with here were regular white folks. Well, maybe irregular white people. And most of them sounded like they'd come down from New York.

We rode on down to Key West the next night. Took a real long time to find a place to park. That didn't used to be the case. We walked around some and worried about our bikes. Went to a couple obligatory bars and had some real mediocre, but hugely overpriced, seafood.

The docks at Mallory Square, where jugglers and whistlers and acrobats and musicians and dancers used to perform in a cloud of marijuana smoke at sundown, them docks now have a cover charge. They also had over-priced, watered down drinks and some real bad little jazz bands and rock combos, a reggae group sounded like they had come straight from Keokuk. Key West, anymore, reminds me of San Francisco, only with better weather and no hills. Duval Street is beginning to look a lot like Broadway, only narrower.

The next day me and my pardner did manage to catch some fish, enough to invite the nice folks running the motel to join us for supper. Still some damn pretty sundowns happen down there in those islands.

I guess the most beautiful sunsets I have ever seen have been from islands. And most of the time, it's hard to get a scooter out to an island. But I have seen the sun go down pretty from high in the Rocky Mountains, and from the level flatlands of The Great Plains, and from the western shore, and from the southern deserts.

Same thing with daybreak. I have personal knowledge that if you watch the sun come up out of the Atlantic Ocean every morning for a couple months, you can regain your sanity.

Need to discuss the moon before I get off this topic. A long time ago a woman pointed out that there was mention of the moon in nearly all my poems. Powerful force, the moon. Years ago I told an arthritis doctor that my hands seemed to hurt worse during a full moon. And he said, well yeah, it moves the water all the way from Africa.

Besides that, there is something about riding under a full moon that brings the whole damn thing into pretty clear perspective and realistic corporeality. Sometimes I think my Grandfather, the man in the moon, keeps an eye on me from up there. One time, when I was a small boy, he explained to me that the moon is like hopes and dreams. It comes on full, and then it fades, and then it comes 'round again.

And as this progresses, I have less fear of repeating stories from the first book. That probably means I will get cocky and wind up telling the same story twice in this one.

The worst bridges are, of course, the ones that open up and block and close the road—drawbridges. I've been at it for over a million miles out there, and I still don't understand drawbridges. Rather than open the damn things every few hours on a schedule, they open them every single time a tall boat, or a short boat with a tall mast, wants to go through. Talk about fucking up the passin' through.

Let me try that a different way. They block highway traffic, people trying to get to their jobs, people who are working, ambulances and fire trucks, truckers with loads and deadlines, school buses, longriders in the rain. And they do this at the periodic whim of some rich son of a bitch in a big-assed boat, a yacht probably. Probably one of them where they tell you "come aboard," instead of "hop in." One guy who ain't at work gets to fuck with hundreds, many of whom are trying to go to work, for no reason that I have ever been able to figure out.

As long as I am on the subject of stuff I don't understand, a full list of such things would include double overhead cams, computers, credit cards, debit cards, ATM cards, calling cards, identification cards, business cards, name tags, guys in suits, women, all team sports, Houston, the fashion police, Michael Jackson, voice mail, most movies without horses in them, e-mail, Seinfeld, the fitness campaign, faxing, the internet, the anti-smoking crusade, helmet laws, seat belt laws, censorship, self-appointed authoritarians, political correctness, self-esteem, running other than as a form of self defense, rap music, Madonna, yogurt, and bunji jumping.

And another mystery I need to spend some time and space on, one of the greatest highway mysteries of all, is tunnels. Way I figure it, you got to have a lot of gopher in you to be comfortable about riding into a hole in the ground. The trouble is that riding a motorcycle is basically an outdoor activity, and tunnels are seriously indoors. It's one of them things, like eating oysters, that makes you wonder who was the first guy tried it, and what the hell was he thinking?

One thing I am absolutely certain of is that he wasn't wearing sunglasses. And I always am when I head into a tunnel. I wear sunglasses most of the time, and all the time when I am riding, unless it's at night or in a rainstorm. And you can't see much in a tunnel if you're wearing shades, even prescription ones. Even if it is real well-lighted, as some of the longer tunnels tend to be, you can't see much. Even if everyone follows the directions to turn on their headlights, you can't see a whole lot as you pass through.

Not that there is much to see, but it's comforting to know where the centerline and the walls of the tunnel are.

And there is never a place to pull over and change your glasses or your mind in a tunnel. There is no backing out once you have entered into the dark hole.

In the well-lighted tunnels you get to see the great hoary appendages of greasy moisture, thickened with exhaust fumes, clinging to the sides. The sides are invariably made of the same tile they had in the barracks showers in basic training. And these same lights illuminate the road surface, which is inevitably pock marked with holes big enough to make you want to ride around them, and covered with the same slime that's on the walls, and stained with enough oil to kill a whole bunch of sea otters.

The tunnel under the river between Detroit and Windsor is like that. And no matter which way you are riding it, when you come out of the hole and into the sunlight, you get hassled by the border authorities. Or you can ride the bridge and be blown about in the chilly wind between the lakes and then get hassled by a similar but different group of border cops.

Worst tunnels are, of course, the long ones. The worst one of all is the Chesapeake Bay Tunnel. That might also be the most expensive. It takes courage to charge someone money to ride through a hole. But the state of Virginia has plenty of balls, and gets ten bucks a pop for the privilege, no discounts for having only two wheels. At least this one is a relatively straight tunnel. You also get to ride out over a pretty scary bridge too, all for the same ten dollar toll. And, if you are going the wrong way, you get to come out of the hole into Norfolk. Seems like to me they ought to pay people to do that, but they don't.

There is another pretty creepy tunnel down in Alabama under a portion of Mobile Bay. There is a sign just before you get into the hole itself, after all chance or hope of turning around, with emergency instructions for the trucks carrying toxic nuclear waste.

I guess you got to have a mountain or a body of water in order to have a tunnel. Maybe that's what's wrong right there. There are some places that just ought not be easily got past, and over bodies of water and across mountains are two of them.

Years ago I took a woman with me on a ride from the Atlantic to the Pacific Ocean. She had never been that way and was real appreciative of the passin' through and all the beautiful scenery she got to see along the way. Until we got to the Rocky Mountains.

I recall it was early one morning just some west of Colorado Springs when she damn near came apart on me. Now you got to understand that this girl rode her own motorcycle some, that she had been up behind me from the Canadian line down to Key West, that she had ridden behind me the whole length of the east coast, and a whole lot of other places. Tough girl. She knew I wasn't going to hurt her, least of all with a scooter or on a highway. On this ride she had already braved some of the worst wind on the planet out across Oklahoma.

And she did not like the idea of riding among, into, over, and through obstructions that stuck up ten thousand feet or more in the air. The fact that it was getting much colder, by the minute and by the mile, as we ascended the leeward slope also troubled her sense of reality and perspective. She made me pull over awhile in order to compose herself. She questioned my sanity in taking her to such a place. She commenced, "Tiger, you dumb bastard..."

I mean this girl wasn't scared of much. But them damn mountains just stone overwhelmed her. She kept asking who was the idiot who had built the road, and how could he be so stupid and vain as to think he could get away with it? She made a compelling argument there at roadside.

She figured that some things ought to be left alone and let be, like rattlesnakes and armed teenagers, and that these mountains were one of those things. She actually talked some about finding an airport and riding on the airplane out to the west coast and meeting me there. Think about that. The highroad through the mountains scared her more than riding on the airplane.

Like I said, this was a tough woman. And she stayed with it, including two lethal blizzards, one godawful rainstorm, three closed passes, many floods, forty miles of mud and the legendary and damn near deadly McClure Pass Detour, and Death Valley, all the way to San Francisco, and back. Although we did come home the southern route and avoided high mountains and bad weather all together. Well, all the way to Port Arthur. Turns out the local laundromat is a good place to hang out in a rainstorm. And we were about out of clean clothes anyway.

Well, one of the reasons we stayed south and down out of most of the mountains was that I had gotten a really bad ring job before leaving out on that trip. And the bike was using oil just damn near faster than I could find it. I knew it was the bad ring job, so I wasn't spending my time worrying about it.

No, I had to worry about finding another quart of oil every three or four hundred miles or so. Keep in mind that this was in the high heat of the summer. It was also a real long time ago, back before there was a giant Mart-Mart store every three miles and a convenience store that sells air and water every three blocks.

If you want to amuse some people, cause some of them to guffaw and shriek with laughter, stop and ask if they have any 20w50 oil in Ocotillo Wells or Geronimo or at Exit 42 or Terlingua or Grand Chenier. If you want to see knees slapped, and hear peals of uproarious laughter even as you ride off, ask them that in Vidal Junction or Seadrift. It was like I was some kind of highway sideshow come passin' through their town.

I had small groups of guys falling down laughing at that question all the way back to the east coast. The general answer was, "Not in this town," chuckle chuckle chuckle, "No, not around here." Hee hee, Haw haw. On to Goliad.

Some places, they'd go out back and thrash around in the store room and come back apologizing. Other places they'd just look at me funny. I think they sold oil exclusively for Ford and Allis Chalmers products.

But in Marfa, a man made five phone calls on my behalf in pursuit of the elusive lubricant. Found me some too. Turns out they had gotten a case of some brand I had never heard of before or seen since by mistake down at the feedstore. And the kind lady who ran the feedstore wouldn't even talk about letting me pay for the three quarts I took.

Anyway, some mountains, like tunnels and bridges, are the sort of things that cause you to pause and wonder some. They are all also the kind of places that test your riding skills. And most of them really do get you to wondering who the hell was the guy who had this idea first, and what the hell was he thinking?

On this same ride, out there in some western mountains and tunnels, we kept encountering a guy with a big Winnebago, who had him a horn that played "Hi Ho, Hi Ho, It's Off to Work We Go." And he played it through every tunnel we got into. I bet he has windmills made of beer cans and yard gnomes in his lawn.

While I'm on the topic of Winnebagos, you ever notice how the damn things tend to run in packs, thereby assuring that no one is able to pass them as they roll along eight miles under the speed limit. That many scooters got together in a group, they'd have us on the roadside in a matter of minutes.

Had a kind of neat thing happen recently. Young man asked me if, in order to get a motorcycle endorsement on his license, he would have to take a practical test in the saddle as well as a written test. And I told him I didn't know. Then he asked me what did I have to do to get my endorsement. I told him I was born with it.

And then I remembered moving to Florida years ago and having to switch state driver's licenses. And the kid at the license bureau saw my helmet in my hand and asked me did I want a motorcycle endorsement. And I said yes, please. He looked me over and asked if I had taken the AMA safety course, and I told him no. Then he asked how many miles I had ridden in the past several years. I didn't say a word, just looked at him over my sunglasses. He said, "Oh," and stamped my license.

5 - WIND, MATHEMATICS, AND MINORITY GROUPS

I made mention of the wind in Oklahoma back there someplace. That was one of the all time killer winds. There were four of us riding together on that run. I had that woman with me. We were westbound on U.S. 64, which is a real fine road, right up there with U.S. 50, U.S. 61, and U.S. 98. And out there in the Oklahoma Panhandle, the winds came upon us from the north. We rode for miles tilted at about a forty-five degree angle to the right.

Then, somewhere out there around Mocane, some prudent rancher had planted a few thousand pine trees along the north side of the road, and they had formed a windbreak. We rode upright for awhile. Then, down the line a long ways, we saw a break in the trees. You can see a long way down the road on U.S. 64 in the Oklahoma Panhandle. The break looked to be a road. And, having seen nothing but windbreaking pine trees for the last long time, we all looked that way as we passed. We talked about it later, and none of us had seen what was up the road. All we knew was that all the wind in west Oklahoma had funneled itself through that gap and damn near knocked us down.

Later that day we found ourselves huddled in the lee of a dumpster outside Lamar, Colorado, home of the Lamar Savages, or so it said on the water tower. By now we were riding directly into that vicious north wind. And we were damn near freezing to death. We discussed setting a fire in the dumpster to get warm, but decided against it in favor of using the downwind side of the dumpster to put on lots more clothes.

That story about the bad ring job and running through all that hard country to find oil put me in mind of another ride when I about worried myself to death. Typically, it is both amusing and pedantic. That run when I was going through all the oil was a pain in the ass, but I really wasn't worried. I knew exactly what was wrong with the bike. I knew the guys who had done the bad ring job would fix it right when I got it back home.

And I knew I wasn't going to hurt my machine as long as I kept pouring oil through it. Like I said, it was an inconvenience, but not a real bad worrying thing. And a real bad worrying thing can make a mess of a ride and the passin' through just every bit as fast as spending time in the emergency room at the local hospital.

One time I took off on a ride a couple months after having had a pretty serious wreck. The details of this wreck aren't very interesting. In fact, it was a real boring wreck, one that I had already had about ten years before this one. I was riding too fast and too close to the senile fool in front of me, and he stopped short and fast for no apparent reason, and I had a choice of decorating his tailgate or putting the bike down.

I went for option B. Made a mess too. My handlebars were bent and twisted like some kind of surrealistic sculpture. Tore a mirror clean off. Punched a hole in the fairing where the mirror was mounted. Ripped the windshield in half. Bent a footpeg. Twisted the crash bars around my right saddle bag. And the clutch lever was wrapped around my left hand like a pair of cheap brass knuckles.

The bike slammed down hard to the left with me astride it. Then it shook me loose and bounced, then it turned over and slammed down again, and then it skidded. I don't bounce worth a damn anymore, so I didn't have much road rash other than on my hands. But I was bad bruised from my ankle to my neck on my left side. Another one of those dreaded hip pointers. And, I somehow managed to loosen two or three teeth.

But I was able to get up and pick the bike up and ride it home. And if there is such a thing as a good wreck, it's one that you can ride your machine away from. But that was the last time I was able to stand for the next three or four days. And it was a whole while longer than that before I could move around much. My pardner, Ron, having been down a time or two himself, he brought me TV dinners and chicken pot pies. But this isn't about a wreck.

Turns out it takes longer for an old man to heal than it did when he was younger. It also takes longer for back-ordered parts to get to you. By the time I had me and the motorcycle both back together in a mobile manner, two months or more had passed. I hadn't been fifty miles on the motorcycle between wrecking it and saddling it up to head out for a couple months.

And when I crossed the line north into Georgia and stopped to get some of their considerably cheaper gas, I sort of superficially checked my mileage. It was low, around 40 miles per gallon, when I usually get 45 or better. I passed it off to bad math and high interstate speeds and a less than totally full tank to begin with, but it bothered me. Then I rode on up to Marietta and spent a couple days with my niece and her family there. I hit Marietta in the rain, sat out some of it at a convenience store, filled up on gas there even though I didn't need to. Again, my mileage was still real poor. And I was mildly troubled by the poor mileage occasionally during my visit.

The next time I got gas, I checked my mileage again. It was worse, down into the thirties this time. Again, I tried to pretend it was bad math, or maybe evaporation while the bike was set up at my niece's place. But I fretted about it on and off all the way to the next tank of gas. The next time I checked, my mileage was in the low-middle thirties, a number I had never before encountered on a motorcycle. Now I began to worry in earnest.

By the time I got up the road to a friend's place, my mileage had gone down into the mid-twenties, and I was beside myself with anxiety. I mean it had been ruining my ride. The bike was running just fine, but I couldn't even appreciate the scenery for concern over this mileage thing.

So I rolled it into his garage and tore the carburetors apart to look for diaphragm leaks and stuck needle valves. Nope. That wasn't it. Then I pulled the air filter out and poured some sand out of it. But I live on a sand road, and I always pour some sand out of my air filter. Then I pulled the spark plugs, and the damn things looked better than when I had put them in. I checked the gas lines for leaks, even though I knew that wasn't it. I have had such leaks. You can smell them, and I hadn't smelled a damn thing.

More than anything, I didn't want to open the bike up and check valve clearances and so forth, not unless I was at a good BMW shop and had help available. So I saddled back up and headed back out on the road, and I worried. I got good at it. And the next time I got gas, I checked again. This time I had managed twenty-one miles to the gallon. I get almost that kind of mileage out of my beat up old pickup truck. So, I worried some more.

When I crossed the Michigan line, I had three different BMW shops in mind to go to. I had gone from worried and fretful to fearful to crazed with anxiety. And while I was gassing up there, I did my math again. That was when I realized it was more than fifty-seven miles from Columbus, Ohio to Dundee, Michigan, that the eleven miles to the gallon I had just figured out was an invalid figure, and that it was my odometer that was fucked up. "Tiger, you dumb bastard." Sometimes I talk to myself out on the road.

Yeah, the force of that wreck a couple months earlier had broken some tiny internal instrument parts. And I hadn't ridden it enough to know that. The only good part of this one was that I was alone, and there was no one around to share in and enjoy my stupidity and shame. As my Grandfather, the speculator, used to suggest, "Nothing quite as satisfying as a good private failure."

Still, the only thing I know of more embarrassing than confidential humiliation is a public one. So I was grateful my Grandfather, the mathematician, the man who was certain that there is a number between six and seven that they aren't telling us about, he wasn't there to see my mortification.

But this wasn't about stupidity, this was about mountains and bridges and wind and tunnels. The bottom end of The Blue Ridge Parkway has several, mostly pretty short, tunnels. Later on you get a few of the ones with curves in them. The kind that get you to thinking about why the hell would they go through a mountain instead of over or around it. Passin' through is passin' through. And that gets you back around to thinking about that first guy again.

Wind. A couple years ago I came upon another old rounder in a roadside rest area, and we discussed, among other things, the nature of just passin' through, and the wind. We talked about the wind down in the ditches, and the wind out over the water. We discussed the wet wind across the Everglades and the hot wind out in Death Valley. We spoke of the cold wind down off the Rockies, and the salt wind on the Pacific Coast Road, and the wind out across the Great Plains and the prairie. We reminisced some about the Tehachapi wind and the windmills up and down I-5.

We talked about Bob Dylan's song "Idiot Wind." And we reviewed the way the wind screams down in the desert around Organ Pipe, and the way it whispers soft in Southern cypress swamps, the way it moans in the Redwood trees along the Avenue of the Giants, and the way it cries out across the Llano Estacado. We even talked of catching a good tail wind. Those first several are all real and sometimes serious things.

That last one is a damned myth.

One time in between Ann Arbor and Flint, Michigan, four of us got into some of the wickedest wind I ever encountered. We had started south, I believe our original intent was to ride down to Cincinnati. Well, the weather dissuaded us of that idea some south of Ann Arbor. Michigan has some of the worst weather on earth, and southeastern Michigan has some of the worst weather in the state, and we got into some.

First, the cloudless blue sky we had left under turned an ugly shade of Michigan Industrial Gray. Then the wind came upon us sideways, damn near put us into one another. Then the rains came, similarly sideways, and with similar force. One of the guys later claimed he got bruised from some rain drops.

Well, it couldn't have been very many of them hit him, because we got off the road at the very next opportunity and spent the next couple hours up under cover in a convenient abandoned building of some kind. We alternately discussed the merits of retreating homeward rather than pressing on, trying to figure out what kind of business used to occupy the building, and playing cutthroat buck-a-point Scrabble.

We made coffee and took turns walking to the door to check the sky and the rain. They were both still there, every single time. One guy had a little transistor radio, and he found a weather report that confirmed our earlier suspicion about retreating being the better move. One of those one-word weather reports: deteriorating. So we waited until there was a slack period in the rain, and then we got back on the road north toward home. And we almost made it.

There were about seventy miles between us and home, and disaster waited for us until we were five or ten miles out. Disaster took the form of the wind. It came up suddenly, while all four of us were bunched up going under an overpass. We entered the protection of the overpass at about sixty miles an hour. There was some wind as we went under, nothing serious, but some wind. It had begun spitting some rain again as we went under the bridge. And, of course there was no wind at all in the protection of the overpass. No rain either. Gave new meaning to the phrase Between The Winds.

And as we came out the other side, we entered the maelstrom. Wind hit us from the right side so hard that it just drove all four bikes, almost in formation, over into the passing lane, where, fortunately, there was no other traffic. The reason there was little traffic was that many of the vehicles had been blown off the road earlier. We saw several in the median and more along the sides of the road. Others apparently had more sense than we did and had headed for cover.

I say *fortunately* not because the wind put us suddenly sideways ten or twelve feet, but because the wind snatched my glasses right off my face. They sort of danced about briefly in the couple feet between my face and the windshield, and then they took off downwind. Gone. And I don't see well at all without my spectacles.

A moment later I really resented not being able to see, because when I glanced in my rearview mirror, the guy riding last was upside down a few feet off the ground. I mean he was still on his bike, and still going probably forty, but the whole thing, bike and rider both, was a couple feet in the air off the pavement, upside down. At first I thought it was my handicapped vision, then I began to think it was the fault of my mirrors. When I saw him come down and bounce a couple times, I knew it was real.

Yeah, he lit on his head. Later he claimed that was what broke his fall and saved his ride. The bike somehow bounced and landed right side up in a medium deep puddle. And other than bad bent handlebars and a mashed mirror and a scraped up front fender, it wasn't hurt at all. The guy riding it had made a mess of a pretty good helmet and a mediocre rainsuit, but aside from that he wasn't real bad hurt. The backs of both his hands were scraped up, and he had some road rash on one elbow. He had a stunned expression, like a guy who just had his bike picked up, turned over, and then dropped back down on him by the wind. But he was able to ride his own ride home.

As soon as we got him and his cycle upright and determined the extent of the damage, I figured that as long as we were stopped, I might just as well organize a search for my glasses. By now I had dug my extra pair out of a saddlebag, and I was able to see again. It was a valiant effort, but to no avail.

Like I said, it wasn't but about five more miles home, but as I recall, we stopped several times on the way. Mostly at bars. To discuss and analyze the events of the day, especially the last one.

Got into some wind one time up in the Canadian Maritimes. At that place called the Canso Causeway, which I have mentioned before. It runs between Mulgrave and Port Hastings in Nova Scotia. Go get a map.

The predominant north wind is channeled through a draw there at the narrows. It is much the same effect, only with wind instead of water, as is found in the Bay of Fundy to the west of there. The Bay of Fundy has the fastest, highest tides on earth.

And the Narrows there at Canso have similar winds. Wasn't nothin' to do but lean left into it and try to stay upright. Fortunately, it's a short run of maybe ten or twenty miles. But the wind was bad enough that we went to some lengths to insure that we would return that way at night, when, we hoped, the wind would lay down some. We did. It did. Some.

Way too many contemporary interstate expressways, mostly the ones built down below the level of the surrounding ground, are filled with mean, dangerous winds. For openers, they fill up with wind, just like the narrows up there at Canso in Canada, and then funnel it down the road. Then there is a different wind created by heavy traffic, especially fast-moving heavy traffic, especially fast moving, heavy semi-truck traffic. It creates a warm wicked wake. People driving vehicles notice some of this, but on a bike you get to appreciate all of it.

Sometimes an expressway can be like a damn wind tunnel. And other times, that same highway can be all cross winds and updraft winds and blasting gusts of wind from the heavy traffic going both ways. Gives you one more thing to concentrate on and make decisions about, along with the road surface, the traffic, the weather other than the wind, and the speed.

I mentioned the Waldo Grade back there in reference to the Golden Gate Bridge. That bridge is a scary span. The Pacific Ocean and San Francisco Bay churn and boil beneath you. The wind whips at you. Joggers line the sides. The local traffic tries to kill you. And you know that if you survived the fall, you would surely freeze to death in those cold unfriendly waters that surround Alcatraz in about a minute. Then, when you have survived and escaped that bridge, you get to ride the Waldo Grade. Wicked wind there at the Waldo Grade. I'm not sure what the meteorological or geologic configuration is that causes it, but it's a bitch.

The north end of the Outer Banks of North Carolina, especially and specifically the area around Kitty Hawk, has some real serious wind. It figures. Old Orville and Wilbur probably could have flown a large kitchen appliance off those sand dunes in that wind.

And the sand is as much a problem there as the wind. It often is along shoreline roads. Damn stuff is in the air, so it gets in your eyes and your air filter. It gets up in your helmet in your hair, and in your beard, and your ears, and often invades saddlebags and fairing compartments. Worst of all, it gets all over the damn road.

There is a myriad of bad things that can get on a road surface, but sand is one of the worst. It swirls and shifts and changes, sometimes while you're in it. A good hard rain will wash a road clean. A light mist will mix with the oil and exhaust smoke on the road surface. It results in a thin layer of slick slime. Most of these places I've mentioned with real bad wind always make me wonder what it's like there during a storm.

But back to more political incorrectness. I am getting pretty damn tired of the ethnic folks who seem to have taken over damn near all of the cheap and/or non-chain motels, and many of the motel franchises in the various chains as well. Apparently I ain't the only one, as I see a lot of "American Owned" signs on motels anymore.

The dot-headed bastards got me twice last summer. First time was in Virginia someplace. Little town on a two-lane somewhere. It had been a real nice day, and I had already done seven or eight hundred miles, and I was ready to quit. So I stopped at a motel on the south end of whatever town it was, and was welcomed by a lovely lady in a beautiful sari. Her English was probably superior to mine, and her manners were beyond reproach.

I was told that the room would cost me thirty dollars for the night, plus tax. And that was too much. It was too much to begin with, but most states have motel taxes in the double digit area, so now we were up to thirty-six bucks. To make it worse, the damn place was nearly deserted. It was a shabby room in a run-down motel, in a noplace town, and even if there had been a swimming pool and free in-room movies, it wasn't worth no thirty-plus tax dollars.

And I told her so. She smiled and explained that that was the price, no matter the value. I tried to get a deal by telling her I would pay cash and that I required no receipt. That one will sometimes get you a discount. But not at this place. I pointed out that she wasn't exactly turning customers away, that there were only three other cars in the lot, and that twenty dollars was more than nothing. But she really wasn't much interested in bargaining.

So I thanked her for her time and trouble and rode on up the road to the other motel, this one at the north end of town. I was greeted by a rather surly Hindu gentleman with bad halitosis and a worse attitude. He, too, had rooms for thirty dollars. Again, it was a pretty sleazy place, windows that wouldn't close, bad smell in the room from the damp carpet under the window. Mediocre water pressure. Rotten TV reception. Lumpy bed. Lots of highway noise.

As I said, this guy was a prick with bad breath, but I tried to offer him twenty bucks, and he decided to get offended by my kind offer. Before we were done talking to one another, he had threatened to call the local police, and I had threatened to stuff him in a pot of curry. Somewhere in the middle of our discussion, I caught on. He was the husband or brother or something of the sweet lady at the first motel. They had the town surrounded, owned both motels, had built themselves a damn monopoly. And his co-conspirator had called him when she saw me head north out of the first place. Sometimes they run a pincer movement on you as you're trying to pass through.

I wound up spending a medium bad night on a picnic table in the wilderness, counting fireflies and stars, and being moderately paranoid every time a car slowed down like it was going to pull in there. Used to be that you could crash a few hours in a rest area, or a scenic pull over, or a picnic area, in relative safety and some comfort. Anymore, I am about half fearful of mobile teen gun thugs deciding that old scootertrash would make a good drive-by target. Although there don't seem much sport in it to me. And, if the armed and mobile urban underachievers don't get you, the damn rest area police will. You can't build a fire anywhere anymore without having a license, a permit, a fire extinguisher, and a promise of rain.

But that's another rant. This one was about various peoples of Asia Minor, the Middle East, and the Indian subcontinent taking over many of the motels in America. I have discovered that oftentimes when an ethnic minority takes over a particular occupation, they make some improvements and work hard for the general betterment of the field. But that has not been the case with foreign motel keepers. As my Grandfather, the Skinnerian psychologist, explained it to me—You ought to trust them to do what you've seen them do.

I heard a strange phrase at work the other day. That happens to me a lot, working as I do, for people in suits, and working, as I do, with eighteen year old students. But this one came from faculty. The phrase was "The Hospitality Industry." I guess that is what they are calling the hotel/restaurant business management major anymore. Or at least this week. Anyway, the phrase struck me as oxymoronic and generally moronic as well.

These things, these linguistic anomalies, happen to me a lot. I recently spent most of an hour in a meeting listening to a high priced girlsuit talk about an interim transition logo. She used phrases like "visual identity" and "graphic image." She showed us various cartoons as she talked. Confusion and disinterest competed for my attention.

But if hospitality has become an industry, then the Iranians and Pakis and Iraqis and Afghanis and Indians and Bangladeshis have done to that industry what AIDS has done for getting laid, or what New Coke damn near did to the soft drink industry. And if you don't want to spend fifty bucks to lay down awhile in a Holiday Marriott Quality Hilton Best Hyatt Howard motel, your chances of staying cheaply at the Iranian Inn are just about fifty/fifty anymore, especially if you're looking for shelter away from an interstate highway.

And I had yet another example of Middle Eastern American hospitality last summer. I think I was in Georgia, but it might could have been Tennessee. Saw a sign that there was a nineteen dollar motel down the way a few miles. It was getting late, and it was already raining. And it wasn't going to stop anytime soon, so I decided to shut it down and spend the night.

A swarthy, dark-eyed youth smiled at me from behind the desk in the lobby. He spoke with a local, Southern dialect. There wasn't a trace of anything other than Native Redneck American in his speech. I assumed he had been born right around there somewhere. He was probably the valedictorian at the local high school.

When he told me the rooms were twenty-six dollars, I pointed out that I had seen a sign some north of there that said they had nineteen dollar rooms. He grinned and told me it was an old sign. But he did have the good sense to accept my twenty-dollar offer and not even pretend to give me a receipt.

A few years back, I believe it was in Virginia, but again it could have been Tennessee, I came across a similar hospitality hustle. The signs, and their number was several, all advertised their rooms for $19.95. It was, of course, a trick. But it was a complex one. The Afgapakaranian owners had hired an indigenous black girl to explain to folks that, according to the laws of the state, they could legally advertise the price of the cheapest six percent of their rooms.

Yeah, now we had gone beyond story problems and on into ratios and proportions. While the local lady explained all this to me, the owner, his turban slightly askew, stood behind her, smiling and nodding. I rode another sixty miles before I stopped that night.

As best I am able to understand such historic, cyclic occurrences, there will soon be a different minority group of oppressed immigrants who will take over the motel business while the current crop goes on to become doctors and lawyers. My research has determined that early on in this century most professional baseball and basketball players were Jewish.

But in the meantime, we are apparently destined to overpay for lodging as we pass through.

6 - OLD BROKE DOWN RIDES,
AND NASHVILLE IN THE FALL

Once upon a time in the late 1960s on the highway between Columbia and Charleston, South Carolina, I broke a Yamaha down. Warped a crank and rolled slowly to roadside in a cloud of smoke, finished. It was the fault of the silly oil injection system, but there were no Japanese engineers around to scream at. And I didn't feel like pushing it the fifty miles back to Columbia, or the near twice that on through Charleston to the beach on the Isle of Palms. And I didn't much feel like leaving it unattended beside the road either, so I wound up pushing it off into the woods and hitch hiking back to town.

It took two rides. The first guy was drinking Jim Beam and insisted I join him. We put away most of his pint as we rolled down the road. The next guy was drinking beer, and by the time I finally returned to Columbia, it was late, and I was drunk. I was also apparently pretty persuasive, because I somehow convinced the girl I was hanging out with that she should help me rescue my broke down ride with her little Comet car. I went out and got more Jim Beam and beer as part of my persuasive technique. Provisions.

The details pretty much escape me now, but I do remember that another couple joined us, and that there were four of us, and that we were all real drunk by the time we started back to the forest primeval for my cycle. And then I couldn't find it. It was dark, and I was drunk, and, although I had put it there, I could not find the damn thing. What we did do was almost manage to lose one of the other people who was helping look for the bike with me. Like I said, it was dark, and we were loaded.

It was near dawn by the time we finally discovered my scooter. We were still pretty drunk, and we took the back seat out of the Comet, and somehow got the bike mostly in the car. I had to take the handlebars off to get it in the back seat. The damn thing was a lot longer than the Comet was wide. As I remember this, I also took the front wheel off to make it shorter. Then we tied the rear doors down some with our belts and a set of jumper cables. Then we somehow all maneuvered ourselves into the front seat and got home. We managed to engineer that without incident. Took most of the next day to go back out there and find the rear seat from the little Comet car.

That Yamaha was cursed from the very first time I got on it. I don't remember the particulars. But it was 1969, and I was in the army, and it was what I could afford, given the nature of my bar bills and what the army was paying for conscription labor.

Before that machine was finished with me, it had hurt me bad a couple different times, burned my first ex-wife all about her inner thigh, and damn near tore several toes off a good friend who refused to change his sandals for boots. It had also cost me so much money in repairs that I had to finally just give it to the man who had been working on it.

I got even. On the night I got discharged, on my way out of town, I stopped by the place where it was now housed, and I shot it. Oh yeah, I was drunk again. It was out in the guy's yard, and I just leveled a pistol through the fence and put six into it at close range. And I never have felt any remorse at all. A friend of mine was with me. When we stopped for refreshments later, and when his hearing had recovered, he said he didn't know I kept the gun loaded. He prefaced his comment with, "Tiger, you dumb bastard." And I had to explain it to him the way my Grandfather, the gunfighter, had told me—If it ain't loaded, it ain't nothin' but a pretty club.

An incident involving a similar machine in northern Michigan years later also resulted in no remorse. I was in a pickup truck, I suspect hunting or fishing, and I encountered a broke down biker beside the lonely road. A kid on a Yamaha like the one I had shot. I was understandably empathetic. So I stopped and drove down into the ditch so we could load his bike on my truck. The kid was elated at being rescued in the wilderness. A few miles down the road I finally got around to asking him what was wrong with his ride. He told me he had snapped a chain.

And I asked him why he hadn't fixed it. He confessed that he wasn't carrying an extra master link. I speculated that such an omission was pretty fucking stupid. He grinned like a kid and said yeah, but, he went on to explain that it wouldn't have helped any because he didn't have any tools with him either.

And I made a U-turn and drove him and his broke down Yamaha right back to where I had found them, unloaded the bike and the kid, and told him I hoped he'd learned a lesson. I should have told him about shooting that Yamaha. No remorse.

I do have some regrets about a couple things. Charlie Syms, who ran the finest BMW dealership in the entire Free World for a long time, once called me and told me to come on up to his shop and talk to him. So I did. At the time I was riding a 1971 750 BMW. And Charlie had found one just like it, only a '72 with real low mileage, that had a sidecar strapped to it. He had bought it real cheap, and offered to pass it on to me cheap. It would have been ideal. A lifetime of parts, and a sidecar.

So I rode on back home and told my woman about it. And she killed that idea before it even got discussed. She figured out that with a sidecar, I could carry my dog and a shotgun and a rod and reel with me, and that I might never come back home. She was probably right.

On the way to Nashville, running up I-75, I kept encountering another longrider on a Honda. We finally wound up at the same rest area together. So we sat a minute and smoked cigarettes and drank coffee and discussed it all. I told him how thrilled I was to be on the road in October. Told him I was going to ride the interstate superslabs all the way up to Nashville because I was in a kind of a slow hurry about getting there. And then I was going to ride the back roads and take my time going home.

We began talking about Atlanta and how it was a hard thing to avoid. And he told me that it was legal for a scooter to run in the carpool lane in Atlanta, on the interstate through town, the one that is way shorter than the beltway go-around road. He said a cop had told him that. The man said you could ride legally in that lane even without a passenger. He also turned me on to the cheapest gas and cigarettes in all of south Georgia on an exit after he was getting off. I gave him a copy of the book I was on my way to Nashville to tout as a means of thanking him.

Then we left together and rode about fifty more miles before he bailed off. It saved me well over an hour going through Atlanta. There were all the usual wrecks and break downs and slow downs and heavy urban traffic. And I blew around most of it in the carpool lane. Had a cop nod at me as I went by him at one point. And the gas the guy turned me onto was eighty-three cents, and the cigarettes were twelve and a quarter a carton.

As a school teacher, I am seldom permitted to go out on the highway anytime other than summer. So this run up to Nashville in mid-October was a treat. Not only was I authorized to be off work, but the suits were paying for it, too.

I made the turn west out of Chattanooga, and a couple hours later up there in those mountains, up by Monteagle, it began to get late and chilly. Then it got dark and cold. So I dropped off the interstate and found a motel room. The guy running the place was a pro. He had dealt with scootertrash before, even had a biker-preferred room he put me in. Ground floor, quiet room out back facing away from the highway, covered parking place a short step from the door. Then he told me two places I could walk to for supper.

It was cold enough the next morning that I put my long underwear and gloves on for the hundred and fifty miles into Nashville. It was just beginning to warm up some when I got into the city. I had good directions to the big deal whoopie-do hotel they had put me up in, so I only got lost once and not real bad at all.

I knew I was in a big city right away. While I was stopped at a red light in the shadowy canyons among tall buildings, a local wino ran over and grabbed a public telephone receiver and began shouting into it. I was pretty sure the phone hadn't rung, and he confirmed this when he walked away with the receiver, still screaming into it. As best I was able to tell, he was talking to someone named Leon.

A couple nights later I had another urban wino incident. As the only sober person for blocks, I was dispatched to the liquor store. Designated gopher. I noticed the small crowd of resident winos in the parking lot. So that's where I parked my cycle. Winos will watch your bike for you, hoping you'll give them some money or a cigarette when you return. As I approached the door, the littlest wino of all broke loose from the group and confronted me. He held out his hand, palm up, as he walked up to me. I could see some coins in it.

Before the tiniest wino in Nashville had a chance to go into his shuck and panhandle routine, I told him I didn't have no extra money. And he got indignant, got right up toward my face on his tiptoes, and told me he didn't need no goddamn money. I had a cigarette in my mouth at the time, so I stepped back away from the fumes and asked him what the hell did he want if not money.

He remained offended, but told me they wouldn't allow him in this store anymore, and that he had his ninety-four cents together already. Again he showed me the money in his hand. Asked me if I would go in the store and get him his bottle of fortified something or another for him. I was so damned humiliated I bought him a pack of Slim Jims, too.

Then, coming back out of Nashville three days later, it happened again—Highway Help. This time they had shut down I-24 eastbound. I mean it was down to a crawl, and there was a Sunday crowd of recreators hard at it clogging the interstate. I hadn't taken my feet off the pavement for several miles when a couple on a Harley pulled in beside me from the right, from the closed down construction lane that was full of orange cones and barricades to keep the cars out. For no apparent reason.

We discussed things as we walked along. And we decided that, as it was Sunday, there would be few workers out there constructing, and that there should be fewer cops out there policing. And the lady pointed out that she was little and cute and could plead immediate tampon necessity or something.

So we dropped over into the right hand lane, the construction lane, and went ahead on past everyone. Me and the couple on the Harley were clipping along in third gear, going maybe thirty sometimes, while the rest of the world was gridlocked hard. We did this for about thirty or forty miles. Then we saw the bottleneck and the cop. The cop saw us, too, and he smiled as we dropped back into the legal line of traffic and rode past him. I'm confident that if I had stayed in the legal lane of traffic, I would have been several hours getting through it all. I said my farewells to the folks on the Harley and rode south the rest of the way home on two-lanes.

Now, some medium neat things happened up in Nashville in between those two highway incidents. I had been invited to The 10th Annual Southern Festival of Books to do readings and signings from *Longrider.* When I rolled into the Quality-Howard-Holiday-Hilton-Marriot-7 or - 8 that the festival folks had me booked into, the guy in charge of valet parking dashed over to me briskly.

They try to get rid of scootertrash quickly at such places, so the regular citizen guests don't even see us. But before the professional car parker even got wound up, I told him I had a goddamn reservation and that he should be nice to me or I was going to make him park my ride for me. He smiled and apologized, and then he showed me to the special place he had just for motorcycles to park. It was a great place, protected and covered and well-lighted and well-watched.

Just to make sure this is on the record, that giant chain motel that I was put up at there in Nashville, that was one of the worst temporary housing episodes ever. And, there was no one about but local corporate white folks running the place. Not a sniff of curry, a turban, or a hint of tinkly banjo music anywhere. Cost somebody damn near a hundred bucks, eighty-seven dollars, plus the Tennessee tax, per night, for me to lay down in a lumpy bed and listen to noisy revelers drunkenly stumbling and screaming their way past my room on the balcony walkway, and past the inn on the sidewalk, and past the sidewalk in their cars. Noisiest goddamn place I was ever in that didn't involve small children or heavy artillery.

But a couple days later, when I was scheduled to do my little reading, I caught a break. The clever festival folks had strategically scheduled my little appearance at an outdoor venue. I got there some early and made friends with the sound crew.

Years ago I did some radio commercials and learned the value and power of the sound guys. Easy thing to do, as these were real nice boys. One of them decided I could get my bike up the nearby wheelchair ramp and park it next to the stage. Then he decided it would be cool if I just sat down on the stage to do my reading instead of standing at a lectern. Was a good gig.

And then, once I got loose of that traffic mess, I got to drift home on some real pretty mountain highways. A few of the leaves were changing colors at some of the higher elevations. It got pretty chilly up high, and I was into my leathers and gloves. But most of the traffic was still up there stuck on I-24. I just rolled on easy south the whole way. Passed on through.

7 - ZEN AND THE ART OF MOTORCYCLE RIDING

Sometimes you catch a day out there when your mind isn't so busy with traffic and weather that you get to thinking about it all. It usually takes me most of the first day to get settled into a ride. You know, figuring out which way it leans, adjustments and readjustments, repacking and shifting and balancing the load around, getting my gear where I want it, hitting a stride.

But the next day out, I try to spend some time alone in my mind thinking about, reflecting on, figuring out, what has happened in the year or so since the last ride out. Sometimes, if it all comes down right, this turns into a very Zen experience. One day a few years back I did it righter than I ever have before or since. Passing through while passing through.

And I spent most of ten hours thinking about motorcycles and how very much cycles and a road to ride have meant to me, how much they have enriched my life. I thought about the sky, and the road, and about the boxer twin engines.

My ancient memories were distinct and clear. I thought about rides to the Canadian Maritimes and to the west coast back in the seventies and eighties. I remembered details of rides from a million miles ago. Somehow I was capable of recalling the very first time I was ever on The Blue Ridge, and The Outer Banks, and The Natchez Trace, the first time I ever saw that other ocean. I was able to focus and concentrate on individual scooters, and certain incidents, and particular people I had met along the way.

Somehow I remembered specific roads and places, some of them from thirty or forty years and a million miles ago. There were memories of places without names that I have rode through, and remembrances of stretches of highway between those places.

And, rolling slow upriver through the warm sunshine, I thought about U.S. One, Route Sixty-six, and A1A. I recalled Going To The Sun, and The Million Dollar Highway, and U.S. Two in the snow, and 170 down in Big Bend, and the road in Canada from Sault Saint Marie to International Falls. And I had remembrances of the California Coastal Highway and The Ridge of The Rockies and The Cabot Trail.

Memories of once buying a tire in North Las Vegas, and another one in Spokane, and one in San Francisco came to me. I got ripped off all three times. Recollections of a welder named Arky in Oakland who had me remove my gas tank and battery so he could hang my cycle upside down to weld the center stand flooded over me. Remembrances of things past, like the guy at the scooter shop down in Del Rio who fixed my front brakes for me. And memories of the broke down long haul trucker up in De Funiak Springs who bought me supper after I spent a couple hours running parts for him came to me out there along The River.

And I thought about a longrider I encountered at a scenic overlook on The Blue Ridge one time long ago. Big, burly kind of guy. He introduced himself, said his name was Bear. I told him I was called Tiger. And we both got to laughing so hard we damn near couldn't get back on our bikes.

I continued northbound and had distinct memories of a road out in the Indian Hills of east Oklahoma. And I also thought about a rest area in Blythe, California in a hundred and fourteen degree heat. The sun sucked our eyes dry going west that day. And then I recalled another day between Havre and Medicine Hat when it was twenty-eight and snowing hard. And a time down along the Gila when the humidity was six percent.

I remembered the way the salt marshes on the Gullah Islands smelled, and the odor of paper mills along the Gulf coast, and the aroma of feedlots in Texas in the Summer and citrus groves in bloom in Florida in the Spring. I recollected clearly the way the hot wind smelled in Death Valley, west of Stove Pipe Wells. And I remembered the distinct scents of several women who had ridden up behind me. And I recalled the odors of scorched brakes and burned rubber, and blood.

It was out there in motion in the warm sunshine along the Mississippi River that I remembered The Storm From Hell that came upon us in the Kettleman Hills one summer. It lasted all the way to San Francisco and pinned us down there for five days. And I recalled riding from Harlan to Hazard the hard way, uphill on a curve. And I had memories of being permitted to listen to the Spanish angels down in the canyons of the Rio Grande.

And then I got to thinking about my old highway blood brothers from back when them old times seemed new. I reflected on old Hank. He could hang on a scooter just like he was meant to do nothing but ride. And I remembered the big Frenchman. He wasn't no good at it at all, and he finally had to put it aside. And I recalled Fast Eddie rollin' out to meet us on the highway between Chinese Camp and Big Oak Flat. I had memories of how me and Zaff, we beat the heat and the cold concrete. Hell, we beat the odds a time or two. And how me and the Mexican Bandit had picked each other up after a fatal fall.

I reminisced about riding to the far left coast with Michael one year, and then back east with him a few years later. That second time, that ride east, that was during the Drought of 1988. The pavement on some of the roads in the Dakotas was buckling and erupting like little asphalt volcanoes. Damn sun got around behind us and into our mirrors and burned our arms up like meat.

And there were memories of Clarkie, who had survived the army and Woodstock and that damn Yamaha with me, and taking the Blue Nose Ferry from Bar Harbor, Maine to Yarmouth, Nova Scotia with him as our bikes swung gently below deck in rope harnesses. Then we rode up the east side of the Bay of Fundy and all around the Maritimes.

And I also recalled how me and Captain Zero had rode along this river, on this road, from New Orleans on up to Natchez long ago on the beginning of what became The Perfect Ride. I thought about running with Scotty on through the Rockies and the Smokies and in the Ozarks some too. As I remember it, we did it for the view. I recalled how we would all saddle up and just get to it for no other reason than just to be doin' it.

Before this ride was done, I even remembered coming back in off the road in my youth and having my Grandfather, the intrepid traveler, insist upon hearing where I had been to, what I had seen. He'd want to know all about the places and sights and names, and about my highway machine. I finally figured out he was doing that, at least in part, so I would review and remember it all better my ownself.

My Grammaw used to do the same thing. Once, when I mentioned being down around Okracoke and The Outer Banks, she taught me that Virginia Dare was the first child born of English settlers in the American colonies. And she tested me, as she was prone to do, on that historic fact several times afterward.

For several hundred miles and several many hours, I reflected and pondered and analyzed. I developed a highly increased understanding of how motorcycles have defined and fulfilled me, made my life better, made me a better man. I was afraid to stop for gas or a drink of water for fear I would break the spell. I was concerned that if I stopped, I would lose the charm and be unable to recall and savor these memories. I hit my stride, rode slow and easy to maintain the enchantment.

And I was also able to clearly recollect particular women, ex-wives and stray girls who had been up behind me out along the way. I remembered Katsy burning herself real bad on a muffler, and I had memories of Lizabeth's wonder at seeing the Atlantic Ocean the first time, and recollections of Nancy's skepticism upon initially seeing the Rocky Mountains.

I recalled a woman named Kathy, who tried hard enough to almost understand. And then I thought about a girl called Jane, who knew what she was doing, and another one named Nan, who actually understood what I was doing. And I remembered Judy, who knew what everyone was doing. And I thought about Susan who kept the scooter upright for me after I had killed a huge groundhog and harmed myself with it. And it took me awhile to think of her name, but I finally remembered another woman, she was called Nora. She was the kind of woman men get killed over, but she didn't have a clue about any of it. And for a minute, I thought about a girl named Mary, and how I'd trade my place on the Lost Highway to get her up behind me again.

I rode upriver through the flat fertile fields of the upper delta remembering the way the snow looked on the Northern Cascade Mountains, and the sound of the Pacific Ocean surf down along the Mexican line and on the Olympic Peninsula. And I remembered distinctly the time the sun dropped down a dime slot in the western clouds up in Idaho.

I rode past cotton and rice and recalled Los Angeles smog and San Francisco fog and Seattle rain and the lights of New Orleans. I dredged up long lost memories of a day I rode around Chicago when the light rain was evaporating at about eye-level before it hit the ground. And I thought about another time, in West Virginia down along the Cheat, when the rain drops were bouncing back up eye-high off the pavement.

The muddy river beside me carried tons of silt down to the Gulf, and I remembered an ice storm in Kentucky, and Kansas in the mud, and the time when three of us came east through Big Thompson Canyon in The Medicine Mountains in the summer after the killer flash flood. I recalled riding out along Cripple Creek, and the time we spent an afternoon playing hide and seek with the Texas Highway Heat. I thought of the McClure Pass Detour when the North Fork of the Gunnison covered the road. And I remembered a time up in the mountains above Truckee when we all just damn near froze.

A breeze came up off The River, and somehow it put me in mind of Thunder Bay and the way the sun went down in Monterey. I remembered passing through Durango, Deadwood, Dodge and Abilene. I thought about the Alamo and Carson City and the streets of Laredo and that corral in Tombstone and a few other places in between. I somehow managed to remember times so long ago that I was still a kid and too young to care.

A man on horseback was going the other way, downriver. We smiled and nodded at one another as we passed by. That caused me to recall some other longriders I have rode with. I shared the road with Hickock and Bill Cody, Doc Holliday and all the Earps, Kit Carson and Jim Bridger, Chief Joseph and Geronimo's ghost. I remembered riding with eagles in the air and with whales out along the coast. And some of the miles involved Daniel Boone and Davey Crockett and old Narvaez, too. I blazed a few trails with Lewis and Clark, and I traveled awhile with Coronado and DeSoto, with LaSalle and Marquette. And I once rode awhile with William Bonney and some with Frank and Jesse James. I recalled some others I have ridden with. I remembered them each one by name.

I had memories of the Chisholm Trail and the Spanish Trace and the Cumberland Gap and the Wilderness Road and the Llano Estacado and the Northwest Passage.

Once I did some time and miles with Coleman Younger and his brothers, and some with the Daltons, too. I recalled the Pony Express and how I rode with Osceola along the Trail of Tears. And people wonder why old riders are so few. I remembered a time I rode through a hurricane with one of the Legendary Highway Witches. The tempest was named Erin. The witch was called Carol. We came out the other side of the storm upright and stone righteous into clear blue skies and a beautiful day. She told me that the sky is the color of dreams gone bad.

Visions of the Cape Breton Highlands and that cold dark sea they rise out of came to me. Memories of riding along the Columbia inland to Grand Coulee Dam and riding beside the Trinity inland to The Avenue of the Giants and riding back along the St. Lawrence to the big lakes.

It was in motion that I remembered the very best times I have had in this life.

I thought about how the desert blooms in the Spring and how the hardwood hills come to color in the Fall. And I remembered a time in the east of Kansas one dark night when about a dozen huge John Deere combines harvesting wheat all crested a hill beside me at the same time. The headlights nearly blinded me. Their sudden appearance damn near scared me to death. And that caused me to think about another dark night, running east on Highway 2 in west Massachusetts along the Deerfield River. There is a tight hairpin curve on that road that they don't really warn you about very well. I damn near lost it all. Curve hooks to the right when you are going east.

My face damn near cramped up from all the smiling as I remembered specific full moons I have ridden under, and the colors of the water under the Seven Mile Bridge, and Mount Shasta with the sunlight on the snow. I thought about the east shore of the Chesapeake and the east shore of Lake Superior and the coast of Texas. I thought about Organ Pipe and the desert sky at night and about the time I saw the Northern Lights, real close.

Even after I stopped in Onward to get some gas and coffee, I was able to continue my reverie. I recalled other rivers and other rides along this one. I remembered rides up and down both shorelines, and rides along and between both coasts, rides across and beside this river and others, the Ohio, the Feather, the Gila, the Walker, the Snake, the Columbia, the Monongahela, the Pecos, the Tombigbee, the Russian, the Trinity, and along the Brave River of the Borderline.

A railroad train went by beside me awhile. The engineer waved and blew his whistle long and loud. And that touched off memories of other trains. I remembered riding beside the Santa Fe, the Orange Blossom, and the Wabash Cannonball. And I thought about running along with the Silverton, the Rock Island, beside the Seaboard Line, and I remembered The Hummingbird's call. Then I had memories of the Union Pacific and the Conrail Line and where the old L & N used to run, and how I've about memorized that Chessie cat. I remembered riding the grade from Lynchburg down to Danville. And then back up it, just in case.

Even when I got shut down for about an hour for road repairs in

Panther Burn, I didn't lose my concentration. I recollected a run from thirty years back across southeast Arizona one real dark summer night. The smelter fires from the mines threw crazy shadows and made it seem like a ride through the outskirts of Hell.

I was somehow able to isolate and reflect upon specific years and particular rides along individual portions of and places on The Blue Ridge and The Natchez Trace, in Rocky Mountain Park, and Big Bend. I remembered coming into Miami, late at night, the back way from Lake Okeechobee that brings you in past the airport and along Calle Ocho where you can get a quick espresso coffee at a sidewalk stand. This time, a small group of heavily armed Cuban youth surrounded my scooter as I was having my pop of espresso. They were impressed by the Michigan license plate and the odometer numbers.

When I pushed the water chaser back, one of them, their leader I presumed, he smiled at me, raised his fist in a salute, called me 'Hombre,' and led his associates off into the night. I have always wondered what would have happened if I had drank the damn water.

And I recalled dawn on Jekyll Island and sundown in Stinson Beach. Memories of former bikes and old highway brothers and old scootershops and highways along the way just kept coming. Memories about riding around Lake Winnebago and Lake Superior and Lake Huron and Lake Michigan and Lake Tahoe and Lake Okeechobee. Remembrances of two shores of The Great Salt Lake and all around Lake Champlain. Memories of Mendocino and St. Augustine and Pismo Beach and The Isle of Palms flooded over me.

That touched off memories of waterfalls. I remembered my awe at seeing Niagara, the beauty of Bridalveil, the majesty of Looking Glass, the size of International, the cold mist from the falls at the Upper Tahquamenon. And I remembered other waterfalls, most of them without names, that I have stopped to admire. I continued with memories of thousand mile days in the sunshine and moonlight, and a few hundred mile days in the rain. Recollections of waitresses and mechanics and motel inn keepers and other riders from back down the line.

Like I said, I stretched this day out about as long and far as I could. But eventually I had to shut it down in Greenville for the night. I rode down by The River and just sat there watching the water run south for awhile before it got dark. Guess I just wanted to make sure it was still running right. But the day was done, and so were the memories.

8 - MORE WIND, NICHE MARKETS,
AND RECONSTRUCTED RIDES

Worst wind I was ever in my whole life was on U.S. 26 someplace between Wyoming and Ogallala, Nebraska, down out along the Platte. There was whitecaps in the ditches, and everything else was laying flat. Including me and my scooter before it was over. This is one of them stories that you are too embarrassed to tell about until a few years have passed.

The nice lady at the motel desk early that morning in Sheridan told me not to go out in that wind. She explained it was going to get worse and told me they were already talking about closing down the interstate highways. She pointed out that there were no birds in the air, no trucks on the road, and even the local prairie dogs were remaining subterranean that morning.

And I said something stupid, like about how I have ridden in blizzards, and I have ridden in rain. I've rode through tornados and out among hurricanes. Might have mentioned typhoons and cyclones. Thanked her for her concern, and then I rode out south on I-25 before that interstate shutdown thing she warned me of.

Sometime later, the sweet people at the bar I stopped at in Dwyer so I could put on more clothes, including long underwear, they too, encouraged me to remain with them and not go out into the vicious wind again. A beer truck driver who was there told me that the temperature was dropping as the wind increased, said it was ten degrees colder than it had been a couple hours ago. He mentioned something about air-borne chickens to the north. And these folks confirmed that the interstates had, indeed and officially, been closed.

The wind was steady at around sixty miles an hour, gusting to over a hundred. There is nothing to break the wind in this part of Wyoming and Nebraska. You can see for about three days in every direction it's so damn flat. Only by now there was enough dust and debris in the air to limit vision. The people in the bar wouldn't let me pay for my coffee, and they all stood in the window watching as I saddled up and got gone. I noticed the window steaming up and figured the beer driver was right about it getting colder.

And, like an idiot, I pressed on east away from the wind on toward Torrington. I used to know a woman taught at the college there in Torrington. She said her whole damn classroom was full of cowboy hats and kids named Clete and Hoss and Hoot. So I stopped there for breakfast.

And then the waitress at the place just outside of Torrington, Janet May Matilda Jean, she damn near begged me to set and drink coffee with the dozen truckers who had quit for the day. A couple of the drivers joined her in beseeching me to stay. The wind was howling, and my bike was wobbling and shaking on the center stand even in the lee of the restaurant. They pointed out that it was an especially poor day for passin' through.

But, as you already know, I ain't real bright, and I went back out into it. As my Grandfather, the broncbuster, once told me—We wouldn't ride them any different if we had the chance to. He used to tell me to Hang and Rattle, too. So off I went again, out into the malicious wind and the swirling dust. The river, off to my right side, looked angry and torn apart in the wind that was blowing the water downstream harder than normal.

About an hour later I came up a rise to a stop sign. I damn near couldn't stop, as the wicked wind was at my back. But I got into first gear and made the right turn. And the sideways wind nearly tore my glasses off my face. I've had this happen before, and I wasn't much interested in doing it again, so I grabbed them up against my face. When I got them back on my nose, I took my hand away. That's when the wind tore my helmet off. The strap, as it sang through the jump rings, made an awful noise in my left ear. As I turned to see which part of Iowa the helmet was headed for, I almost lost my glasses again. I did manage to poke myself in the eye pretty hard.

I made a U-turn, no mean feat in all that wind, and rode back to about where I thought the helmet had gone. The road was built up on a tall mound of dirt, in order to get more wind, I guess. Maybe it was so they would have someplace to push the snow in winter. This was one of the few times a tunnel would have been welcome. There were no birds in that air, not a cow standing in a field. And I had not seen a prairie dog all day. At the bottom of the mound of dirt the road was on, there were four strands of barbed wire running from horizon to horizon.

I parked my scooter, leaned it into the wind, and headed down the embankment, probably twenty yards, hoping my helmet was jammed under the bottom wire. It was almost eerily serene and quiet on the lee side of that mound of dirt.

As I reached the bottom of the grade, I heard a noise. I don't know how, but I knew what it was. It was the sound of the wind blowing my bike over. I turned to watch it come down the grade at me, and, for reasons that no one but scootertrash would begin to understand, I ran uphill toward it to catch it. I caught it. Then me and the bike wound up at the bottom of the grade together. I remained underneath it to break its fall.

It took me about fifteen minutes to find my helmet. It had blown much farther than I had imagined. It took most of an hour to get the bike out of the bottom of the slope and back up on to the road. I was fighting the grade, the loose dirt, gravity, and eighty-mile-an-hour winds. But I finally muscled it back up to the road. It involved laying across the seat, with my feet on the down-slope side, and easing it along in second gear at a long angle up the grade. Then I leaned against it into the wind for a long time while I caught my breath.

The wind got worse between there and Ogallala. Some of the harder gusts were a lot like being slapped sideways. That was where I tried to get on I-80. Nope, the interstates were all closed, and according to the state cop blocking the entrance, I was a stone retard. He started out, "Tiger, you dumb bastard." I kept at it on the major two-lanes toward North Platte. The wind increased.

I found myself thinking of my Grandfather, the meteorologist, who had once explained that the wind wails for what might have been. There was a whole lifetime of busted fantasies in this wind.

Sometime later, I stopped in North Platte, mostly to get out of the gale for a minute, but I needed gas, too. Turned out I had leaked a little while my scooter was sliding downhill. Before gassing up, I got the bike parked up against the building so it would not fall over, and I did a quick duct tape repair on the mirror that had taken the brunt of the fall down the slope. Then I got some gas and went to pay for it and stand inside out of the wind a minute. Enough wind in your helmet will drive you stone mad. There was a real nice kid running the place. He suggested it would be prudent to seek a motel there in North Platte and wait a couple days until the wind calmed down.

Instead of taking his sound advice, I made him turn on the TV, and we watched the Weather Channel together awhile. The only way out of this mess was south. So that's where I went. First I talked the lad out of some distilled water and topped off my battery while I had the lee side of the building to work in. Turns out gas wasn't the only liquid I had leaked.

Then I hit it hard down U.S. 83, The Yellow Brick Road, down into Kansas. Yeah, that seemed surrealistic to me at the time, too. But this wasn't my first eastbound nightmare, so I kept at it. Looked for Toto, in vain.

The problem, besides that surreal feature, was twofold. First of all, the wind was blowing from the west and some from the north. It had been at my back, either as a tailwind or at a quarter, all day. When I turned south, it came at me sideways. And it increased and blew harder.

It blew so hard and put so much dust in the air that I honestly could not see past my high beam. Oncoming local traffic, most of it going lots faster than I thought judicious, was literally on me way before I could even see their headlights. And the wind was doing its damndest to blow me over into that lane. This was easily the worst wind I have been in since that time up in Montana when I wore the chrome off a crash bar leaning into the gale. Long haul truckers had escorted me off the road and into a bar that time.

Somewhere between McCook, Nebraska and the Kansas line, the wind began to slack off a little, and it began to get warmer. That was when my gas line ruptured. And damned if it didn't happen as I was riding past a John Deere dealership. I parked in the lee of the building, and by the time I had my gas hose replaced, the wind had abated even more. By the time I got to Kansas, I had to peel my leather off. By the time I got to I-70 to head east it was close to a hundred degrees, and I sort of missed the wind.

The part about running uphill to catch my bike reminded me of another such incident, many years ago. And, like the previous tale, I am sure it ain't in that first book. Although it should have been.

This one happened down in Coconut Grove. Friend of mine there, an old Honda rider, offered me shelter for my ride while I took off to Bimini. He had a sort of elevated shed in his yard. You had to ride the bike up a short ramp to get into it. So I did. Left my scooter there beside his Honda in the shed and headed for the Bahamas.

I was gone awhile, probably a month or two. Long enough for a big heavy branch from a nearby tree to grow heavy with fruit, droop down and stretch across the top of the doorway to my side of the shed. I believe I was told it was a loquat tree. As I was backing my bike down through the doorway and onto the ramp, it became apparent that this new limb was going to tear my windshield off. There wasn't time to stop the bike, so I quickly reached out and jammed my hand between the limb and the windshield. Didn't even think about it, wasn't one of them deciding things.

Saved the windshield. But I broke two fingers and bled all over everything and lost the nails on one finger and my thumb. And again, only scootertrash will understand and appreciate that story.

One June I got rained on most of the way east across Iowa and on into Wisconsin. I mean I got into some real poor riding weather out there. The Buffalo River was raging hard and so was the sky above it. The English was a flood. There was deep water in most of the cornfields, and mud became an element like rain and thunder and dark. I finally crossed east across the Mississippi at Dubuque in the rain. The River was boiling muddy below me. Then I checked the TV weather radar at the Welcome Center there near Hazel Green. My best, hell my only move, was to head for the ferry boat at Manitowoc and beat it east across Lake Michigan in hopes of getting out ahead of the weather.

To make a real long story sort of brief, it cost me sixty-six American dollars to damn near freeze to death while surrounded by dozens of inconsiderate, screaming, pre-socialized children. There ought to be some kind of law preventing such children from being taken out in public. Or maybe they could only allow them out during specific hours or alternate days. If an adult was to make that much noise, they would surely put you in jail.

And then it cost me another dollar and a half for a cup of coffee. But the little coffee counter girl, Jennifer Jillian Julia Joy, told me I could come back and get a refill for free. I didn't bother. I did piss off a couple deckhands when I went back down to my bike to fire up my propane stove and make myself a pot of decent coffee. But I gave them each a cup, and we became great friends before the voyage was over.

There were two incidents that almost made up for the expensive boat ride. The first was when we boarded the ferryboat there in Wisconsin. A guy and his old lady on a brand new multi-thousand dollar Harley was the only other motorcycle involved. They were wearing more Harley leather and other after-industry apparel than my bike was worth. Motorclothing. They had ridden all the way up from Chicago, and the guy was bragging about it to me when his lady walked behind my ride and saw my Florida plate. He wasn't even embarrassed, much less ashamed. And I don't think the son of a bitch even thanked me when I helped him get his hog parked and strapped down in the boat. I believe he was a lawyer.

The second good thing was that, in spite of it being really cold, the boat ride got me out ahead of the storm front a little. When we docked in Ludington, it was obvious to those of us with bad arthritis that the storms were imminent. And I rolled into the first non-chain motel I saw. Lady running the place was out front amidst an untidy pile of lumber and tools. I shut my ride down and inquired about a room, and after a brief conversation, we struck a twenty-four dollar deal, cash money-no receipt, while I was still sitting on my bike. Then I asked my hostess if it would be OK with her if I pulled up under the overhang to protect my ride from the storm.

She looked up at a basically clear sky, and asked, "What storm?" So I told her it would be upon us soon after dark, and I suspected it would be massive in its intensity. I held up my arthritic hands of death to show her my source of information. She frowned and inquired about how sure was I, and I told her I would bet her the price of the room, double or nothing, that by an hour after dark she would wish her new lumber and electric tools were under cover.

She looked at me like she didn't think I had forty-eight dollars and then countered by offering me the room for half if I would help her put the lumber and tools and all up. I told her I had a pile of dirty clothes to take to a laundromat, and if she had a washing machine and dryer and would let me wash my clothes there, that she had a deal.

Her husband had heard this last part, and he walked out and looked up and didn't believe me about the rain, and took my bet. The storm came in off the lake just at full dark. It was intense, really serious lightning and near deafening thunder and about two or so inches of rain in the first hour.

We had all their stuff put up, I got my laundry done, and the husband brought me a plate of chicken and biscuits later that evening. The rain was past by daybreak, and I rode north up the Lake Michigan shoreline in one of those beautiful, Northern, post-storm mornings. The whole world looked freshly washed and clean.

These are the days that make the ones like the day before worth it. There is a reverence comes to the highway in the morning sometimes. If you do it right, you can get out there by yourself, be the first one. It's so quiet sometimes you can hear your tires heat up on the cold concrete and listen to your exhaust smoke softly caress the road.

And once in awhile, you get to it like this in the evening, just before you and the sun quit for the day. You find an elevated place with a view and a perspective, and watch the sun fade on down as you drink the last of the tepid coffee in your Thermos. Gives you a quiet moment to reflect upon the day and the miles. Permits you to appreciate some of the passin' through.

Then, if you're lucky, you locate some gas and a cheap motel and a nearby restaurant. If you're real lucky, you find a pretty waitress and watch her walk around while the locals all sit and frown at you while you eat.

Once upon a recent summertime, I reconstructed a ride from twenty-five years ago. That first one, that time back in days of yore, that one was just dumb luck. We just sort of came upon it that time, trying to work our way east to The Blue Ridge. This time I knew how. Hell, this time I even knew when and rode it of a Sunday.

What you do is you catch State Highway 15 east out of Lexington, Kentucky. You ride beside a superslab, I believe it's 402, and you are real glad you ain't on it because Highway 15 is empty and full of easy curves and short hills, another one of those graceful roads.

At a town called Campton, I stopped and asked the boys at the gas station which way to go. They explained how the road breaks south into serious foothills. They were right, it was beautiful and some of the finest two-lane running I know of. You can't go real fast, but that's good because you can smell the Sunday chicken as you ride by the farmhouses. You can smell the wildwood flowers. You're going slow enough to wave back at the people on their front porches.

At Hazard, Highway 15 sort of ends. So I caught 421 through the Daniel Boone National Forest and on into Harlan and then on east to Virginia. It was my intention to cap the perfect day off with the perfect end, to get on The Blue Ridge Parkway, and ride it south to someplace to spend the night.

But first, I rode some more really spectacular two-lanes from the Virginia line south to eventually Boone, North Carolina, where I got on The Parkway. Boone was full of bikes. I mean full. That should have tipped me off, but I figured this was of a Sunday, and I was in a hurry to get on The Parkway. Yeah, I ignored all the omens and portents.

The Parkway was wall to wall scooters. It was weird. I don't think I saw a vehicle for the first ten miles. Many of the bikes were giant overdressed highway machines of various and assorted brands and models. I mean some of them were tricked out with electric fringe and neon lights, a bar-b-que pit in one saddlebag and a swimming pool in the other. Whole bunch of sidecars and even more trailers. Everyone seemed to be riding double. Many of them had out of state plates. And most of these riders weren't worth a damn at riding a narrow serpentine mountain road. There were some groups of them seemed to think it should be done in formation. Told you it was weird.

Interspersed among these overdressed wide body scooters, there were all manner of Ninja racing rice rockets. And these people were doing their very best to blow the big old heavy clumsy highly decorated road bikes off the pavement. It wasn't pretty.

These people had all come up there to be seen by one another, not to ride among the heights. They had less understanding of the passin' through than did the forest's trees there on the mountains.

Finally catching on, sort of, I bailed off at the first inhabited exit and looked for a motel. The third-worlder motel clerk at the second motel told me the same thing as the first one. They wanted eighty-eight dollars for a twenty dollar motel room.

As I wandered, confused and forlorn, back into the parking lot, it finally all began to make sense, sort of. The whole damn lot was jammed to gridlock with new pickup trucks and vans with bike trailers. Lots of out of state plates. A festival. So I finally found a local cop to ask. They were out in force, too.

He laughed hard and commenced, "Tiger, you dumb bastard." Told me I had blundered into the Honda Hoot. There were tens of thousands of bikes and probably that many trucks with trailers that had brought them there. The festivity stretched from above Boone to below Asheville. The participants, they called themselves Hooters. I eventually managed to engage the by now way too mirthful cop in enough conversation to find out that the thing for me to do was head west as far hard and fast as I could. He was glad to have one of us just passin' through anyway.

I wound up in Newport, Tennessee, and even then it wasn't easy. The first place, the one by the interstate there, was jammed with trucks and trailers and overdressed bikes. But I went ahead on in and asked the English-speaking desk clerk how much farther I was going to have to go to get out of it all. He smiled and made a phone call to a motel across town. Told them to hold a room for me. It was too expensive, and it was Iranian-owned and operated, but they turned out to be real nice folks who made sure I got a place to put my cycle under cover and suggested a pretty good nearby restaurant for supper.

I will address festivities of this nature, Bike Week, Sturgis, et. al., derisively, and in some detail, on a later page.

9 - OLD UNRECONSTRUCTED RIDERS, AND OLD ROADS

I pay cash as I go. My Grandfather, the economist, saw his first credit card sometime in the middle 1960s. I recall that because it was the first time I had ever seen one, too. The Old Man examined it thoroughly, discussed it with my aunt, the owner of the new credit card, at some length. Then he said, "Well, hell, it ain't nothin' but the company store again, is it?"

So I pay cash as I go. I used to have a credit card. I carried it on me like I used to carry a rubber in my wallet when I was thirteen. Only the damn plastic charge card from hell got far less use. Similarly I don't have a checking account, a business card, a debit card, an ATM card, a calling card, or anything else other than cash money. This appalls and disgusts many people, especially young people. But then most of what I do and what I am horrifies and offends somebody.

In no way is any of this meant to encourage anyone to follow my lead or my fiscal example or imitate my behavior, or anything else other than laugh some. This is not a missionary rant. Girl explained this one to me long ago. She said—You weren't made to lead or follow either one. Told me I was born to be lonesome.

Anyway, I think credit, the very concept of having and using things you haven't paid for, is illogical. The idea of spending money you ain't made yet is just disturbing. The notion of being able to spend money faster and easier than you made it goes right on into foolish.

But, I digress. Back to some scooterstories. I live on a real crowded sandbar. And, as most sandbars tend to be, Florida is pretty flat. There are no mountain roads or coastal cliff highways to ride, but there are a couple hills up north of my house. The Pasco-Hernando Alps. I suspect some are as high as two hundred feet above sea level.

And, if you keep looking hard, there are some pretty neat roads through them. Back before The Freeze of 1984, there was one stretch that ran for about twenty or thirty miles. There were some easy curves, and some easier hills, and some places to run hard. And, if you did it in the Spring, you could see and smell grapefruit blossoms the whole time.

The profusion of white flowers would about tear your eyes out, and the aroma of the blooms would near pull you out of the saddle.

The Freeze took the citrus, and the developers took the land and made horrible little subdivisions and plaza malls and such out of it. The developments took the road. Now it's full of traffic and stop signs and convenience stores. Much the same can be said of most of America.

But there are a few classic old highways left in the country. U.S. Highway 27 runs north from Miami on up to eventually Michigan. Biggest place it goes through in Florida is Ocala. There is some fine scenery along the way. And, if you look for them, there are some interesting roadside attractions and good places to stop and eat. And anytime you can get through Florida and avoid Orlando and The Black Rat, you're ahead.

Then U.S. 27 goes north some more through west Georgia and on up to Chattanooga. There are some real pretty sections to this part, too. Along the way it runs through Columbus, but there's a way to avoid that. And even in the less scenic portions, you can feel that this old road has some character and history to it.

The next portion, above Chattanooga is a four lane mess. But after that, it clears out pretty good, and some of it real pretty, all the way up to Lexington, Kentucky, where it goes to four lanes again. But there are lots of ways around this. Same deal in Cincinnati, but you got to cross that river somehow. Then U.S. 27 cuts an angle over into Indiana and on up to Fort Wayne, where they combine it with I-69 up to Lansing where it becomes four lanes. Later on, up above Lake Higgins, they hook it up with I-75.

But there are some fine alternatives, like the shoreline of Lake Michigan and the shoreline of Lake Huron. And in the interior there is Michigan 37. And around The Thumb of the state, Highway 25 makes for a real fine ride.

These cross-country roads are lots more fun than interstate highways. They aren't everything Old U.S. Route 66 used to be, but you can find things on these roads that you don't on expressways. You won't make good time, but you will encounter historic sites and old stores in little towns that will take you back to your childhood. You'll eat better, too. You might not get the food as fast, but it will be better food. And friendlier service.

If you want to do an east to west, coast-to-coast run some to the south, try U.S. 82. You ride west out of Brunswick, Georgia. Try to get a bowl of Brunswick stew before you leave town. And then be careful through Waycross because some of the local police still have a 1950s speed trap mentality. You might want to stop in Tifton and check out the Georgia Agrirama there. Then you cross the Chattahoochee River into Eufala, Alabama. U.S. 82 runs through Montgomery, which is full of history and Hank Williams' grave.

There is a portion of 82 in east Mississippi where it is a divided four lane, but not for far or long. Then you cross across the Natchez Trace around a place called Mathison. After that, you can pay tribute to B.B. King in Indianola before you cross The Mississippi River at Greenville. That area in east Arkansas there where 82 runs is real pretty and pretty interesting. It runs across the bottom end of Arkansas all the way to Texarkana, mostly through the pine forests and past the paper mills.

I just ran U.S. 82 across east Texas nearly all the way to Amarillo last summer. It's a pretty ride, and I found the rural folks out there to be among the nicest in the nation. The problem is that U.S. 82 kind of ends there in mid-Panhandle and is taken up by I-40. A good alternative is to drop south and keep running west on U.S. 60. Some fine burritos out there on U.S. 60.

There is, or at least there used to be, a scenic turn out or something such as that out on U.S. 50 around Salida, Colorado, someplace on the banks of the Arkansas River. Actually I think it was more a big, flat, high spot that sort of evolved into a place to pull over and look east and west than an official rest area. There are no facilities. I've not been through there in a long time, so maybe it has become condominiums and strip malls. Most everything else has.

But there is a view of the majestic Rocky Mountains off to the west that will just make you want to stop and take pictures. And you can orient yourself and look east downriver just nearly all the way to the melon fields. You can see just damn near every direction for about a half a day.

Last time I was through there, the weather to the west was dark and threatening. Lightning tore through the purple gloom that covered the mountains. The wind was from that direction, and you could smell the rain off that way. To the east, it was clear and cloudless. The sun shone warm on the flat country beyond the foothills.

About forty bikers were piled up in there, in that half acre flat spot beside Highway 50. Those headed west were getting into their rain gear, those going east were removing wet rainsuits. I was, of course, westbound. It looked like some kind of weird, outdoor costume change at a highway sideshow. I recall some of us laughed at one another.

U.S. Highway 50 is a fine and noble road. It is the old Lincoln Highway, a pretty famous road, like Route 66. These old highways used to be The Roads for cross-country travel. Besides often being pretty empty and having some character and history, they run through some real old places. Little towns where you need to stop and mail a post card at the local post office and maybe get some gas.

Much of U.S. 50 goes through scenic country. It runs from the top end of the Chesapeake Bay Bridge Tunnel on east into and then through D.C. and eventually up into the scenic mountains of Virginia and West Virginia. This portion of the highway is real pretty, lots of fun to ride.

Last time I was on it, it rained, and I sought cover under the overhang on the side of a giant discount drug store of some kind. Think it was around Front Royal or Winchester. I hadn't been there two minutes, and the assistant manager came out the door and toward me. It was raining hard, and I didn't want to argue or go back out into the weather either one.

But damned if the guy hadn't come out to see if I needed help or anything. I thanked him and told him no, all I was lookin' to get was dry. But a few minutes later he brought me a cup of coffee and stood there and talked with me awhile. Turned out his daddy rode a Harley.

Highway 50 cuts across a pretty portion of West Virginia, the west end of Maryland, and then crosses the Ohio River at a toll bridge at Belpre. Then it goes across Ohio, and some of it, around Chillicothe, is pretty scenic. Then it eventually runs though Cincinnati, and that ain't pretty or fun either one. Few cities are. But at least you can stay to the north and avoid crossing the Ohio River again.

Then Highway 50 continues across Kentucky, and Indiana, and Illinois, through some real pretty rural parts of all three of those states, and then on across The River and into and through St. Louis. There is no good way to get through St. Louis. I've done it east and west-bound, from north to south, and vice versa. I've even tried to sneak through on surface streets. I've done it on motorcycles, and in pickup trucks, and once in a nasty under-powered Ryder rent-a-damn-diesel. I've even tried to sneak through at night.

Much of St. Louis, but especially the roads and the infrastructure generally, is under constant repair. The rest of it is growing and being developed. I can't recall ever getting all the way through St. Louis without being held up by a wreck or a construction mess. And I can't remember ever going through there without getting my kidneys beat and my teeth rattled.

But this wasn't about St. Louis. It was about Highway 50. After St. Louis, that road kind of parallels I-70 across Missouri to Kansas City. Parts of it are real pretty. Then they fuck it up, and 50 and I-35 are the same four-lane nightmare from K.C. down to Emporia. U.S. 56 is a good alternative. But then you can get loose of it and head on west to Newton and Dodge City and on into Colorado. They have some real serious tourist stuff in Dodge City. Kansas, while having some magnificently attractive portions, is not known for its scenic beauty. Wheat. But there are some seriously pretty parts to this ride on this road. Incidentally, U.S. 36, which runs east-west across the top of the state, has some truly beautiful segments.

Anyway, they hook U.S. 50 up to Interstate 70 over beyond Grand Junction, and the roads stay combined, along with U.S. 6, across about half of Utah over to Salina. Then 50 runs to Ely, Nevada and on to Carson City. The whole of that portion is just scenic as can be. And then the highway continues through some more real pretty country and runs down some of the east shore of Lake Tahoe and on into Sacramento. I guess it quits there. Guess it has to someplace. But mile for mile, it's one of the best roads and best rides I know of.

There is a magnificent view, this one of Mobile Bay, from a rest area on the east side of the Bay where U.S. 98, U.S. 90, and I-10 all come together. U.S. 98 is another real fine ride. It begins down south of Palm Beach. Runs west off A1A. Then it sort of cuts across most of the peninsula of Florida up to the panhandle where it runs along the Gulf of Mexico all the way to Mobile.

Then it goes north to Hattiesburg, Mississippi. I don't know why. Actually it's kind of a pretty run north, but when you get there, you're in Hattiesburg. But then you can ride west on it across some beautiful country and on in to Natchez, where the road ends.

The part along the Gulf is the best part of this road. If you can catch it when the traffic is light, and you're not working hard to stay alive, you get to behold some things. There are some of the most beautiful beaches in America along this highway. So you get to see the regular beach stuff, water and waves and boats and underage bikinis and an occasional jumping fish. There are also some wonderful sand dunes and barrier islands toward the west end of the panhandle.

Me and Captain Zero once spent a couple hours setting out a rainstorm on this highway someplace around Mexico Beach. We found some shelter and watched the dolphins put on a show in the warm Gulf waters. And some of the finest seafood in the entire Free World is in this area and along this road.

In the center of the state of Florida, where U.S. 98 sort of forms the southern boundary of The Green Swamp, I've seen turkey and alligators and deer and bear along this road. Saw an otter once, too. He scurried out of a cypress head that was being logged off and ran right under the semi-truck running ahead of me.

The Green Swamp is a hell of a place. Five major rivers rise in The Green Swamp. Osceola took his people into The Green Swamp and hid for months undetected. I was once bad lost in The Green Swamp. And the south end of 98 runs along the east shore of Lake Okeechobee for thirty miles or so. You have to cut west on a local road to see the lake. The rim ditch and levee are in the way of such a view from the highway. The sugar fields stretch for miles around you.

The problem with this road up north in the Panhandle is that it runs through The Redneck Riviera there along Panama City and Mexico Beach and on into Pensacola. That stretch, during the tourist season, is like a huge amusement park with a two-lane, traffic-jammed highway and an ocean. I've come through there in mid-summer and gone for miles without ever taking my feet up off the ground. Fortunately, there is a way around it inland a little.

Yeah, them old roads, they're the best ones. You can run at your own pace without a semi-truck up your tailpipes and a minivan going twelve under in front of you. You can eat local, indigenous, non-franchise food. You can pull off into a rest area, or a scenic pull out, or a little picnic park, or a historic marker and make a pot of coffee and learn something. You can meet some local folks and find out something about that place. And if you need help, you're going to get it faster and better than anyplace else I've ever been.

10 - THE PERFECT JOB, MULTIPLE BREAK-DOWNS, AND WOMEN

Old friend of mine moved to Idaho in pursuit of work years ago. Had to leave his old lady and her kid here. When it came time for them to follow him and move west, talk turned to old truck drivers. And I wound up taking a huge load of household stuff to Pocatello in a Ryder Rent-a-Diesel. I cleverly put my cycle up in the front end of the load.

I will be brief about that truck: What a fucking pig!

But it was a fine trip west in spite of the equipment. Took most of six days. Took most of a couple days to load the damn thing. Little kids sure have a lot of stuff. And it turns out a full loaded truck and a car with a woman and a small child and another load in it travel way slower than a man alone on a motorcycle. They remained faithfully in my mirrors the whole time. And along the way, at rest areas and gas stations and scenic turnouts and truck stops and restaurants and motels, I told old highway stories to the woman and her girlchild.

Unloaded the load and my scooter and abandoned the truck in Pocatello, where I hope they shot it. Spent a couple days there. Then I headed outbound on my cycle. Did a few days in the local mountains, on up to the Craters of the Moon and on toward Salmon. Ran into some late snow up there in the mountains. I smelled it a mile or so before it hit me in my face. Took me a minute to recognize the odor, as I had not smelled snow in many years.

So, to escape the weather, I dropped south and east. I gave some thought to doing such a thing every summer. Drive a load someplace with my motorcycle on it, drop the load and the truck, and ride on home. The almost perfect job.

I came down out of Idaho and toward Salt Lake City. It was high summer, and I didn't see much point in getting involved in the traffic and recreating mess around Glacier or Yellowstone. Then I cut down and across Colorado below Denver. Anymore, Denver is one of them things, like Atlanta and L.A., that should be avoided if possible. Seems like I rode 64 and 13 and down to around Gunnison somehow.

I kept at it, mostly east down out of the mountains. Ran through Salida and Canon City and Pueblo and on to Rocky Ford on Highway 50. At Dodge City I dropped south some.

So anyway there I was, homebound. I came across Kansas, sideways, on Highway 54, a really fine road. It was up near a hundred that day, so I continued on some into the evening, across Missouri, just to enjoy the cool. Eventually I crossed The River at Caruthersville under a sky full of stars. The next day it was well over a hundred when I made the turn southeast on Highway 280 out of Birmingham in the hot afternoon, thinking of Gulf breezes and fireflies and how I would be home sometime that night.

That was when the bike quit. And I mean the rascal just stone quit running. No sputtering, no nothing. I grabbed a handful of clutch and looked for shade. There was some just down the way across the road in front of a house. So that's where I coasted to. Parked it, so to speak, at the end of the driveway out near the road under the live oak trees.

Then, helmet in hand, I walked toward the house. It was a pretty nice house, well kept yard and all. A young man with a baby infant child in his arms answered the door. There were another couple little bitty kids running around in the house. The air-conditioner was on full tilt, and I bet it was thirty-five degrees colder in the house than it was on the porch. I nearly swooned in the doorway.

But I recovered, and I introduced myself and apologized to the young man for bothering him and explained that I had just broke down a motorcycle. I gestured back toward the road.

He stepped out and shook my hand, told me his name. Man's name was Beau Davis. We called one another mister and sir. I asked if I might be allowed to use his shade to work on my scooter. And he assured me that I, indeed, could. Then he asked me if I would like to come inside, into the air-conditioning, and have some iced tea and maybe something to eat. He asked if there was anything he could do to help me. I thanked him, passed on the tea, and told him I would let him know if he could help.

He went back inside, and I went back to my broke down ride. It took me a little while to determine my problem was electric. The battery was done. I'd never had a battery go on me suddenly like that, but things electric baffle me generally, and I have come to expect mysterious phenomena of an electrical nature.

I pushed my bike up the driveway next to my host's truck, and then I went to the door and apologized for bothering him again and asked if I might be allowed to try to jumpstart my scooter. I gestured out toward his truck. He apologized to me for being unable to come help me because he was watching small but mobile children, but told me to help myself to his jumper cables and gave me the key to his truck.

I was able to start the bike off his battery, but it wouldn't take or hold the charge. So I figured it must be the battery was past dead. Sometimes I'm very clever with such diagnoses.

Anyway, I shut the truck down and returned the jumper cables. Then I made my way back to Mr. Davis' house, returned his truck keys, apologized for continuing to bother him, and asked if there was anything even remotely like a motorcycle shop around there. He laughed politely and insisted I come in and wash up and cool down and look through the local phone book while I had some iced tea.

The local phone book was more a pamphlet than a book, and the closest thing to a scooter shop was a farm implement dealership. I asked Beau if they sold little riding lawn mowers, and he said sure. But the problem was the place was ten miles off, and Beau couldn't take me because he was watching small children. He felt badly that he hadn't been able to solve my problem, so he called the place and told them to bring me a battery. And they did. Cost me twenty-two dollars, and I gave the kid who brought it out five bucks. And I still got the damn thing in my lawnmower.

The point of this is that I was really glad that I broke down in Alabama. People make fun of Alabama, but for manners and just plain nice, helpful people, I'll take the Heart of Dixie any day. My Grandfather, the lexicographer, knew this, and used to refer to Florida as Baja Alabama. There are places in the North where they'd have called the cops when I knocked on their door. There are some places in New England where they have.

Anyway, the damn lawnmower battery was just about a millimeter bigger than the ruined one, and I had to remove the whole entire bracket to get it in. But I did. Took about an hour. And when I finished, Mr. Davis came out on the porch and insisted that I come back in his house, wash up again, set a spell in the cool and have another cold drink. So I did.

I thanked the man for his kindness and hospitality and help. Gave him one of those little poetry tapes of mine. And then I got back to it. A hundred miles later, on the outskirts of Opelika, as the sun was dropping behind me, the bike quit again. Just like it had last time. This time there was no nearby shade.

There wasn't much other than a Motel 6 sign in the near distance. So that's where I began pushing. It was a long mile or two away. I had to push my ride up a pretty steep grade just as I got to the motel. At the peak of the grade, I paused briefly to catch my breath, leaned on my bike a minute, and then I climbed on and coasted downhill the last fifty yards into the parking lot.

That's when the applause began. The second floor balcony of the motel was literally festooned with happy people laughing and smiling and clapping as I rolled in. I realized they had been watching my progress up the road from their gallery.

Two other things struck me. All these cheerful people were black. And they were all very, very formally attired in some regal and elegant outfits. They continued to applaud, some stood in ovation, as I coasted to a stop. So I climbed off, put the side stand down, and bowed deeply. They cheered. And again I was glad I was broke down in Alabama.

I hollered up at one of them, asked him why the hell didn't four or five of the young and strong among them come and help the old boy push the damn thing. He laughed even harder and explained, (Tiger, you dumb bastard,) that they were all of them in their good clothes. More laughter ensued. Fortunately, I am used to being a source of such merriment, especially on the highway.

Me and my pardner, Tommy, once drove from Tampa, Florida to Belize, Central America, through Mexico, around the Gulf. And along the way, we amused an entire population of foreign speaking people. They'd take one look at us, say "Old Gringos," and then the laughter and merriment would begin. It got to where Tom thought we would surely be declared national treasures. But that's another book.

It was about then that the pretty Motel 6 desk clerk walked out of the office through the parking lot and up to me. She was also black, and she was smiling, too. Then she handed me the key to the room on the ground floor that I had coasted to a stop in front of. She smiled some more and told me to come pay her for it when I got settled and rested. As I was unloading my gear into my room, I analyzed my electrical situation and figured out it was a magneto or a circuit board or a rotor, or something else mysterious that I didn't understand and couldn't fix if I did.

That caused me to remember the time some years back when my headlight had quit working. Luckily, I was up north in Michigan where many of my relatives are. And, as I am the one they wonder and worry about, they always take good care of me. Anyway, that time, the damn headlight just kind of suddenly quit, not unlike what the whole bike had done this time in Alabama. So, I had found a place to get out of everyone's way and changed bulbs. Nope, that wasn't it. Just to make sure, I tried another light bulb. And now I was sure it was something I didn't understand.

Most states, anymore, insist that you turn your headlight on while in motion, whether it's dark or not. Most newer cycles have a built in automatic switch that turns the headlight on when the bike is turned on to make sure you comply with the law. I think all that is right up there with helmet laws for an un-American activity, but this seemed a poor time to protest.

My Uncle Keith, for whom I am named, lived nearby. Uncle Keith, being the second son of my Grandfather, the predicament resolver, knows some stuff. And when he doesn't know it, he can figure it out better than most anyone I know. Besides that, Aunt Doreen is a superb cook, and she always makes sure I get fed when I am around her. So that's where I headed.

The headlight switch is combined with the turn signal switch on the model bike I have. To make it all worse, the choke lever is situated in the same housing. And just to insure confusion, the damn horn switch is in the same mess. Yeah, now we got springs and cables and extra connections and potential disaster.

Uncle Keith, screwdriver in hand, grinned at me and announced that he had never been inside of such a thing before. It took him awhile, and he had to make a couple parts, but by the time Doreen had hot food on the table, I had a headlight. And he made sure I understood everything he had done in case I had to do it again. Gave me a couple backup parts. And people wonder why I ride North in the Summer.

I paused in my memories to smile and wish I had a headlight switch problem this time in Opelika. Then I wished my uncle was there to solve this problem. Then I began to get hungry and wished my aunt was there.

Some of the other motel guests, my previous audience, came by to offer me a cold beer and some conversation. I learned they were all Shriners and Eastern Stars and such as that in town for a big deal Shriner gala to-do. Now since this incident, I have been told there is no such thing as a black Shriner, especially in the South. My source, who is a some kind of poo-ba in the Masons, referred to these African-American folks as the "Prince Hall Lodge." But that might be a disparaging appellation. And I just wanted to get that all in before someone got bent out of shape by a careless detail. For all I know these folks might have been Mystic Knights of The Sea. Whoever they were, they were real nice to me.

During my chat with these people, I also discovered that it was Friday. I often lose track of such things on the road, and the point that it was Friday didn't really surprise or bother me. What did was the fact that it was the eve of the Fourth of July weekend, the Fourth falling of a Monday that year.

When my new friends went off to their festivity, I wandered to a nearby restaurant, where I began to study a map over supper. And again, the entire staff and clientele were black. And friendly. Word had gotten out, and they already knew I was the funny old broke down biker.

And there was nothing even like a BMW shop from back way up above Birmingham to way down to Tallahassee. And they would all be closed for the next three days. So I made a short list of friends I could impose on. And I got lucky, and the first guy I called went and got my truck and came the nearly four hundred miles to retrieve me.

When I told him I was in Opelika, he asked how would he know how to find me. I told him to just stop and ask anyone, that I was the only white guy around, and I had already made friends and thoroughly entertained just about everyone in town. He showed up the next morning, and we were back home before the holiday traffic got into a hard thrash. It was the rotor.

I disremember exactly where this happened, but it was way up in the northeast someplace. I had gotten my motel room and took a shower. And then I had gotten gas, and I'd found a local eatery and had supper. All I needed was some milk and Oreo cookies, and then I was on my way back to the motel. I usually buy a quart of milk in the evening, and then there is some left come morning so I can make *café con leche* for breakfast.

So I pulled off into the nearby convenience store lot. The parking lot and the store were both empty. As I was parking and climbing off my ride and unbuckling and removing my helmet and checking to make sure I had money in my pocket, I noticed the pretty little girl working the cash register.

I saw her through the big window. Little tiny girl, she looked to be about something-teen and was just cute as could be. Light brown hair down her back and eyes the color of good, store-bought whiskey. And she was leaning on her elbows on the counter, smiling real big and looking back at me through the window, checking me out as thoroughly as any grown woman I've ever had check me out. Oh yeah, their number is legion.

This happens so infrequently that I turned around and scanned the parking lot. Then I looked in the store to see if she was looking at a television. It turned out that she really was looking at me. It confused me.

As I walked in the door, she sort of jumped up and down and squeaked, "You look just like Sam Elliott."

I've heard this one before. Ain't true. Not no more than them Oriental tourists thinking I looked like Willie Nelson. And the reason I know I don't look like Sam Elliott is because I ain't married to Katherine Ross. Had a woman tell me once I looked like Charles Bronson with a beard, only lots more beat up and run over. But if that one were true, I'd have got to hang out with Jill Ireland.

But instead of being honest and modest, I stepped up to her, leaned over the counter and whispered to her in her ear, "Little Darlin', it's better than that. I sound just like him, too."

Well, it turns out I do kind of sound like Mr. Elliott, more than I favor him anyway. And that just caused her to squirm around and sort of make little damp spots on the stool she was sitting on. So I kept on talking. Her name was Martha, it said so on her little name tag. She asked me what I was called, and I told her Tiger.

When she asked was I married, I explained frequently, but neither currently nor for a real long time.

And that made her giggle. Girl was a good giggler, and the sound of a woman's laugh has always been one of my favorite noises, so I tried to be funny some more.

She asked me what I did for work. Most people don't believe me when I tell them I teach school. I suspect I look more like an aging unemployed felonious serial suspect than a professor of English. Well, young Martha didn't believe me either, and I had to show her some I.D. She paid particular attention to the fact that I worked at a college in Florida. I could see visions of palm trees and sandy beaches dancing in her Northern eyes.

As I was the only customer at the little convenience store, I wound up taking most of an hour to get my cookies and milk. Yeah, of course it made me feel guilty, old and dirty. She thought Oreo cookies and milk was pretty funny and laughed about that some, too. Finally, I had run out of funny stuff to tell her, and my milk was about to go sour, so I bid her farewell.

And damned if this pretty young woman didn't right away ask which motel I was staying at. And I told her. She said she got off work at 11:00, and did I want some company later on.

It was like when I was a kid and the sheriff car would pull in the yard. My Grampaw, the legalist, would, invariably, turn to me and ask, "What you goin' to do now, Boy?" In fact, when this girl asked me about where I was staying, I had a quick flash of cop cars at the motel and me being taken off to the local jail for child molestation or baby napping or white slavery or elderly stupidity or something such as that.

So I prudently asked her how old she was. She said twenty-one. And I said bullshit, let's see some of your I.D. She was two months short of twenty-two. And I explained that I had boots older than that. Made her laugh some more.

Martha showed up at a quarter after eleven, had an open beer in her hand and another in her coat pocket, a cigarette hanging from her lips. My kind of woman. Girl was a damn Midnighter. She offered me the extra beer. And she was somewhere between surprised and amused when I told her I had had to give it up, back about when she was born. Told her I just wasn't no good at it at all.

She spent some time walking around and looking over my bike before she came into my room. That Florida license plate had her attention. When she got in the room, she took note of my gear. She asked about a couple things, smiled at the little propane stove and coffee pot.

Now she was pretty well taken with that Sam Elliott look and sound alike thing, but she was even more enamored by the idea of climbing on behind me and crossing the country southbound. She wanted to see

Florida. I think she just wanted to get warm.

For the careful reader, it has become obvious that irony looms large in my life. If it weren't for irony, there would be little humor at all. Yeah, here I was with a girl who was born between of my second and third divorce, and she was almost making sense.

For a whole lot of reasons, some of which I still don't fully comprehend, I tried to tell her about one headlight in the dark of the night, about the stress and the steady strain. I spoke some of regret and remorse, of gettin' off course and putting it all sideways in the rain. I told her of the blood on the saddle, and the blood on the road, and the blood all over the sun. I showed her scars lots older than she was.

She wanted to hear about orange trees and warm Gulf waters. She wanted to hear stories about beaches and suntan oil. Hell, she wanted to know about Cape Canaveral and rocket ships.

And I tried to explain about how I had been to the Highside, about the motion and the bein' free, and about The Lost Highway. I told her about the Highway Call and about the freedom and the runnin' like a refugee, about the price we have to pay. I said something about Mother Earth and Father Time coming together out on the road. I spoke of the Road Songs. Told her I had rode with the highway witches and with the ghostriders and with Satan himself.

She giggled and asked about sunshine and unfrozen rivers and flowers and birds and butterflies in the air. She asked about alligators and the Southern Cross and the Spanish moss. And she wanted to know about manatees.

But I told her about the heat and the cold, about just gettin' old, and about thousand mile days. I tried to tell her about border towns and the local citizens' frowns and about how the highway will wear you down out there between the Mohawk Valley and Tampa Bay. Tried to tell her that the highway will either kill you outright or break you up a little at a time. I went on some about living out of a damn saddlebag and about the nature of the wind.

She asked about Key West and Daytona Beach and Panama City. She wanted to know about coconut trees and cypress swamps. She inquired about Mickey Mouse and Shamu and the Budweiser Clydesdales and the mermaids at Weeki Watchee.

But I told her old highway stories until around three o'clock in the morning. And then I sent her home. And if I don't go to heaven for that, I am going to be one pissed off dead guy.

However, one other time, this one involves a waitress out in the middle of the country, little nothing town somewhere on the west bank of the Mississippi River, I did succumb to a young girl's charms. I rolled into town on the two-lane main street sometime in the middle of a hot mid-morning. There wasn't a building over two stories anywhere. Heat shimmered on the asphalt, made it look like liquid in the distance. And this girl began smiling at me the minute I walked in the cafe. I sat at a booth near the door where I could keep an eye on my ride.

Then she continued to smile at me. That confused me. Pretty women really do tend to make me stupid, but when they smile at me, it thoroughly baffles and perplexes me. And this was a beautiful woman, retardation pretty. She brought me a cup of coffee before I even asked for one. And she kept on hanging out and talking to me and smiling a lot even though there were other customers. Girl had a world-class smile. I mean she smiled pretty enough to give a man hope.

While I was eating my eggs and grits, she sauntered over to the jukebox and dug into the pocket on her waitress apron. Slammed a quarter in the machine and played "Take It to the Limit." The Eagles. Twice. Walked back past me and smiled and winked. By now I was too bewildered to even begin to pretend to be able to think about figuring it out.

And then she continued to smile at me even after I had tipped her. So I finally asked her what was the joke. I was kind of waiting to be told I looked like Sam Elliott so I could tell that Katherine Ross thing to her. But instead, she had to explain that she had been flirting with me for the past half hour, but now she would settle for just making me smile. So I did. By the time this one was over, my face hurt bad from all the damn smiling.

If you look up "willowy" in a good dictionary, there is a picture of this girl. She stood close to six foot tall in her flat heeled waitress shoes. It was a privilege just to be allowed to watch her walk around. And I observed her stroll to the door and go out into the parking lot and walk slowly around my bike, and examine my load. She smiled some more when she saw the Florida plate. Girl had long dark hair and darker eyes. Her hair swung from side to side when she walked, thereby confusing the onlooker as to where to focus.

She strode back into the restaurant, checked the clock, took her waitress apron off, got herself a glass of iced tea and some more coffee for me, and came over to join me in my booth. She asked my name, but she didn't inquire about my age or marital status. She either didn't give a damn or she didn't want to know. Told me her name was Amanda. When I asked, she said she was twenty-six.

I explained that she was born the year I got drafted. Made her smile even more. She told me her shift was over now, that she had the next two days off, and that it was too hot to ride far anyway. Young Amanda said she had lived right there in that little nothing town her whole life. She looked at me right in my eye and told me a whole bunch of things.

Girl said she had heard of me in campfire stories, from tales the old men still tell. She said they talk of me wherever there's a highway, told me I was a recurring rumor. This pretty woman went on that no one could anymore remember what my mother called me, but they all knew my highway name.

She said she knew all about me. She told me her mother had warned her. She said she always knew I'd ride through there one day. She said she had heard all the myths and most of the legends, and she knew that I couldn't stay. She told me she understood about the passing through, but she figured to give me one good reason to drop my sidestand down.

I followed her back to her place where I unloaded most of my gear to make room for her on the cycle. Then we went to somebody's house so she could borrow a helmet. Then we went for a long ride to a place she knew where we could swim and cool off. We swam.

Two days later, she had to go back to work, and it was time for me to leave anyway. Amanda cooked me some breakfast, filled my Thermos for me. And she told me to think about her all the way downriver. I did. Made me smile some more.

Writing about The River made me recall another such incident, almost. Years ago, coming back from California, I found me a boat launch and picnic area on the west bank of The Mississippi someplace in northern Louisiana. It was already up near a hundred in the mid-morning there, and I was looking for a place in the shade with a breeze. Damn picnic area was stone empty, and I had taken over the most shaded table with the best view of The River. Having found some shadows for me and my machine, I made a pot of coffee. Got my book out. *The Good*

Brother. Chris Offutt. Hadn't been there long enough to drink a cup of the coffee before a little sporty convertible car drove in.

The woman who got out of it was stunningly beautiful. Girl had honey colored hair that hung down below her waist. Eyes the kind of green you see in jungles. She had one of them waists that make you want to see can you get both your hands around it. She was dressed for the weather, and she parked nearby and got right out of her little car and smiled at me as she walked over and sat down beside me.

I can still remember her downriver accent as she asked, "What you doin' down here by the river?" I told her I had come to the river to water my cycle. She looked at me real strange, and then she got up and got back in her little sporty car and drove off.

11 - FESTIVALS, MORE NICHE MARKETS, AND MORE WOMEN

The boy who edited and published *Longrider* told me I had centerpunched the Mother Of All Niche Markets with that book. I still ain't sure whether he meant that scootertrash are too damn cheap to buy a book, or that we ain't real literate, or what. And I disavow that niche market thing because I know of several people who ain't never even been on a cycle who said they liked the book. Hell I know some people with Ph.D.s, and a medical doctor, and two veterinarians, and an eighty-two year old Midwestern mother of eleven who all liked that book a lot. Ain't none of them related to me neither.

But I am about to piss off a whole bunch of people here and probably narrow that niche some more. And please try to remember that this is in no way a missionary effort. It's just me.

But I was asked awhile back about Bike Week. It happened at a bad time: Bike Week. Just in case somebody picks this up who doesn't know, every Spring, Daytona Beach hosts Bike Week. Hundreds of thousands of riders attend, and probably that many more erstwhile and wannabe bikers show up. And there is the regular vehicular traffic, too.

It's a mess. So is Sturgis in the summer when probably even more such folks show up for that festivity. So is the Honda Hoot. And Biketoberfest. And another twenty or more such gatherings that I don't even know about. Notice I didn't say that they ain't fun. Note I didn't say that they're not great places to meet new folks and connect with old friends. Nor did I say that they're not good places to find parts and other swap meet bargains. And I can't argue that they aren't places to get drunk or get a tattoo and a pierced something. No, I just said they're a mess. And remember the part about vehicular traffic, too.

Permit me to preface this by saying that my idea of a big crowd is me and two other people. I am uneasy in large groups. Last time I was comfortable in a big crowd was at Woodstock. I think that is much of why I ride a motorcycle. Solitude.

I went to Daytona once, back twenty years ago when I first moved down here to Florida. It was an error. It was then and remains now the only time in my whole life that other people on motorcycles ever tried to kill me. And then there was the regular vehicular traffic trying to kill me. I mean it was lots more dangerous than trying to ride through downtown Atlanta at rush hour.

I wouldn't have felt safe in a tank with a suit of armor and a magic charm. Drunks on bikes. Idiots on bikes. Drunk idiots on bikes. Idiots on bikes other than their own. Fools on rental cycles. People lost and badly confused on bikes. People in groups on bikes who were intent on remaining in groups. Intent. Elderly, senile people on bikes. Youthful, inexperienced people on bikes. People who had been awake for four or five days on bikes. People who had trailered their cycle several thousand miles to unload it and ride up and down Daytona Beach. People who don't belong on bikes on bikes. In short, everyone who has ever vaguely considered getting on or near a motorcycle shows up at these things. And all the regular vehicular traffic. Gridlocked with scooters. What a weird concept. Right up there with seeing how much tread you can burn off your rear tire in a puddle of bleach and a cloud of toxic smoke.

And as often as not, the whole extended gala jubilee area is gridlocked even worse because many, if not most, of the festive participants really have brought their bikes there on trailers. A few ride thousands of miles, but most don't. I've researched this. The trailer people drive anywhere from a couple hundred to a few thousand miles, dragging their motorcycles behind them. Then they unload their shiny clean bikes and ride around in the immediate area of the happy merrymaking, often with great fervor, for several days. Then they load their rides back up and go home in their trailers and trucks. What a weird concept.

And many come, in part at least, for the camaraderie. Some come to drink beer. They come for the races sometimes, or for the weather. Some of them come to buy and sell their assorted wares. I got a hunch most come out of some bizarre herd instinct. Many of them attend because that's why they got a motorcycle to begin with. And all of them show up to be looked at. And you get looked at enough on a bike without drawing extra attention to yourself.

And then there is the regular vehicular traffic. This year at Daytona the regular vehicular traffic killed thirteen bikers and wounded another several dozen. The highest death toll in the history of the event. One of the worst ways I know of having attention called to yourself is when the cops and ambulances show up on your behalf.

Speaking of personal attention, this is another one of them things that somebody ought to try to get down on paper before we all go senile. I went and found me a woman who wanted to ride up behind me. But that ain't the point. Point is, the girl set a scooter so damn good that it just made me want to keep going. Short girl, but she could stand flat footed on the ground and get a leg up over the seat. Knew enough to do it from the left side, too. And then she snuggled up tight behind of me and put her arms around me, and all I wanted to do was point it at a place on the horizon, get out there and listen to it rattle and watch it burn. Seems like I'd learn, don't it? I should know better by now. Pretty women really do make me stupid, and I ought not be allowed around them. Like I ain't allowed to take a drink or have a credit card.

OK, get ready for the moral. Turns out this girl lives in Spain, Europe. Figures, don't it? I finally go and find a woman who knows how to set a scooter, and she lives on a whole different damn continent. And, as further fortune would have it, some real good friends of mine also live in Spain, and I had planned on going over there to visit them before I even met this girl.

In the past, I have always said I would go to Europe when they built a bridge. But I had some time off and some money saved, and I knew those friends of mine would take care of me over there in Spain, Europe. So I had me a cheap plane ticket and plans before I even met the woman. Met up with her again when I got over there. And I did have a real good time in Spain.

Incidentally, I saw an old Bultaco over there. It was locked up inside a jewelry store in Segovia during siesta, so I didn't get close to it. And this thing with the girl, that actually served to reconfirm what I should already know about women. My Grandfather, the marriage counselor, explained women to me when I was a small child. He said to me—Boy, they different from us.

Boy are they. And I have further concluded that not only don't we understand them, they don't understand one another, and for the most part they don't understand themselves. Most women, it turns out, enjoy change. Some thrive on it. Many create it.

The minute you think you got it, they change the game, the deal, the ante, the stakes, and the direction, and their mind, and their hair style and color, and often, their size and shape.

But this wasn't about women. It was about Bultacos. Seeing that old bike there in Segovia was one of the highlights of my European trip. Later, in Madrid, I was introduced to a young woman who had read my *Longrider* book. She began talking about Bultacos. Seems she went to school with or knew one or some of the Bulto daughters. Said it was a family business that had folded sometime in the early seventies, before she was born. She told me the references to Bultacos were her favorite parts of that whole book. Niche market, my ass.

I saw a whole lot of bikes in Spain. Lots of big Moto Guzzis and Ducatis. The Guardia Civil, which are sort of like national troopers, all ride BMWs. Bikes are green and white, and these troopers ride in pairs with high boots and bad attitudes. Saw a whole bunch of European BMW models I was unfamiliar with. And I saw some Italian and English bikes. And a whole bunch of Japanese cycles. Damn few Harleys. Saw more goddamn little bitty scooters than I ever wanted to. Vespas and Velocettes and Lambrettas and Mopeds and such.

If I ever go over there again, I intend to spend some time on a bike somehow. The mountains to the north, and the whole northern coast are magnificent places, especially for a motorcycle. The drive up there from Madrid looked like fun on a bike, too. And I saw a lot more places I would like to ride from the train I took down to the Rock of Gibraltar. And, yes, there are Winnebagos over there in Spain. And I sure do wish they'd build a bridge.

The assorted mentions of that damn niche market, and the Guardia Civil and their attitudes, and the rant about of festivals got me to thinking about all that together at the same time. No, I haven't figured out any of it. But my Grandfather, the metaphysician, told me over and over that I wasn't never goin' to confuse myself to death. He also used to claim that the proverbial cat died of stupidity, not curiosity.

But I do wonder why some riders get so damn clubby about it. And again, I am over generalizing like crazy, and this does not refer to nor intend to disparage anyone. I mean I am just delighted that they got The Good News. I just wish they'd keep it to themselves. The Harley people, I saw a reference the other day to "The Harley Community," are probably the worst. But some BMW riders come in a pretty close second.

Really serious, snooty little cliques. Won't even talk to people riding

Jap bikes. And, lately, I've had some folks on giant Gold Wings dragging giant trailers behind them frown condescendingly at me. And I've had kids who ain't as old as the cycle I'm riding sneer and snicker as they go by me really fast, riding in a forward leaning fetal position, on their zippy little plastic Ninja bikes. And we are all out there together trying to do the same damn thing.

Kind of like them boys I heard about who formed an Official Four Corners Club, rode from Key West to San Diego to Seattle to Bangor, Maine, and then back to Key West. And anyone who ain't, don't matter if you been from Alaska to Ecuador, is a weenie. And them Iron Butt people. Man, if you want to get out there and do 3800 miles over the weekend to have a beer with an old friend, I think that's great as long as you're having fun. But I don't want to do it. I been to a jail, and I been to a hospital. And I've been on an interstate highway. I do kind of wonder if the Iron Butt people would even talk to the Four Corners folks. Probably not unless the man had done the Four Corners ride in three or four days.

As my Grandfather, the jockey, once explained, "I'd sooner ride a hobby horse in a claiming race than to keep at it like that at another man's pace."

Kind of like that time I heard about a bunch of guys someplace in Arkansas who see how many holes of golf they can play rather than how well they can play, how few strokes they can take. Long's everybody's having fun, and they don't get missionary about it. I don't get it, and, as young people keep pointing out to me, I ain't supposed to. But, as my Grandfather, the humorist, taught me—If you ain't havin' fun, you're doin' something wrong.

While I was over there in Spain, Europe, I got my bike re-built. Seemed prudent after a couple hundred thousand miles. And this seemed like a good time. Well, of course it wasn't finished when I got back. Wasn't none the fault of Karl The Kraut Mechanic either. Back-ordered parts and the seat reupholstery folks got way behind. And then old Karl had to go up north to watch his elderly father race motorcycles or be in a parade or something up there in Laconia, at the original track. Hard to be impatient in such a situation, so I just went for a "Go Dad!" and settled in to wait.

But I got it back finally, with instructions to go put 600 miles on my new rebuild and to stay under 4000 RPMs. Karl The Kraut is real specific about these things. I worked on it. What I did was I made it rain nine days straight, usually when I was some distance from home and unable to hurry.

When I went down there to Karl The Kraut's Afterhours Scooter-shop and Social Club, Karl told me when I got the first 600 miles on it, to change the oil and filter, and do the next thousand or so miles under 5000 RPMs. He suggested I should find cooler weather and a mountain and then put a fat girl up behind me. Told you Karl was specific.

Anyway, I was off my ride for roughly six weeks. That is the longest I been out of the saddle without I was bad wounded since I moved down out of the winter to Florida, so I could ride every day, back in 1980. Weird time, almost like someone important had died.

Took me the next few weeks in the saddle to get the scooter broke all the way back in. I didn't find a fat girl or a mountain. And I have since lost track of that girl from Spain. But one day while I was breaking my ride back in, I got to watch the sun come up on the Atlantic side one morning. And then I rode west to see it drop down into a Gulf of Mexico tide that evening.

12 - WISDOM AND ADVICE, AND OVERLOADED TEENAGE NINJA BIKERS

Some of my old highway blood brothers read that first volume like this and complained that I hadn't included much in the way of counsel and insight, helpful highway hints. I argued that I had, in fact, incorporated such things into the stories. They seemed to want it all on one page, or in one place, one chapter anyway.

OK, you all. Some of this is common sense. Some of it ain't. Some of it derives from the Wisdom of my Grandfather. Much of it comes of riding a million miles. And damned if I don't still think most of it is already wrote down someplace, one way or another.

Don't never cross the border holding. Neither one. Either direction. Keep your mirrors clean, and consult them often. Don't go where you ain't been invited. Keep your feet dry, and change your socks frequently. Carry extra light bulbs. Blow your nose often. Don't climb on nothing you can't ride. The way to tell if you are fixin' to run into rain is to check the oncoming traffic; if they are wet, you're going to be. Keep your eye on the road. Be particularly careful the first fifty miles or so on a new tire, especially a new rear. When crossing an intersection, look both ways, and then look both ways again. Don't never try to argue or reason with a gun and a badge, neither one. The only way to tell if the upcoming intersection/railroad track/construction zone is going to be real rough is to watch the guy ahead of you or the oncoming car go through it. Wear your glasses if you need them, but never get into a real long tunnel with your sunglasses on. If the guy ahead of you is going ten under, and you can't tell if there is another vehicle in front of him, look for the shadow. Don't carry anything breakable or potentially lethal in your pockets. Don't tailgate; you need to see the road you're about to ride on. Try hard not to stay at a motel with a lot of taxi cabs coming and going. Change your oil and filter regularly. Don't never get in a card game with a man named Doc. Keep your load low, horizontal, and minimal. Mind your manners. Assume the guy pulling out of the bar parking lot is drunk. When it all goes to hell on the roadside, after you've inspected spark plugs and wires and carburetors and the battery, check your air filter. Eat your vegetables. Never presume that there is just one cop. Always sit down real close to the door in case some fools there want to fight. Park in the shadows. Don't make fun of anyone's hat at a bullfight. Avoid riding in storms with names. Take notes. Abstain from eating in places that are playing Lawrence Welk music or that smell like your grandmother's house of a Sunday. Never leave your helmet on your ride, even if you are just going in to pay for your gas. Avoid low companions and bad company. When you get gum on your boot, and then on your footpeg, and then either on your brake or shift lever, use gas to remove it. Works with creosote and asphalt, too. Never take a knife to a gunfight. Pack your rain gear where you can get to it easy and fast. Oil your leather occasionally. If another rider waves at you, wave back; you might be broke down a mile later, and he just might live around there. Be mindful of the wind. If you go down, get away from the bike. Try hard not to lose your bearings if you get to running through the night. Avoid cities. Pay real close attention to the omens and portents; listen careful to the roadsongs. Set just inside the center line; ride left of middle in your lane. Be particularly cautious in a light rain; the road surface isn't washed clean yet. Listen careful to your scooter. Talk to it occasionally. Be reverent of the roadkill. It could be you.

I was also chastised for not recommending specific gear and equipment. So here is some advice on that, too. Find a helmet and a jacket and gloves that fit. Don't worry about brands or anything else but fit. Make sure the helmet isn't going to give you a damn headache after an hour or choke you to death at high speeds. Similarly, assure that the jacket isn't going to fill up with wind or that you can't zip it up after a heavy meal. I've had a DryRider rain suit for about as long as I have ever had anything, and it is still holding up well. I wear Redwing boots, use Castrol motor oil, and run Metzler tires.

One time, a few years ago, I got to lay some wisdom on a group of children. I was coming back home from three weeks out, mostly to the West and North, and I had got up under some cover in a rainstorm someplace in Kentucky or Tennessee. In the mountains there.

Nine kids riding six Ninja rice rockets joined me there in my shelter from the rain. All of them were wearing day-glo racing leathers, full-face helmets, and designer tennis shoes. Brand damn new shiny rides with real low miles. They were, all of them, critically overloaded and badly loaded. Some had gear piled up above their heads behind them. Kids all had giant tank bags with dried fruit and GPS computers, AAA maps and bottled water, cellular telephones and credit cards.

I was older than any three of them. The iron I was riding was older than some of them. It got much darker, and the rain escalated as they parked their rides.

They frowned at my cigarette, like they've been taught to do instead of how to read and write, and got upwind of me as they all parked. They stared at me awhile, like they couldn't imagine what I might be. One of them said I looked like a dinosaur. Another said he thought I might be a pioneer. I told him his friend was right, I was about to go extinct and just finally disappear.

They refused my offer of coffee, but we all sat there in the shelter from the storm and talked. Mostly I told these children highway stories about what they termed The Bygone Days of Yore.

Whole lot of things have changed in the past forty or so years. There are a whole lot more folks out there on cycles. I guess there are a whole lot more people out there doing everything. Anyway, riders seem to have to take less shit than in the past.

One of the things that has changed is headlights. I have no idea who invented the quartz halogen iodized headlight, but he should be eligible for sainthood. Running at night is still pretty dangerous, but used to was it was like blowing through the dark at high speeds with a birthday candle to light your way. And none of the aftermarket stuff helped. I mean we were all out there, in them Bygone Days of Yore, blowing through the night, going sixty and seventy with thirty-mile-an-hour headlights.

One time in the early seventies, back before quartz headlights, me and an old pardner of mine were heading west. We had been shut down by Midwestern thunderstorms most of the day, and we were trying to make up for it by riding fast on an interstate at night. Might could have been in Illinois. When we talked about it later, we decided it was one of those perforated iron poles from a speed limit sign that he hit. Damn thing was sideways across the dark highway, and he didn't see it. He heard it when he ran over it, heard both tires go over it. I heard it when it glanced off my mirror on its way past. He was pretty sure it was a metal post, but I thought it was a spear had been chucked at me.

Besides the evolution of motorcycles, many other things have generally changed in the forty years I been out there on the road. People are less hostile to bikers than they used to be. This could be the result of several things. The outlaw biker gangs have faded into history, obscurity, and organized crime. More regular citizens have cycles, whole lot of weekend riders. Too many of them are yuppies going through some kind of excessive wealth mid-life crisis. And anymore there are so many other weird things and people out there that folks can focus their suspicion and hatred elsewhere.

Even in the few remaining secluded parts of the country, the towns on the two-lane roads and the people who live out there between the towns, the people who have to drive a hundred miles for groceries, they're not near as isolated as in the past. For openers, there are three convenience stores within ten miles; I think that might be a national zoning law of some kind. But overpopulation and TV and telephones and the Internet and such have connected these remote places to the rest of it all. So folks in secluded areas aren't near as likely to be suspicious and distrustful as years ago.

I also think I am personally getting treated some better in my old age than I did in my youth. Might could be respect really does come with age. Or maybe I just look less threatening. These young Ninja bikers didn't seem intimidated, only curious.

Lightning and thunder went off simultaneously, and for a long moment, it was too bright to see and too loud to hear. Before the storm was over, these overloaded teenage Ninja bikers had confessed to me that this was the first long ride for all of them. Then they invited me to join them on their journey when the storm let up.

They asked where I was going to. I told them I wasn't. Said I was going back. Told them I had rode every road that had ever been run as I finished up my coffee. Said I had been to the West and to the North just lately.

Then I inquired about their destination and their route. The response resulted in my delivering about a ten minute spontaneous roadside rant about The Eisenhower Interstate Expressway System. A fine idea for moving troops and freight, but the damn things are all alike. You might make good time, and you can eat McFood and stay at a HoJo's, but that ain't why I got a bike. I bitched about the warm wicked wake of the traffic jam wind, and about how missing all that scenery seemed like such a pity. I concluded that the god damn things don't do much but run from city to city. I noticed the wind had shifted and lit a cigarette.

They asked for some details about this ride I was coming in from, and so I did tell them about how the orange trees turn to peaches, and then to apples, and then cherries of several kinds. I said how the rivers change from broad warm slow and muddy to cold torrents that twist and wind. I told them about how the cotton turns to sorghum, and then to soy beans and corn, and eventually to wheat and clover. I told where the pine and the cypress end, and where the hardwood trees take over. I said how the armadillos turn to groundhogs, and how the jasmine becomes roses. Then I explained in detail how it was that the moon comes full, and some about why the borderline closes. I even revealed where it was old riders go to and told about the problem that poses.

The rain intensified some, so I poured myself more coffee and delivered a brief lecture-demonstration about motorcycle packing and loading. Then I explained about how I was bound for Glory. And I told them about how I had once rode in a hurricane with one of the Legendary Highway Witches, and that I had also ridden some with the Rising Sun's Second Daughter. I explained about times before Chinese bikes and the like, cell telephones, and designer bottled water. I recalled with nostalgia times without helmet laws or computer global positioning systems, or fast food or inconvenient Ghandi Marts and chain motels. Lightning, then deafening thunder, punctuated my fond remembrances.

I suggested that as they roll through the countryside, they ought to try to recall all the things they see. I told them to take stock of the birds and butterflies in the air, and to try to attend to the trees. I said for them to watch for the wildlife and the livestock as they roll through the miles and hours. Told them to be reverent of the roadkill, respectful as they pass the graveyards, and to try to always admire the flowers.

I told them about thousand mile days and about the old and the true ways. I extolled the virtues of two-lane roads and little local restaurants and rest areas without flush toilets and security SWAT forces. I ranted on at roadside about The Code until my good eye got to twitching.

Thunder rolled again, and the rain intensified when I tried to tell them about how a reverence comes on the highway in the morning when you're riding all alone. Your exhaust smoke blesses the road, and you watch the sun come up, and you think—What else could a man ask for?

Then that led to a discussion of how today is a good day to die. After that, I addressed the topic of The Highside, where some of us get to die, and that of The Lost Highway, which some of us will get to ride through eternity. Lightning shredded the rain clouds, and I had to pause in my monologue while the thunder rumbled.

Some of these overloaded teenage Ninja bikers had their girl friends with them. One of the girl-children, she asked how long I had been at it out there. I told her all my life. She was young enough to laugh at that. Then, when she tried to apologize, I explained how it had been awhile since I'd heard a woman laugh, so I really didn't mind.

When she asked, I told her she might better take a good hard look, as I might be The Last Longrider, the very final one of my kind. She said she thought I might be an old Highway Hero. And I had to tell her, no. Then I had to explain that there ain't been any heroes on this highway since about nineteen sixty-four.

But I told her about how I was blood kin to the Enchanted Wind and Heir Apparent to The Stars in the Sky. I said to her that it comes around, and it goes around, and then it comes 'round again. I explained how it comes back around to summer, and it comes back time to take it back out into the wind. I tried to tell about how the highway calls and the distance beckons, about chasing ancient memories and the pursuit of primeval passions. I told her about gypsy nomad wanderlust, all in a scootertrash fashion.

When I got up to the part about how I was there when they invented the wheel, and later, when they made it go 'round, the kids all seemed to think I was fucking with them. Lightning flashed for a full minute, it gave a kind of x-ray effect to everything. Then, when the following thunder had finally calmed down, another of the young women inquired about landmarks along the route to the The Lost Highway. I told her you know that you're there just after you've rode past the Point of Caring. I said that it had taken me a million miles to figure out what it's all about. Told her it was about me, and this old scooter, and one more Blue Highway.

13 - FALLEN RIDERS, TWO-LANE ROADS, AND YOUNG WOMEN

Another rider went down here awhile back. Karl The Kraut BMW Mechanic's brother. Did it at high speed with a curve and a tree. Karl said he was doing pretty good dealing with it until he looked at that highway poetry tape of mine and saw the part about how it was dedicated to All The Fallen Riders. Then he cried.

Years ago I got a phone call in the middle of the night. Was a woman out in Arizona, and it was obvious she had been crying. No, I didn't know her. Told me her husband had wiped out and gone off The Highside, and that they had just buried him that day. She said to me that they had played that motorcycle poetry tape of mine at his funeral. And then they buried it with him. She asked if I would send her a new copy.

And now with Karl's brother gone down, I have one more name to occasionally speak into the exhaust smoke between the winds, one more ghostrider to ask the gods of motion to take care of, one more reason to leave a sacrifice of cool water and warm blood on the cold concrete, to offer the air sage and woodsmoke, one more motivation to ride on two prayer wheels. One more reason to wonder how the hell am I still around.

My Grandfather, the sorcerer, once commented that in the only triumphant alliances, the only truly successful marriages, the only lasting friendships, one person buries the other one.

Old two-lane roads make the best rides. I've found some that are so utterly devoid of traffic that you can roll for an hour or more, and only a couple cars go by. Most of the time it's a pickup truck, and the driver smiles and waves. And I don't mean thirty or forty years ago. No, I mean now.

You mostly can't find such rides near recreational facilities. You can't find them anywhere near a big city, amusement parks and attractions with - World in their name, weekends, state or national parks, a coastline, a festivity, places with a casino, and most holidays, especially those involving shopping. But, if you work at it some, you can still find them, even in Florida.

And these roads are why they made motorcycles to begin with. Awhile back there someplace I wrote about U.S. Highway 98. Need to amend some of that here. Some of 98 is two-lane, some four-lane, and some of it is four lanes and divided. Recently, I rode from my house, which is nearly on U.S. 98, over to and up the west coast of Florida and beyond, much of it completely alone.

I left out northbound pretty early, and the tall, agribusiness pines provided some shade until mid-morning. That road was so very empty that I got to wondering why. Then the sun came up over the trees, and it quickly went up to around ninety degrees even though it was only mid-morning. And I realized most of central Florida was hiding at home in their air-conditioning. Those who weren't were driving up and down the interstate with their air-conditioning on high.

But it continued empty on past Perry where I cut north up across the Panhandle, up there in Baja Alabama, and then up into southeast Alabama proper, where I encountered temperatures up over a hundred and more empty roads. It was so peaceful, even in the heat, that I purposefully wandered west and north on little, minor state and county roads, just to continue enjoying the solitude. I enjoyed it so much that I just damn near ran out of gas someplace west of Dothan.

But I got to see some wildlife, and some wildflowers, and a whole lot of trees, and some pretty neat little towns, and besides the usual livestock, I got to see some mules and miniature goats. There were birds in the air and country people waving from their porches and Spanish moss waving in the wind.

I expect a lot of folks reading this are wondering about the surfaces of these little back roads. My experience is that many of them are in better shape than contemporary interstate highways. But that's about like saying Mel Gibson is better looking than I am. Sure, the little roads that are beat to death by the weather and log trucks and rock trucks and trucks hauling freight, the surfaces of those roads are likely to be messed up. But most of them aren't, so tore-up roads aren't a problem. They really aren't much good for going fast.

And I rode by country churches with graveyards beside them. Some contained the remains of Confederate veterans. Crossing some two-lane bridges, I saw tire swings set up over slow dark rivers. Crossing others, I saw folks fishing in the sluggish brown water. I rode through miles with little other than Southern forest on either side of me. I rode through a small community of about a dozen small houses. They were cooking chitlins.

When I stopped at a remote and empty picnic area to find some shade and have some coffee, I got to see a little snake stalk and catch and eat a big grasshopper. Cattle egrets winged overhead, buzzards wheeled high in the sky. I could smell arrowroot and knew there was water nearby. Then I heard a frog. There were coon and possum tracks in the dirt around the picnic table. Two squirrels scampered through high in a live oak tree. Clouds blew across the sky, bees swarmed a huge magnolia tree, and a ways off somebody's hound dogs raised hell. I finished my coffee, checked my oil, and got back to it.

One of the problems, besides that running out of gas thing and having to go slow, with riding these roads is that there are few places to hide when it rains. There often isn't much in the way of places to stop and buy a soda pop either. Sometimes you have some trouble even finding a rest area or picnic area. But that's all secondary to being exposed in a storm.

The deluge came upon me out there in the wilderness. It was inevitable. I was in the southeast on a real hot summer afternoon. And I had seen the mass of dark clouds building and looming ominously in the west.

As I came around a curve, lightning damn near blinded me, then the thunder almost shook me off the road. It was like the storm had been lurking there behind the towering trees waiting for me. I could smell ozone. The wind went gale force and seemed to come from several directions. When the first giant, fat, greasy raindrops fell on me, I made a hasty U-turn and headed for some buildings I had noticed a few miles back. Lightning tore the sky apart in my mirrors, and the thunder sounded like artillery finding the range on me. The wicked wind tried to lay me down when I made the U-turn.

As my Grandfather, the teamster, often suggested, "It's an ill wind that blows your ass off the road."

The rain came so hard and fast that I was pretty much soaked by the time I got that couple miles back east. The shallow ditches were overflowing. Water was already running down the road. The fact that there was a double gate there and that all the buildings were inside a fence put me off some, but by now I was wet and I was scared and desperate, so I rode right on in. Another bolt of blazing lightning illuminated things for me as I went through the gate.

It worked out pretty good. I had come upon company headquarters and the big equipment shed for a little local logging outfit. The crew was about done for the day, it being late in the afternoon and raining. And by now it was raining so damn hard I couldn't see across the road.

Pickup trucks drove out and disappeared into the increasingly hard rain as I put my ride under cover beside a torn up cherry picker and some stray pieces of a backhoe. Some of the departing drivers shook their heads and waved. A couple of the remaining workers drifted over and talked to me, commented and commiserated on riding in such weather as they put their tools away.

One of them, the last guy out, I suspect he was the yard foreman or the walkin' boss or something, he set and watched the hard rain and smoked a cigarette with me. We introduced ourselves, his name was Nathan, and I apologized for keeping him. Told him I would get back to it and let him go home just as soon as I got my rainsuit and face shield on. The storm intensified as I said it.

And he smiled and said I could stay under the shed roof until it quit raining if I promised to lock the gate when I left. Then he handed me the padlock and ran through the rain to his pickup. His truck vanished into a solid wall of rain. It was pouring so hard I could barely hear him honk his horn at me.

It was obvious, even to those of us who had blundered into this storm, that it was going to last awhile. When the wind shifted, I threw a cover over my ride and got my stove out and made some coffee. Got my Oreo cookies and a book out. Elmore Leonard. *Cuba Libre*.

I left about two hours later. The rain had quit, but steam was still rising from the earth. I sacrificed some fresh coffee to the damp earth, offered the air tobacco smoke, picked a wildflower and put it on my mirror. Shut the gate and clamped the padlock in place on my way out.

And the next hour or so I pondered all that as I rode slow in the rain-cooled evening. Those people didn't have to be nice to me. I ain't kin to nobody around there, and didn't any of them boys even know me. I looked around some while I was there, but I didn't see any evidence that any of them rode a motorcycle. And while I saw a couple white men leave in pickup trucks, the guys I had talked to had all been black. And they had all been young men, at least way younger than me. And I still have no idea why they would trust me like that. Sometimes I think racial and ethnic minorities recognize longriders as fellow outcasts. Some times and some places, the passin' through is easier.

Coming back from this same ride, I wound up all by myself out there on U.S. Highway 98 again. Only this time I rolled along the Gulf beaches between Mexico City Beach and St. Marks damn near all alone. And this was in the summertime, which is The High Season in that part of Florida. Now understand, that road was a damn mess from Mobile to Panama City, but this was of a Sunday, and it should have been heavily trafficked. And it was.

But somehow that far east stretch before the road leaves the coast and then turns south was virtually vacant. Tall pines on one side and sand dunes and beach on the other. The wind laid down and the gentle surf rolled in on unoccupied sand. The Gulf waters took on a copper color in the slant of the late afternoon sun.

Next day I had a wonderful thing happen. It began, as some wonderful things do, with an error. I decided to ride through Gainesville and catch U.S. 441 and 301 south to home. Good idea normally, but this Monday was the day the U. of Florida students show up for the new Fall semester. Whole town was wall to wall traffic, mostly confused parents dropping lost kids off.

So it was slow going. I made the turn south on 441 and right away encountered worse traffic. And I mean it was down to a slow crawl, even the oncoming cars. Brake lights came on, and I feared the worst. But everyone, at least all the guys, was slowing down to admire a group of about a hundred co-eds, most of them in shorts and little light tops, moving in a loose column parallel to the road. Young girls, all of them pretty.

Long hair swung rhythmically above cute butts while every guy in every vehicle on the road went for his brakes. Long, tanned legs strode purposefully as even old men slowed down and dawdled past. Little white tennis shoes barely stirred the dust as they marched on. Those girls knew exactly what was going on, and they responded by straightening up and walking tall and graceful, by smiling. A few guys honked, and at a stoplight, several of us applauded in appreciation and admiration.

Later that day it gave me something to review and ponder while I sat out the rainstorm that was waiting for me down the road. And I finished that Elmore Leonard book.

14 - THE KILLER FEDERAL FOLIAGE INCIDENT, AND ANOTHER WOMAN

The lady came from Baltimore. She flew down on the airplane. The plan was to put her up behind of me and ride on back north to her house. I had put a new rear tire on my scooter for the occasion. Found an extra helmet. We were going to run north up The Blue Ridge Parkway and The Skyline Drive to get her back home.

First day out, we only rode about a hundred miles. Turned out it was her birthday, and her retired parents and her grown daughter all live north of here a little. It was late August, and that day was a hot ride even though it was only a hundred miles.

We left out of Micanopy early the next morning with the low sun still behind the eastern trees. Rode north up U.S. 441 just damn near all day. Some places on that road, they let you run 60 and 65 legally. Mostly lofty pine trees and live oaks with Spanish moss on both sides of the road. Egrets and buzzards in the air. Lots of construction sites, mostly repairing the bridges where small water runs under 441. It was a beautiful morning, the sky was clear, and the road was too. Like the day before, it still being late August, the temperature got up over ninety as soon as the sun cleared the tall trees on our right side, but it was still real pretty.

Even though she is a little bitty girl, we were having some trouble with the load tied on behind us. It was more a space problem than a weight problem. Sometime in the mid-afternoon, she told me to find her a post office. So I did, in Homer, Georgia. Real nice folks there at the post office in Homer, Georgia. And she mailed three or four books, a big work file she wasn't going to get to, and a couple other things her mother had made her take with her all back home. And that fixed all the problems with the load. Perceptive girl.

Right here is a good place to note that this woman also determined that I had been a long time alone, and I wasn't fit to be around most people, and that that's why I cooked my own coffee and carried it with me in a Thermos. The less interaction the better. Such things tend to detract from the reverance for the road anyway.

And she also quickly figured out where a BMW cramps you up there under your left shoulder blade, and she was rubbing it to ease it for me as we rolled along. Smart woman. Tough girl, too, it turns out. This was the first time in a real long time that I have been out on the road with anyone else, much less with someone up behind me. And she made it all real easy.

A couple hours after mailing her stuff home, we stopped awhile there at Tallulah Gorge to admire the mountains and the canyon and put jackets on. It was getting up toward late afternoon, and the temperature had come down some as the elevation went up and the sun went down. We looked down the gorge at the Chatahoochee, where they made the movie *Deliverance*. We looked out across the gorge where the Flying Walendas once did a tight wire walking performance. Then we got back to it.

Some time later I bailed off 441, and we rode east on U.S. 23 and I-40 on into Canton, North Carolina, some short of Asheville, some before of sundown. That was when I began calling the lady Iron Butt. Five hundred and nine miles. Most of it on two lanes with little towns, stop lights, and construction zones.

She is a real upfront woman, and she talked a lot about her feelings about this experience. She was excited by it all, by gaining some understanding of the road, the motion, of the distance and the freedom. It was really neat hearing her brand new perceptions of it all. Listening to her going on about the nature of motion and which way the drive wheel rolls, I clearly recalled a time so long ago that I had to think about which hand the clutch was on.

Next morning it was almost September chilly in the mountains. We got into our leathers and rode I-40 through Asheville to where The Blue Ridge Parkway crosses it. Started up The Ridge northbound. It was a spectacular morning. The sky was clear and close, the haze in the mountains was blue and heavy, like the smokes from many fires. There were still a few flowers in bloom beside the road, a few of the trees were making a half-hearted attempt to change to Fall colors. I had thought about getting my gloves out, that's about how chilly it was.

We got maybe thirty or forty miles, up to Craggy Gardens, and stopped there to get the camera out and buy some postcards. About five or ten miles later, there were orange cones and caution signs on the road alerting us to an upcoming work crew. So I slowed down, and then when we got up to the man with the stop sign, being the literate and law-abiding person I am, I stopped.

Me and the stop sign guy nodded and smiled at one another. He looked my scooter and the lady over. A couple cars went by southbound. Then I glanced over to my left side to where the work crew's double cab truck and trailer were parked, real precariously it seemed, on the narrow shoulder. Beyond that there was a very steep precipice; it dropped a long way down, probably back to Asheville.

I looked to my right and up to see two or three guys in orange vests and hardhats up the sheer cliff probably thirty or forty feet. They were cutting trees. I could hear a little chainsaw whining and buzzing. I thought about how glad I was that I didn't have to do such a thing for a living. Then I looked up the road to see a final car come around a sharp curve to the left about a hundred yards away. When that car had gone by, the stop sign guy turned his sign around and nodded at me. I got about forty slow yards.

I was just about to shift into second gear, I might have been going ten or twelve miles an hour, when the tree came crashing down off the cliff and into the bike. Made a terrible ripping noise as it tore loose from the cliff. The butt end of the tree had come loose, and the top end of it got hung in some vines. The tree came swinging down, trunk end first, so fast and hard that I heard it, and I saw it. But I could not figure out what it was. Damn thing came at me like some kind of weirdly aligned catapult.

The tree trunk centerpunched my windshield, down low around where it is attached to the fairing. Sounded like an explosion. Then the windshield erupted in my face. I blinked as broken bits of plastic rattled off my glasses. Then the tree bounced off the master cylinder reservoir for the front brake that's mounted up on that handlebar near the grip. Then the tree kept swinging and cleaned off my right mirror. This time I got to blink again as glass came at me. The bike shuddered violently, but I managed to keep it upright, and wobbled and quaked and shook and shivered to an unsteady stop sort of sideways in my lane. I didn't exactly ride it down easy, but I did ride it on down.

The girl was rock steady through the whole thing. I mean she hadn't flinched. She asked me was I alright, and I told her yeah, and inquired as to her own personal well-being. She said she was OK, so I asked her to please get down off the cycle. The bike had quit trembling, but I hadn't.

And it took me a moment to make my right hand turn loose of the brake.

I parked it right there in the road where it had come to an infirm halt. Dropped the side stand and eased out of the saddle. As I walked back toward the guy with the stop sign, I kicked pieces of windshield and mirror out of the road and picked them out of my beard and spit pieces of glass and plastic out of my mouth. By now there were a half dozen workers in orange vests and hardhats running up and down the road and another two or three sort of slowly rappelling down the cliff.

In their frenzy, their attention shifted from me to my bike several times. But none of them came anywhere near me or my busted up ride. One of them headed to their truck to get on the radio.

The guy with the stop sign was nearly as scared as I was. He and the others all agreed that I had done nothing wrong, that I had stopped where and when I was supposed to and that I had proceeded with caution when told to. And they all apologized with great sincerity, especially the guy who had cut the tree.

When I asked what the hell did I do now, one of them said he had already called, and a ranger had been dispatched to the scene. Guy said it would take awhile. One of the workers suggested that they could move the tree and my scooter out of road and let the traffic continue.

I parked my busted-up ride up near their truck, and when one of them recommended that they put the tree into the chipper, the girl I was with told them not to, that it was evidence. Them boys set that tree down right away, thereby confirming what my Grandfather, the blacksmith, said when asked what was the strongest most powerful element on earth. He said it was estrogen. Then the girl began taking names and pictures. Told you she was a hell of a woman.

While she was talking to the work crew, I looked for more pieces of my bike. The two knock-out covers in the fairing were gone, as was much of the hardware that attaches the windshield to the fairing. I paced the road, chain smoking cigarettes, occasionally talking to some of the guys on the crew, for an hour or more. Burning off adrenalin mostly. My hands were beginning to stiffen up and hurt worse.

Well, I didn't find the knock-out covers or the windshield bolts or the hardware for the mirror. I did find another few pieces of mirror and windshield when I took my helmet off. I gave up the search and poured myself some coffee. Taking the helmet off and unscrewing the thermos cap showed me that I had hurt my arthritic old hands and arms some holding the bike up through it all. I thought about that a minute. Decided that I had put some extra effort and skill into keeping the bike upright because I had a passenger up behind me.

While I was drinking the coffee, I looked at the scene of the near disaster and reviewed some more. If that tree had been about a foot or a half second later, it would have hit me in my face and torn my head off. If it had been a foot earlier, it would have dropped on or in front of my front tire. Probably would have put me off the edge of the deep chasm to the left side either way. And either way, I would have hurt a real good woman.

For the record, it was a pine tree, about four inches in diameter at the trunk end where it hit me, about thirty feet tall. I am sure in later versions of this story it will be a giant redwood tree that blotted out the sun as it fell from the several hundred foot tall cliff. But it was a tall pine tree. A real heavy one.

The girl, having prevented evidence tampering and taken names joined me there at roadside. She observed my composure, remarked on how I had made friends with the people who had just tried to kill me. She commented on how well I was taking this, how well I was handling misfortune. And I told her about my Grandfather, the alchemist, who explained to me that if they hand you a bucket full of piss, you'd best learn to play like it's lemonade.

About then the Ranger showed up. Federal Department of the Interior Ranger Cody Murphy. He was small, and he was young, but he is a credit to his profession and to the people who raised him. A man that young couldn't have much experience, but he handled things like a skilled professional. First, as he got out of his car, he looked around, surveyed the area of the disaster, and shook his head as he introduced himself. I later found out he used to ride some, a Kawasaki 750 I think, and that he had a pretty good grasp of what had happened, and how fortunate we were to be able to be standing there to tell him about it.

The first thing he did was ask me and the lady if we were hurt, did we require medical attention. We didn't, so he asked us to sign official medical release forms. When I frowned, Ranger Cody explained that we could either sign the forms or he could call an ambulance for us. Gave me a real warm feeling about the federal government. Then the Ranger began filling out several other forms. The lady and I, Otis and

J.C. and them other boys on the tree trimming crew, all had to write narrative accounts of the disaster. The paperwork reminded me of the army.

I finished mine pretty quickly and looked away from the cliff and the road, out into the distance to where the blue haze hovered on the mountain tops. I thought about a wreck north of here, on The Blue Ridge up in Virginia, near the Peaks of Otter, twenty-five years ago. That one had involved trees and vines as well. An old pardner of mine damn near bought it all that time. The Federal Ranger who arrived for that one helped us out and was just about as efficient as young Cody.

As I was gazing down and out over the cliff, one of the workers joined me. He pointed to a place about a quarter mile down, just about where I figured I would have landed if the tree had hit me instead of the front end of my scooter. And he told me that just a couple months ago a group of hikers had discovered a car and body that had been down there several years. He said just about everyone figured it was a suicide.

I was still wondering about it all as I turned back to the road. Then I looked at my bike and at the tree, and I smiled. As my Grandfather, the railroad engineer, once pointed out, any time you can walk away, it's a good wreck. The Ranger was busy collecting filled out narrative reports from everyone.

Various forms filled out and filed in triplicate, with the wheat copy going to federal world headquarters, Ranger Cody next measured the distance I had traveled from caution sign to tree, the length of the tree itself, and then he estimated the weight of the tree and the height of the cliff from which it had come. Then he got his camera out and took the obligatory twenty-seven eight-by-ten color glossy photos with circles and arrows pointing to various elements of the recent disaster. He took pictures of my busted up scooter and the tree and the road and the cliff.

After he had taken the pictures of the tree, the trimmers cut about six inches off for me to have a souvenir and chucked the rest of it into the chipper. Ranger Cody kidded me that now he was going to have to bust me for possession of federal forest products. When we got back home, I cut it in half so the lady could have her own souvenir memento. God knows she had it coming.

I got a Request Copy of Incident/Motor Vehicle Accident Report

Form and damn little hope of recouping any of the money it was going to cost me. Oh, I figured they might pay for the damage done to the bike, but I bet I would eat the price of a motel and an airplane ticket to get the lady back home and so forth. And mostly we lost a ride up The Blue Ridge.

Just as an aside, damn near everyone I have told this story to reacts by telling me that I have a wonderful law suit here. Well, my people don't do such as that, and even if I were prone to those things, I don't think you can sue the federal government unless they let you, unless they want you to. But beyond that, it wasn't nobody's fault, so where's the lawsuit? I mean what the hell am I going to do, claim I have developed an irrational fear of chainsaws?

It was an accident. Some people would write it off to destiny or karma or chance. It goes around, and it comes around. Others would claim it was An Act of God, but I don't know if they'd mean the tree falling on me or being able to walk away from it. Doubt they would either. And there are some folks would say it all had to do with the timing. I figure the ghostriders and the gods of the road and longriders were keeping an eye on me, like they almost always do.

Ranger Cody was kind enough to offer to follow me a few miles to make sure there wasn't any damage to the forks or steering or something else on my bike, that I could ride it and all. Last time I had been on it, the front end had been shaking off a tree. I was as fearful of the crack in the reservoir for the master cylinder as much as anything. It didn't appear to have leaked much after the initial impact. But, as I didn't know what the bike or the brakes were going to do, I proposed that the lady could maybe ride in the cruiser with the ranger while I did my little test run.

Then I put my face shield on and rode back south toward Asheville. It was colder without the windshield, and by now my hands ached like bad teeth. When I stopped, I got my gloves out, but my hands were swelled up too bad to get them on. Anyway, I did a few miles, about half way back to the shop at Craggy Gardens, and, having determined that the bike was OK and that I could ride it, I pulled over and collected the lady. She and Ranger Cody were the best of friends by now. He shook my hand, looked at my bike, shook his head again, and wished us well.

The girl put a pair of goggles on, got back up behind me, and back down The Ridge we went, without a right hand mirror or a windshield, maybe without much front brake. Been a very long time since I have been on a bike without a windshield. Been even longer since I been on one without front brakes. It was sort of perversely nostalgic.

I was hoping for a BMW dealership in Asheville. I can be pretty optimistic when I've just cheated death. Then, as we were about to exit The Parkway, I saw another BMW rider getting on the road. Local plates. I yelled and waved, and he made a big U-turn and came back and pulled up beside me. The man, his name was Tony, took one look at the mess the front of my ride had become and asked what the hell had I done. He had great sympathy and empathy, even though he did seem to sort of over-enjoy the story. Then he told me the nearest BMW dealer was in Greenville, South Carolina. Then he gave us a map and told us how to get there, even led us a few miles down the road.

Once in awhile your optimism pays off. Finding this man like I did saved me a lot. By the time it would have taken me to get to Asheville, find out there wasn't a BMW dealership there, find out that there was one in Greenville, and then get there, that motorcycle shop would have been closed. I did the math.

I asked the lady did she want to go to Asheville or Atlanta or Greenville to get on the airplane back north. She said she'd just as soon ride it out with me. Tough girl.

Like I said, I haven't rode without a windshield in the past thirty years or more, and the run down to Greenville reminded me why. By the time we got off the bike there, my hands hurt so bad from the impact of the tree and from a short hundred miles without a windshield, that there were tears in my eyes. I claimed it was because I was saddened at having messed up my ride.

The dealership there in Greenville, South Carolina is among the finest I've ever encountered. The friendly people there took immediate pity on us and our situation. The parts manager, a boy called André, said he had the mirror and the brake fluid reservoir, but I might have to continue to do without a windshield. OK, the mirror and reservoir are safety features, the windshield is a luxury convenience kind of thing, except, it turns out, for the old and broke down.

The mechanic, his name was Troy, had a tire to change and some other small job to do, so me and the lady went to a nearby fast food emporium and got something to eat while we waited. When we got back, I put the new mirror on, and the mechanic changed out the master cylinder reservoir for me, bled the brake lines and got me some new brake fluid. And damned if he didn't find both those knock-out covers from the fairing. I had given up looking for them back up on The Ridge. Turns out they were wedged in front of the cylinders up against the frame. They were both broken, but I affixed them back in place with duct tape. We looked around for a junk windshield, but to no avail.

The parts manager called the Parabellum Windshield people over in north Georgia to see if I could ride over there and get me a new one. Nope. They were backed up on orders and didn't seem much interested in selling anything to anyone but a dealership. So we took it on south with a new mirror and front brakes that worked, but without a windshield.

We got as far as Athens that evening. In Athens anymore, part of the downtown area has lots of little outdoor sidewalk cafes and such. I thought it was pretty funny and sort of nouveau European. We ate at a pretty decent Mexican place by our Iranian motel, some distance away from the cafes, indoors.

Next day we took it 546 miles on to home here, right straight back down U.S. 441. Well, I got on I-75 for about fifty miles to save a little time. It was another hot day on the road. Told you the girl had an iron butt. And she rubbed that shoulder cramp for me most of the way home.

15 - THE HORROR OF I-75, AND A TENNESSEE TANK OF FUEL

It took longer than it should have to get the new windshield. It took damn near that long to get it mounted. The hardware that attaches it to the fairing was damaged worse than I realized. Fortunately, my pardner, Ron, is as persistent as he is good with such things. So I decided to head out, run north up to Michigan, maybe see some old friends, see some family. I had the time and money.

That was when Hurricane Floyd appeared on the TV radar. I am beginning to suspect that the Home Depot and Scotty's stores sponsor hurricanes. Over here on this side of the state, we didn't get much more than a few sprinkles and some hard wind. But it kept me from leaving for a couple days. I didn't want to fight a rainstorm or a headwind, and the Hurrakan wind was coming down out of the north. And I didn't want to get anywhere near a traffic mess of media-inspired evacuating adventurers. But mostly, my hands hurt from the low barometer. That is often the primary local damage.

So I set to home and let Floyd go on past. Then I got on the road northbound. I did that a day early, on the wrong road. I live about fifteen miles east of I-75. My folks live about two miles east of I-75, twelve hundred and some miles north of me. It seemed the logical choice of routes, and I was in a kind of a slow hurry.

From here to the Georgia line was a nice ride. I cruised on up the superslab without a problem or a care, until around Valdosta, birthplace of the legendary Doc Holliday. Valdosta was where, it turns out, Hurricane Floyd's winds were waiting on me. I had a forty-mile-an-hour headwind the rest of the day.

Most of it was from the storm, but much was generated by the heavy traffic, especially the semi-trucks. The warm, wicked wake of the traffic-jam wind. The kind of wind that moves the whole bike sideways occasionally. There was a constant wall of semi-trailers on my left side. That made the wind worse. Gave me something to read, but that was small comfort.

Then the surface of the interstate went all to hell, from below Atlanta to my dad's house, and probably beyond. I mean it was bad, and it deteriorated as I went north. So did the weather. And the traffic, especially the eighteen wheelers, was bizarrely heavy.

It became the kind of road and ride that has you stopping every couple hours just to get off it. And going through Atlanta, I got a clump of dirt in my eye and damn near had to pull over and wash it out. This happens to me a lot in Atlanta anymore.

In spite of the north wind, I rode this whole day in a t-shirt and a leather vest. I have no idea how hot it was. Wasn't nowhere near as warm as it had been in Alabama and Mississippi a couple months before, but it was a temperate, if really windy, day.

I rolled into a motel in Knoxville six hundred and twenty-five miles north of my house the first night out. Took me eleven hours to do it. I was beat. Hell, I might have been beaten. I mean the wind and the road and the damn traffic had taken a toll.

Remember awhile back there was some advice about avoiding motels with a lot of taxi cabs coming and going? Well, the reason for this is that most of their passengers are local hookers and their clientele. And the last thing you need after six or eight hundred miles of highway is the littlest, lamest whore in wherever the hell you are banging on your door at three in the morning trying to get her cab fare together to get back home.

This motel in Knoxville, it had a panel truck parked near my room. Big sign on the truck said Acme Escort Service. And I thought that was pretty straight up and out front, delivering prostitutes to the motel doors. I saw that once in Reno. They brought the girls on school buses that time. Then I saw the roof-mounted warning lights on the panel truck and realized it was escorting wide oversized loads up and down the highway.

Next morning it was forty-five degrees when I got in motion at about six-thirty in the pre-dawn darkness. Just exactly thirty degrees colder than anything I had seen in months. I stopped at the first rest area and put on more clothes. By then, the sun had come up cold, and the traffic was back up to bizarre, and the road surface continued to decay. Then it clouded over.

There were huge traffic jams, nearly all of them oddly and fortunately on the other side of the highway, all up and down I-75. I rode by twenty miles of stacked up southbound traffic several times. Most of it looked more stop and stay than stop and go. The road surface continued to worsen. The parts that weren't ruined from the weather and heavy traffic and trucks and neglect were bad fucked up with repair work. Some parts of the surface looked like it had been rolled and pleated. Some of it felt like one of those corduroy roads from bygone days of yore. And I don't recall removing any clothes that day either. It remained cloudy.

I rode into the graveyard where my grandparents are buried, after another six-hundred mile, eleven-hour day. Left some used shotgun shells, feathers, a flower, a couple of the stones and sea shells I had picked up over there in Spain, Europe. So they would know where I had been to.

Then I headed to my dad's place. I was even more beat by the highway than the night before. And two mornings later, the temperature was thirty degrees, a local record. I watched Canadian geese go south overhead with a hard wind up their little goose butts and wondered about my own intelligence.

My daddy, being the son of my Grandfather, the sage, has some real pithy and perceptive observations. In part, I blame my dad for my love of the road. Some of the very best times I can remember as a kid were when I got to go to work with him and ride in his truck.

One evening I was studying the Weather Channel report on his cable color TV. He saw my attentiveness, watched the TV with me awhile before he spoke up. He said, "I bet the damn wind is as bad as the rain sometimes."

Well, yeah, sometimes. Depends on the wind, and on the rain. I explained that most times wind don't make a mess of being able to see, unless you're in Wyoming, down out along the Platte.

And I told him about how I have heard the wind roar in the redwood forests, and that I have heard the wind whisper through the pines. I have heard a wind that blows nobody good, and I have listened to it blow just fine. I said how I've heard the wind wail righteous with a gospel truth, and how I've listened to it lyin'. Sometimes I've had the wind tell me fables and secrets. I've had the breeze disclose omens and signs. I told that I've seen the wind blow whitecaps on both oceans, and I have rode with it out along the white lines. I even told him about the Idiot Wind. I believe he understood me.

Had a woman tell me once that I rode between the winds. I tried to explain about how it was a state of enchantment, but she thought it was a curse.

One time I was coming back home to Florida from the far left coast, had a woman with me. I rolled into Perry, Florida in the late afternoon. Perry is a short two hundred miles from my house, so I could easily have made it home. One time, years after this, I did it in two hours and change. Beat the weather to home that time.

But this time it had been a long, hard, hot day, and I still had some money left. So, instead of rolling home in the dark, I made an effort to be a real sport and not hurt the girl with any more miles. I stopped and got us a motel. My Grandfather, the adjudicator, used to tell me that there would be times when fate chose up sides and played Heroes and Pricks, and that I should be ready to decide.

This motel was of a higher quality and price than is my usual highway preference, but like I said, I was trying to be a hero, and I had some money. Took the girl out and fed her oysters and shrimp for dinner and all. Told her she could sleep in the next day.

The rain came upon Perry, Florida around midnight. It came torrentially, vengefully it seemed. It came sideways off the Gulf of Mexico with enough noise to wake us up. I was already up, as the plummeting barometer had alerted my hands to the impending storm. No one called it a hurricane or gave it a name, but that wind was a stone bitch. We waited until noon, the designated check out time posted on our motel door, but it didn't matter.

It rained so hard that it took me damn near until late evening to make it home. Soaked. One of those set and wait out the hard rain and then run twenty miles when it slacks off to a deluge kind of rains. Occasionally someone would pass me, and the first indication I had of that was when I heard them in my left ear. And it was dark the whole time. I mean it rained so hard that not only couldn't I see the road, I couldn't even see my windshield most of the time. I don't think there is much need to review for the moral here.

But even with the geese going south over Flint, Michigan and mocking me, and after the ordeal of I-75 northbound, I spent a real fine week up there in the land of low cold skies and dark winds. I had woman-cooked food several times. First such victuals I'd eaten since Spain. I spent some time in graveyards and other old haunted places. Got to hang out some with friends and relatives I hadn't seen in too long.

One day I rode down to Detroit to see an old and dear friend, Linda The Hawk. I wound up spending the night there. I hadn't seen this girl in way too long, and we set and listened to her music and talked and laughed and drank coffee until well into the night. She had fallen in love recently, and it was a real treat listening to her be happy. Girl's a good laugher. She was leaving Detroit in a month or so to move back out to San Francisco, where she belongs.

Besides more damn fine woman-cooked food and a good time, I found a nearby BMW shop, where I went the next morning promptly at nine, to see could I get my steering tightened up from the beating I-75 had given it. Well, it turns out BMW of Detroit opens at ten, especially of a Monday. I sat out in the parking lot and watched a cold front, complete with real light rain, come in from the west.

But a couple of the guys who got there early let me in and poured me a cup of coffee. I told them what I needed as I wandered among priceless antique BMWs and even more expensive contemporary machines. I got to set on a machine just exactly like Charlemagne, my 1971 R75/5, my first one, the one I had put almost three hundred thousand miles on, the one I paid $2002 for. The one I called Chuck. This one at the shop, thirty years later, it's worth lots more than it was new. And I also got to see a brand new machine that cost more than my first house. I was afraid to set on it.

A mechanic arrived shortly, talked to me while he had his coffee. I figured out these boys were riders, and that they had been at it hard all weekend, and Monday morning was a rough time at BMW of Detroit. Anyway, this guy finally got himself together, and then he took a look at my front end. He said it didn't need tightening. And I told him I had been just before going into a serious tank slapper a couple different times. He insisted I should have another cup of coffee while we waited for the head mechanic to show up to work.

In the meantime a few more bleary-eyed Monday morning riders had wandered in, a new pot of coffee was made, a B.B. King tape got put on the public address system. We all set there and discussed it in the shop there in Detroit as the soft rain hit the windows and B.B. explained that nobody loved him but his mother, and that she could be jivin', too.

The weather went to hell as we sat there. Temperature dropped ten degrees, the wind picked up, and it went from a light mist to a medium drizzle. We set and drank coffee and spoke of old times and old riders and wrecks and old machines. We told of the places that we have and those we haven't seen. Somebody made more coffee, and B.B. King kept on keepin' on.

Most of these boys had spent the weekend riding in Canada. Been a long time since I been in a group of riders. And I had a fine time listening to their recent highway stories and some of their old ones, too. We discussed the absolute horror I-75 had become. I told them the tale about my Downfall In Durango up on Red Mountain, and the more recent one about The Killer Federal Foliage Incident. Wasn't a dry eye in the place.

One of the common themes as they analyzed and discussed the weekend's outing was that the guy who had been riding lead the second day out was a weenie and wouldn't go any faster than 80 or 85 mph. I was glad I hadn't been riding with them. I've got to where seventy is plenty fast. I eventually figured out that there were no hills or curves or anything like that in the area they had spent the weekend riding in. Lot of flat straight between Detroit and Toronto. So they went fast.

The head mechanic got there around ten and got himself a cup of coffee. He'd been on the ride to Canada, and it took him a while to get squared away, too. Then he looked my bike over and agreed with his colleague. He lubed and tightened my swing arm, said that could cause some wobble in the front end sometimes. I had another cup of coffee and went up front to pay my bill.

No, they didn't want any of my money. One of them, I think he was the owner, said, "Hell, it ain't about money, man. It's about getting you down the road." I bought ten dollars worth of historic commemorative BMW postcards to bring home to Karl The Kraut Mechanic. Gave them a twenty. Told them to buy some beer for lunch with the change.

I left in a light rain, which I ran in and out of all the way back north. And my front end was a little better. By the time I got back to my dad's, the cold front had come in. I was back in waffle weave underwear and heavy gloves. Then I got to thinking about them geese, and watching the Weather Channel on the TV some more and decided I'd best get back to it and go home. And I had already decided I'd just as soon walk as get back on I-75.

So I came out southbound on I-69 to Indianapolis and I-65 south from there. Figured to get to Nashville or Huntington and bail off and ride some easy two-lanes on home. But first, I had to stop in Lansing to put on clothes. There was another of those fronts, one the Weather Channel folks hadn't forecast. Then I had to stop just south of Indianapolis, where the front was squatting, to take most of the clothes back off. Rode on in a t-shirt and vest.

People in Louisville, Kentucky are among the worst drivers I've encountered in a long time. They tailgate one another and overuse their brakes and make real poor lane changes without a signal, all at high speeds. I was damn near blinded by brake lights, even though it was daylight.

Up above Nashville, I got a tank of fuel and saw a sign for a twenty-six dollar motel room a ways down the road. Decided to stay in Nashville, there where a mere eleven months previous, I had been one of the attractions at that book festival.

Well, I got to the motel, but I had to push it the last half mile. The bike had been making a nasty noise for a couple miles right after I filled it up, and when I came back off the interstate, it was blowing enough smoke to qualify for pollution. When I got to the stop sign on the exit, I was done. So I got off and pushed it. About a half a mile. Uphill.

And the Hindu son of a bitch running the motel saw me push my ride in, watched me stand a moment and try to breathe before going in to the motel lobby. He smiled and rubbed his hands together as I stood and sweated on his counter, then told me he only had forty-dollar rooms. Velly good. I was again reminded of my Grandfather, the Skinnerian psychologist, who explained that you ought to trust them to do what you've seen them do.

I was convinced I had sucked a valve or torn a piston ring loose from the recent rebuild. And it was late enough that if Nashville had a BMW shop, it was closed. So I handed him the forty bucks, insisted on a room way in the back, way away from everything and everyone, and then I pushed my ride another two hundred yards to my motel room. Uphill. Pushed it right up on the sidewalk next to the window of my room.

By now the bike would turn over, but it wasn't about to start. When I was able to, I checked the oil, and it was up near the top and looked clean. Then I pulled the spark plugs. They had seen better days, but they weren't fouled or anything. The air cleaner was dirty, but not clogged. It didn't appear to be a problem of an electric nature. I checked the float bowls, and they too seemed OK.

So, thinking I had blown something up, I began calling people on the telephone. The boy who had come to my rescue up in Opelika, Alabama years ago was on stand-by alert. But my pardner, Ron, got the rescue call and made it up in my truck in twelve and a half hours the next day.

And I got to spend about thirty-eight hours in an overpriced, lowdown Nashville motel room with a view overlooking the parking lot, a dry creek bed full of shopping carts and beer cans, and the back end of a closed down clinic. Sign said it had been operated by Drs. Sansipore Rajiface and R.F. Pushwar. I suspect they were kin to the guy running the motel, Pollywog Dollyjing. Four channels and bad reception on the TV. A pack of feral dogs chased something down the dried up creek bed. Cost me near a buck an hour for all this splendor.

But then a kind of a good thing happened. Something, some sort of Harley-Davidson gathering, was going on north and east of town someplace. And my motel lay along the route for many of the participants. An all-day, barely intermittent, Harley parade. I sat in my doorway and watched and listened. Awhile back I was told that the Harley corporation people had somehow tried to trademark the sound that their motorcycles make. It's real distinctive.

I had a Harley for awhile years ago, an almost brand new 1966 Sportster. And I enjoyed it thoroughly when it was running right. And I have ridden with Harley riders many a mile over the years and along the way. And, as much as these classic American machines may be the epitome of sex appeal and the Easy Rider mystique, you stay around one of them for more than an hour or so, and you're bound to go about half deaf.

The sound of them going by my motel all day reminded me of a time me and three other guys were in line for something, I disremember what, a toll bridge or a ferry boat or a border or a construction project. We had the bikes running and were alternately walking them and riding in first gear slowly toward something. All four of us were riding BMWs. And a guy on a Harley quietly pulled up and joined us. He smiled and nodded at us as he took his place in the line.

And it just did not register right somehow. We four all looked at one another like dimwitted, confused cartoon animals. Something was wrong, but none of us could figure out what. Vague questions half formed in our minds and died in our mouths. We all were aware that something was terribly wrong, something was not as it should be. We looked all around us for the source of our bewilderment. It was mysterious and scary.

Some of us looked up, others glanced to the road. We were unable to determine the reason for the wrongness, but we all sensed that it was elemental. It was like suddenly the sun was blue and going down in the north, and the water was yellow and the trees purple and the road was made of cheese or something. Only that wasn't it. We stared suspiciously at the new rider and his bike. And we continued to look at one another, confused, forlorn, and stone bewildered.

Then suddenly and simultaneously we all figured it out. The Harley didn't sound right, didn't sound like a Harley. It did not have that distinctive, patented noise. Having finally figured out the question, we all turned to the rider for the answer.

He shook his head and smiled like he was used to the inquiry, and said, "They don't HAVE to sound like that." I remember we all just about broke up laughing at that, but I can't recall where the hell it happened. But sitting in the doorway of that lowdown motel room in Nashville, listening to the Harleys go by, I had some fine memories of other times.

Then the prick running the motel noticed I had been on the phone a lot, and he called my room to tell me I had a four dollar phone bill. Fuck I did. I got pissed off and told him I had been making all the calls on a pre-paid card that I had bought just for this very occasion at the next door convenience store, which his family also ran. Oh yeah, them folks had a lock on the whole damn intersection.

A while later he called back and angrily told me to move my motorcycle off the sidewalk and into the parking lot. This gave me a chance to sit in the doorway and watch the shadow cover my bike as the sun ran west. Listened to Harleys roll north and east. Read the *Nashville Tennessean* from one end to the other. There was a story about a beauty pageant in a women's prison in Colombia or someplace in South America. Girl from the Netherlands won. Did the crossword and jumble.

As it grew dark, I reflected on riding at night. I've seen some tremulous things out on the highway at night, most of them in the sky. If I had a hundred dollars for every shooting star I've seen, I wouldn't have to promote this book. One time, running north through the dark night in the interior of Florida, I saw a shooting star go over at a couple hundred feet. You could see the damn thing coming for miles, it went from northwest to southeast and passed right over me. I pulled over to the side and turned to watch it head toward Miami. It never did seem to lose altitude. And one time up north, the Perseids Meteor Shower went on overhead most of the night as we rode on toward Saginaw.

I've rode under several lunar eclipses and two blue moons. And one time down in the Keys, I saw a rainbow in the full moon light. One time in the U.P. of Michigan I saw the Northern Lights so damn close it almost blinded me. And you see all kinds of animal eyes at night, most of them in the ditches and roadsides and woods beside the road. But sometimes in the middle of the road. Seems like there is always more roadkill during a full moon. Two saddest things I know of are roadkill and failed romance.

Speaking of roadkill and animals, one time me and an old pardner of mine, a Honda rider, got into some animals. We were someplace in the south of Florida, it was in the heat of the summer. And we were slow running down an empty two-lane through a dense forest and swamp, mostly to get into some shade.

And a chipmunk broke from the cover on one side of the road and ran across it. We both came to an abrupt halt right there in middle of the remote thoroughfare. To begin with, chipmunks are not native to this part of Florida. Secondly, this one was about three feet tall and scampered on its two hind legs. And it was wearing what appeared to be smaller chipmunks on its feet.

As we sat in the road and looked at one another in confusion, another animal, a skunk this time, followed the chipmunk and darted across the road. Damn skunk was about the same size as the chipmunk and also ran upright on two legs. Then we heard music, la la la la Disney cartoon music.

Then someone screamed, "Animate! God damn it all, animate! You're HAPPY animals!" A fifty pound rabbit danced after the chipmunk and skunk. Then a second giant bunny of similar proportions broke across the road right behind the first rabbit. Both were upright and bipedal with smaller rabbits on their hind paws. The cartoon music played on. My companion and I feared this was the dreaded flashback we had heard about.

When no other science-fiction-sized beasts appeared, we rode on a few yards, around a bend in the road, and found a picnic area full of such creatures. Must have been a dozen or more gigantic woodland animals there, including a turtle, a couple enormous squirrels, and what I suspect was supposed to be a gopher.

And then we saw a sound truck and the several huge speakers playing this la la la HAPPY animal music. Guys with video cameras were everywhere. And a small yet loud woman, who was honest to god wearing jodhpurs and riding boots and a pith helmet, was running around with a bullhorn pushing and screaming at small children in animal costumes. "Animate, damn it! You little bastards are supposed to be happy and glad about the fucking slippers!"

Turned out they were making a TV commercial for some kind of child footwear. It was up in the nineties that day, so I don't know how happy a kid in such a costume could be, even with matching slippers. Before we got the hell out of there, my pardner looked at me and said that he had been hoping it was a flashback.

One time in the twilight out on Alligator Alley, back twenty-five years ago, a futuristic looking jet plane blew by me going the other way. The pilot was running about fifty feet or so above the ground following the canal that runs beside the road there. He was blowing the water out of the roadside canal. He damn near blew me off the road.

I've seen dolphins play in the light of the moon and the phosphorescence glow in the shallow breakers near shore. And when I was living in my truck over on the east coast of Florida on the beach that time, I saw a flying saucer out over the ocean there one dark night. As I recall, I hid from it behind my tailgate.

I was in mid-reflection when my relief showed up at the lowdown Nashville motel. It only took us about twenty minutes to load the bike and exit the motel and the town. I drove it back home in thirteen and a half hours.

Then I took it down to Karl The Kraut's After Hours Scooter Shop and Social Club. Karl took it apart, and it took him just about that long to determine that I had paid high test gasoline prices for a tank of diesel fuel. Come right out of the high test pump and all. Dead serious honest. Somewhere above Nashville.

Karl began, "Tiger, you dumb bastard..." But it wasn't my fault. If you are ever asked, a motorcycle will run for just about twenty miles on diesel fuel. When I found out what had happened, I didn't know whether to be enraged, or really frightened, or relieved. So I went for all three.

I will remain pissed off, probably forever. I doubt anyone did it on purpose. I really doubt the tanker driver did it intentionally, and I am sure the nice lady who took my money didn't do it with putting me on the roadside in mind. But being incompetent and inept is near as bad as being evil. Hell, sometimes it's worse. I might stay scared forever, too. And I intend to carefully and thoroughly sniff every tank of gas I buy from now on.

And I am real relieved that I ain't goin' to have to have a long distance fight with the catalogue parts people about inferior components. I already knew Karl The Kraut had done a good job with the rebuild. He always does. And that gives me great faith and optimism. Them old boys, Charlie Syms, and Doc Baum, and Coach Robinson, them boys are all dead and gone. But there are a few new ones like Karl.

16 - SUPERSLABS, INCOMPETENCE, AND THE PERILS OF CONVENIENCE

One of the by-products of the expensive diesel fuel episode was that Ron and I got to have a lengthy, uninterrupted conversation on the way home. I delivered a long rant about interstate highways that lasted damn near to Dothan. Besides all my usual complaints about the federal interstate expressway system, I have recently begun to conclude that the worst weather on earth tends to form along these roads, even though the TV weather reading news-puppets lie about it. But that wasn't the point of the rant.

Interstate highways permit the inept to drive. Hell, they encourage the incompetent to travel cross country. Think about it. To drive, or ride, the interstates, you don't need to know anything. They tell you the direction and where you are on a mile-by-mile basis; they provide more information about what's next than most people need. No, you can't get even mildly disoriented. And if you can't read the multitude of signs, many interstates suggest you tune your radio to a special station that will tell you what to do. You don't need to know anything. And you don't ever need to figure anything out either. It's a real mindless activity, and it can be done by the mentally deficient.

You don't even need to calculate about gas or food or lodging. The mile or so before most exits is festooned with official signs and advertisements of upcoming business. It has become a lot like TV. And, anymore, if you break down, there is a convenient roadside emergency telephone nearby, just in case, God forbid, you do not have a cellular telephone with you. No damn wonder contemporary kids are devoid of feelings of accountability or responsibility or resourcefulness.

An angry old long haul freight driver showed me the GPS computer thing the company had installed in his tractor awhile back. He showed me how this device made it literally impossible to get lost, how it took him mile by mile and block by block to his delivery. The computer screen displayed his speed, direction, fuel consumption, and estimated time of arrival.

So I asked him what he thought of it. His first complaint was that the damn thing permitted someone with an inflated salary and a job title unrelated to trucking to sit at a computer at the company, back a thousand miles off at corporate headquarters, to determine if and when his butt was in the seat. Then he frowned at the machine and said a good brawny six year old child could do his job anymore.

He's right. You don't have to do much, least of all drive well. The occasional lane change in traffic is about as demanding as it gets, and sometimes with the three and four lane highways, you don't even have to do that. Few curves, fewer slopes or serious inclines, no downshifting at all. Easy, convenient roads.

Interstate highways allow the incompetent to drive, much like computers permit the inefficient to have jobs. This is why and how we get people who are just flat unable to count or make change operating cash registers, people who don't know a fuel pump from a lug nut working in parts stores, employees who don't know what or where their inventory is, folks who don't know enough to check to see are they putting diesel fuel into and out of the high test tank, a lot of people who are fundamentally illiterate and completely unskilled running computers all over the place.

This is how we get the maladroit idiots in giant Winnebagos, and the unprofessional in semi-trucks, and bad angry commuters in little zippy plastic cars and minivans. And inattentive people messing with the remote control to their nearby CD player, fiddling with their climate control, eating their lunch and putting their make-up on and rifling around in their purses and pockets for change for the toll and reaching around in the back seat to smack their kids and watching a video on the TV in their van and talking on their god damned cell telephones while they are driving.

This is how we get most of the wrecks and fatalities. Two thirds of the people driving around out there on the roads ought not be. We should take the homeless and unemployed and give them serious training in proficient professional driving, teach them to drive competently and efficiently. Take the licenses away from those who can't and provide them cheap transportation with a professional chauffeur. Ought to do the same thing with jobs.

Damned if it don't seem like to me that driving and riding a cycle, like work, ought to demand some skill and competence.

Ron, he agreed with minor portions of my rant, but then he pointed out that I think you ought to have to harness a horse to go to town for provisions in the wagon. And he is kind of right. I do firmly believe it should be harder to spend your money than it was to make it. I am confident we were better off with sword and pistol than with cell phone and laptop.

Like telephones, I just don't get it. My Great Grandmother, on the occasion of my Grandfather, her son, the plumber, installing an indoor toilet in her home, inquired—Why would anyone want such a nasty thing in the house? That's about the way I feel concerning telephones. Anyone can harass you at their convenience. And then there is the additional amenity of answering machines and voice-mail, wherein anyone can fuck with you whenever they feel like it, even though you ain't even there. And again, I just don't get it. But, once more, Ron hastily pointed out that I thought the Pony Express was the absolute zenith of high tech telecommunication systems.

More than that, I think contemporary life is infested with false conveniences, the sort that permit the unskilled to hold down jobs, and the inept to drive, and the unqualified to raise children, and the illiterate to graduate from college. Years ago an old friend of mine, man who taught me a whole lot about teaching and learning and life, Ed Calver, told me, "Beware convenience." Now I know what he meant.

And apparently having a computer and a webnest and access to the Internet is like having a license to bore. It's like the yammering cell-phoners. Most of what passes for communication along the Internet is semi-literate at best.

My idea of a real good computer program is one that would destroy the message as soon as a run-on sentence or a fragment appeared on it. And immediately upon badly misusing punctuation or horribly misspelling a word, the whole thing would just blow up in the faces of the authors. Make them start over and keep at it until they get it right. Maybe the computer people could devise a program that reaches out and slaps the users if they make the same error twice.

The other fallacy of contemporary computerized life is the irrational emphasis on unnecessary speed. I still think that if you can't step outdoors and holler, then you ought to go get yourself a stamp. Yet I see people on cell phones talking to other people who they are going to see in three minutes. Students "chat" with one another from dorm rooms a few yards down the hall. And the bad jokes that mock humor on the Internet would be just as un-funny if sent by mail. Most of the fax messages don't need to be instantly transported; many don't need to be sent at all.

The folks who employ me insisted that I get on-line at work awhile back. So now, in addition to wasting my time and effort checking my god damn voice-mail for unnecessary communications, I have to also check my computer for such messages. E-mail. Few contain any real knowledge or useful wisdom, just lots and lots of worthless information. Data—the most treasured commodity of The Information Age. My tendency is to use a pencil rather than a ball point pen. Fewer moving parts.

I kept track for awhile; ninety-four percent of such communications had nothing to do with me or my job or my life. What they had to do with was with some self-important fool in a damn business suit wanting to spread the gospel of his importance and share his mundane ideas with others. I quit checking. I figure if it really is important, they will send a runner.

Before we got all the way back home, I told Ron the story about the time three of us made a pit stop in the middle of the dark night as we were running through the wilderness between of DeRidder, Louisiana and Livingston, Texas. It was a real black, moonless night, just like the one we were driving through back from Nashville. We'd been at it for around twenty hours that time in Texas. As I recall, we were westbound, and we were all beat and about half out of it. So we found a place to stop and make some coffee and rest a minute there at the roadside. We hadn't seen a town or a house or a car or a light for some time.

We were all about half asleep, waiting for the coffee to perk, when we first heard the noise. It was a weird sound. Sounded like the giantest bowl of rice crispies in the world. Snap, crackle, pop, and crunch. It came, forebodingly, like a huge bowl of breakfast cereal, from the other side of a nearby fence, from an area where pine trees had recently been cut. Earlier, we had remarked on the pine scented air as we waited for the coffee to brew.

The noise grew closer. The noise got louder. It became ominous and menacing. It got just creepier than hell. One of the guys got into his saddlebag and dug a pistol out, the other boy picked up a nearby limb. I was poised to throw the propane stove and the hot coffee. Snap, crackle, pop, crunch, crunch, crunch.

Then a car came around a curve, and its headlights illuminated the area where the sound was coming from. Suddenly hundreds of eyes shined back at us briefly as the car went on. The sound came even closer. Snap, crackle. Before we could take cover or get off a round or throw incendiary devices, we smelled them and heard them moo. Turned out to be a herd of cows stomping through pine cones and mast and small branches. Snap, crunch.

Ron chuckled and said, "Tiger you dumb bastard" just before he fell asleep.

17 - MORE ZEN STUFF, LITERARY CRITICS, AND DIRT ROADS

A long time ago, I had a whole bunch of old highway blood-brothers to ride with. Hell, a real long time ago, I was cute. But lately, last ten years or so, I been riding alone.

Mostly it makes for a better ride. I am reminded of this because awhile back, one Sunday, I kept running into huge groups of scooters, twenties and thirties and forties of them. Looked like old times.

Speaking of old times, and the lack thereof, I have a really scary statistic. A little while back, I was up north in the post-industrial urban tundra visiting my people. And I grabbed a phonebook to see if there was a BMW shop closer than Detroit. Not only wasn't there, but there wasn't but about six or seven motorcycle shops in the whole entire book. And there were about eighty-seven pages of doctors listed. Think about it.

While you're thinking about that, consider this, too. Although I avoid doctors like I avoid darkly neurotic women, I have noticed something lately. Contemporary doctors' offices all look like Las Vegas—real bright and no clocks.

Anyway, I rode with one big bunch of motorcycles for a half hour or so that Sunday. It's hard enough to predict what the lead rider is going to do when you're three bikes back. Doing it from twenty-eighth is impossible.

And more recently, I have dropped in behind two or three other riders, had a couple fall in following me, rode awhile together. It was kind of fun temporarily. Most of it was on interstates, so at least it gave me something to do.

Although sometimes, like when you've bought an overpriced tank of diesel fuel, or used up two batteries and a rotor, or when the federal forest employees have just dropped a tree on you, you kind of wish for some companionship.

And mostly, back in them bygone days of yore, I rode with the same four other guys. I mean we hung out together, socialized and hunted and fished and rode local together a lot. Then, come summer, we would synchronize vacations and head out down the road. Turns out, you put in enough miles together, and you get to where everybody knows what everybody else is going to do before they do it.

But riding alone you don't have to compromise or agree on anything. You just have to decide. Dedicated to independence, in a state of solitude and isolation. Maybe grace. You don't have to interact at all, just act and react. It don't matter when anybody else has to go to the can or eat or get something to drink. You don't have to consider anyone else at all except the other traffic. And if you get lucky, you are so alone that there ain't much other traffic.

If you do it right as it can be done, all you have to do is find food, find shelter, find gas. After that about all you got left is figuring out when to drop back and when to come out and pass. Get it right down to the basics. Motion and isolation. It's as free as I know of. If we are bound for Glory, we're destined to ride there alone.

Sometimes I am convinced that is the essence and nature of motion, the very purpose for the road, the reason the exhaust smoke caresses and blesses the highway, at least for longriders. Woman once told me that I had gone stone crazy from all the goddamn solitude and freedom. I tried to explain she had it backwards, but she wasn't much of a listener.

Speaking of listening, you ever notice how a certain song will flood you with memories? Like you'll be sitting drinking coffee in the all night truck stop, and someone will play an old Willie Nelson song on the jukebox, and you suddenly recall something from so damn long ago you thought you'd forgot it. Or you're hanging out in a scooter shop in Detroit, and they put on a B.B. King tape that takes you back to the time six or seven of you rode most of a day to see him live back in 1972 or '73. Or maybe you're waiting for a red light, and the car that pulls up beside you has the oldies station on, and they're playing a Buddy Holley hit from nineteen fifty-something, and you immediately begin thinking about Bultacos. Speaking of wondering, you ever wonder why all shop cats are named Scooter, and most shop dogs are called Harley?

Years ago, I rode some with a man who seemed utterly intent on passing everything in sight. He didn't insist on riding fast, he just seemed to deeply resent having anyone in front of him. So he passed them. It made riding with him somewhere between a job and an ordeal. One time the woman behind me inquired as to whether he had also taught his dog to chase cars.

Anyway, whenever I see a big group of riders, or when I see a guy with a sidecar and a trailer, a passenger and walkie talkies, a radio and tape player, a beeper and a cell telephone and a laptop, I get to wondering about the solitude, about the very nature of his ride. But, as my Grandfather, the cryptographer, pointed out to me—there's more than one way to ride a horse.

More than one way to write a book, too. Although some of the folks who wrote reviews of that first one of mine sure didn't seem to know that. Wish I had kept a list of things people, professional critical literary reviewers most of them, complained about. But before I get off into a rebuttal rant, permit me to say that the assorted critics all taught me something. And I'm grateful.

Organization was one of the main and frequent complaints. And I said right out front in that book that I was too burned out to even try to organize any of it. Wasn't a damn novel with a plot and all, anyway. Neither is this one. In fact, I was told by a number of people who know, that these are great airplane books. Took me awhile to catch on that that was a compliment.

The other compliment I got was from people I know who said they could hear me, hear my voice, tellin' my old highway stories as they read the book. Good. That's just what I was goin' for.

Had several of those reviewers take offense at that first book because it was fraught with political incorrectness. Yup, and thank you. If the Politically Correct Movement don't ruin us, the Personal Self-Esteem Crusade will.

And all the P.C. crap has done no good really. Kids now call one another gay like they used to call each other queer. A condom is still a rubber, and a penis a dick, and a breast is a titty, even if you can say all the former ones on regular TV and in mixed company. I guess a nipple is a nipple either way.

And the second assistant double under associate vice dean for flush toilets, pay phones, parking lots and chuckholes is still the damn janitor. No, changing the language into some kind of goofy government-inspired institutional doublespeak won't do no good at all.

Some of my personal favorites are the ones with initials. Screwed up kids are ADD or SLD or EMH or HRD. If somebody don't knock some sense into them, what they are is SOL. Makes me wonder when was the last time anyone determined a kid was stupid or lazy, or both. And if they did, they would call them specially endowed underachievers. Someone told me awhile back that I was a recovering alcoholic. Told her the fuck I was; I was a dried-up drunk. I got plenty of excuses without making any up.

A few critics wondered about what had happened to my ex-wives. Well, I don't keep in close touch with any of them. I suspect that they've all had enough of that. And it ain't like they have them a rally every year or nothing. Ain't like I'd get invited if they did.

But that first one, that girl I wed briefly while I was in the army, I heard she got married two more times after me, had one child by the second guy, two by the latest, and since then has found Jesus. Chinese Lizabeth is still the finest woman I have ever been permitted to spend time with. She is still living and working up North. Nancy remarried and is living around here someplace, or so I'm told. I suspect none of them has ever gotten back on a motorcycle.

Them ex-wives, and several other women, they taught me a whole lot along the way. For example, one of the book reviewers wondered if I would go for a fourth ex-wife. Just because I'm funny looking, don't mean I'm stupid. I might be a slow learner, but I ain't that dumb. No, I ain't about to do that again. I see no reason for a potential fourth ex-Mrs. Tiger.

Devoted to independence. Them girls enlightened me that I ain't much good at anything else anyway. They discovered that I don't clean up or tame down worth a damn. I have little potential. Beyond that, it would seem that I am an unappreciative son of a bitch and an insensitive bastard. And finally, I have real high standards for no apparent reason. Told you they taught me a lot.

Another thing they all taught me is that I am the Best Weekend Date around, the Finest Rebound Guy available, and the most Definitive Get Up Behind Me and Let's Go Little Darlin' Man that there ever was. This information is in the Girls' and Women's Handbook. Look it up. I managed a personal review of all this last summer briefly; she quickly moved on and did better. Nope, ain't likely to be another full-time woman in my life.

And all of them girls and several others have told me that if things ever went all to hell, and we all were to become refugees, that I was the guy that they'd want to be with. They all spoke of my resourcefulness and primitive skills. But other than that worst case scenario there, they agreed that I wouldn't never amount to much.

Once a girl has done heard all my stories and seen all my magic, well, I get pretty boring. And, as my last ex-wife told me, I'm too old and ugly to take out in public and too damn weird to hang out to home with. One before that explained that I could somehow manage to piss a whole roomful of people off just by walking through the door.

Words like "soul mates" and "kindred spirits" terrify me. I've got to where when I even hear the term "relationship," as a reference to anything other than blood kin, it makes me just want to head for the woods. Same thing with "commitment," especially if it refers to incarceration in a mental facility. Romance scares me near as bad as technology. I just don't want to disappoint no more people, especially women.

I have no children. That may be the only thing I ever did right on purpose in my whole life.

Some of them reviewer people thought some of my stories were exaggerated. One of them, I disremember which one it was, used the term "hyperbole." Another went for B.S. Had one boy even suggested I had invented the names of the various savior waitresses in the book. That ain't the case at all. All those names and stories are gospel truth, just like these here.

Some of the literary critics pointed out that I had made some mistakes with the technical motorcycle portions of that first book. Well, yeah. The technical part only took up about two pages and was followed by a disclaimer anyway. Like this one, that book was a tale of just passin' through, not a damn repair manual. I hate it when people read what they're looking for and then quit. And these guys were looking for something to bitch about. And that was too easy, just no sport to it at all.

But there were some good things got said about that book, too. One boy said he wished he'd written it. He's a damn fine writer, and I consider that high praise. Got one review of my epic motorcycle poetry tape in *rpm*, a real good trucker magazine. Guy said that tape might have been about motorcycles, but that there was a whole lot of trucker in it, too. Ain't the first time I've heard that. Again, yup, and thank you. Like my Grandfather, the Taoist philosopher, taught me—We are all out there on the same road.

A couple others agreed that book of mine was real politically incorrect, but one guy said it wasn't mean-spirited at all. Some reviewers commented on my views regarding change. My opinion on change is that most of it don't do much good. Different for the sake of different just costs time and money. It's a lot like trying to engineer and manipulate the language.

The term, "niggardly," no matter the context or audience, in no way refers to people of color, any color, disparagingly or otherwise. The word "retarded" indicates quite clearly that an individual is slow or limited in intellectual development and abilities. I used that word, correctly, awhile back in conversation. People acted like I had said One-Eyed Psychotic Bastard Child. They told me I was supposed to say "mentally challenged." Told them that particular expression referred to me trying to do long division or figure out women. And the phrase "to queer the deal" has no reference to homosexuals, negatively or otherwise.

I read a while back that in the past thirty-five or so years, the average vocabulary of high school graduates has dropped from 30,000 down to around 10,000 words. See above for some of the reasons.

One of the other primary reasons is that anymore education has become an industry and an institution. Many students graduate from schools bigger than the town I came from. Hell, some contemporary high schools field bigger marching bands than the total students in my high school. Quite obviously bigger doesn't mean better.

And most of these places have about .9 administrators per faculty member, including the senior sub-assistant to the third associate superintendent for marketing, spin, statistical deceit, and data obfuscation. And it's a school; you need teachers and students and some chalk.

But, enough social criticism, and back to more literary critic criticism. There was one assessment of that book of mine in a motorcycle magazine where the guy said it was real politically incorrect of me to tell them old stories with drugs and alcohol involved. First of all, refer to the first page of this. Secondly, it was the 1960s and '70s. Thirdly, those, like these, really are true stories. And finally, with everyone denying that they inhaled or even ever saw any drugs, I am beginning to wonder who the hell I used to get high with.

But then I also wonder about George W. Bush being a war hero in the National Guard. I mean I kind of understand about that cocaine thing. He was just doing it because he thought it smelled good. Wasn't to get high. But it seems like to me that most of them rich guys wound up in the National Guard back when they were drafting regular poor boys. If I'd been a rich kid, I sure as hell would have made my wealthy powerful daddy secure me a position among the weekend troops.

All this damn revisionist history is starting to scare me pretty badly. That incident when Jimmy The Greek Snyder got ostracized, censured, fucked with, and fired for commenting on a pretty heinous part of American history was an important bellwether event. I suspect eventually there will never have been anything like rebellion, slavery, protest, losers, drugs, repressive government, lynchings, smoking, dissenting opinions, perfidious politicians, immoral wars, individuality, genocide, tolerance, or ugly people in U.S. history. Say No To Drugs. Drop a Prozac, drink a Bud.

I mean they made some kind of weird museum monuments out of Auschwitz and them places. But at Sand Creek, there is a small sign. There are no signs at all where we slaughtered the buffalo and starved the natives we had already infested with syphilis and smallpox. The Battle of Bear Paw Mountains, where Chief Joseph told he would fight no more forever, remains uncommemorated. There are no museums along the Trail of Tears, no monuments at Moultrie Creek, no memorials along the Guadalupe.

We killed damn near as many Indians as Hitler did Jews and Gypsies. The extermination took us lots longer. Maybe that's why we don't call it a holocaust. Makes me wonder what my Grandfather, the pundit, would have to say about all this cleansed and modified history.

There were a couple partial stories in that previous book that a couple reviewers thought I should have finished in spite of the potential legal ramifications. That incident with the yard gnomes in Poison Springs, Arkansas, that was the result of frustration. Girl I was with had secreted about thirty pounds of quartz crystals from up north of there, up in the Blue Ouachita Mountains, into one of my saddlebags.

And besides causing a medium serious list to starboard, it pissed me off. I was still angry and frustrated as she was boxing and mailing the rocks home from Poison Springs. I was angrily pacing around my motorcycle in the parking lot of the post office when I located the croquette mallet, mounted up, and charged the nearby yard gnomes. Based on that brief, but enjoyable, experience, I really don't think polo would be all that difficult.

That petting zoo episode out in Kansas, I checked with one of my former students who went on to law school, and she told me to maintain my silence on that one. When I asked her if I could write about setting out a rainstorm one time with the devil, she said I should refer readers to my tape of epic motorcycle poetry.

Satan rides a red Harley, and he drinks his coffee black. Me and him, we had some time to talk while we waited for the storm to abate. He told me I was just an old ghost story. The Devil said they made me up to scare children. He promised me I would haunt a highway when I die.

Ran across him one other time since then. That first time, he was alone, and we set out some rain together. I disremember where. This other, more recent time, the Devil was riding lead with a pack of ghostriders that went by me in some real bad weather. Satan waved and hollered at me, called me by my name, as they rode past in the storm. Their faces were gaunt, their eyes were red, their leathers were all bloody and torn. I recognized several of them.

There were a couple articles in which the reviewers wondered why I was called Tiger. I honestly don't know. It happened real early on. I suspect because, even as a small child, I was so damn charming and agreeable. I am certain it was not my Grandfather, the christener, who first named me Tiger. The Old Man always called me Boy or Runt, because he could. Either that, or he called me Pardner, because we were. And my Father, the firstborn son of my Grandfather, the genealogist, he still calls me Punchy. And if I'd had anything to do with it, I would have nicknamed myself Lance or Buck or Duke or something cool like that.

One of them reviewers said the book made him want to know more about me. That seemed kind of oddly flattering. So I sent him a biography, but I doubt he got much past the part about how I was abandoned as an infant and raised in the woods by gerbils.

For the record, I was born and raised mostly in the industrial North, mostly by people from the rural South, in large part by my Grandparents. I enjoy long rides in the moonlight. My favorite colors are faded denim and black leather. I've broken most of the major bones in my body.

Along the way, I've worked jobs washing pickled bologna jars, sweeping floors, selling shoes and selling grave plots and selling sausage products, and making flywheels for Chevrolet V-8 engines, driving a truck, and delivering sports cars to rich people, training dogs, and soliciting easements for a township government kind of briefly, and teaching school.

I've settled in on that last one, been teaching English at colleges the last thirty years or more. A couple of the literary critics wondered about that. Somehow the idea of a scootertrash/professor, a biker/teacher seemed to bother them. It's bothered some of the folks I worked for over the years, too.

I got lucky and had the G.I. Bill and some small scholarships and one big fellowship along the way and managed a B.A., an M.A., and a D.A., all from the University of Michigan. Doctorate is in rhetoric and linguistics; I teach mostly writing classes.

And then I worked real hard and got good enough at that teaching thing that they let me come to work on my scooter in my leather and a black t-shirt and blue jeans. I don't own a suit or a pair of shoes.

So, I have been to a college and I been to an army and I made it to Woodstock. I've been to a wedding, and I have been to a divorce, and I been to a funeral. I been all three points of a love triangle and most of the places along all three lines. I been to both oceans and to both borders. And I been down a time or two.

One of them literary critical reviewer boys, he was some upset at the quality and formality of the grammar in that first book. So I wrote him back. Referred him to my doctoral dissertation and most of the works of Geoffrey Chaucer, Mark Twain, Woody Guthrie, and Johnny Cash.

Anymore, I live with my dogs and cats and horse out here at The Redoubt. I might have mentioned them dogs earlier. I been breeding and training my own cross-bred dogs for a long time. And I am now down to the last two of their line, a spayed thirteen year old bitch and her neutered ten year old son. About the only hobby I have besides writing is hunting. And, as I involve myself in both them activities mostly to maintain mental health, I ain't sure they count as hobbies. Not any more than motorcycles. But I have an unpublished manuscript about the dogs. It's called *Dog-stories*. I ain't worth a damn at titles, or endings.

It had been my intention to call that *Longrider* book either *Scootertrash* or *Scooterstories*. Guy who edited it thought that was pretty funny and laughed about it. He said, "Tiger, you dumb bastard." Then he renamed it. That dog book begins with The Legend of Milford The Dog, the first of his line, back in 1975.

I try to maintain my diet within the five basic food groups: caffeine, nicotine, sugar, grease, and aspirins. I smoke Winston cigarettes, and I take my coffee black.

I ride a seventeen year old scooter, a twelve year old pickup, and an eighteen year old horse. Horse is named Nokomis, and she is about the sweetest Cracker Cowpony a man could ask for. Dirk the Cat, who I have come to love like a dog, is near as old as the horse. Itty Bitty the Kitty ain't but about five or six. Them cats, they were both foisted on me. Horse was on purpose.

But enough about literary criticism, and far too much about me. Awhile back there I mentioned how much motorcycles have meant to me, how much they define me. Yeah, I been a wild young rounder, and I been an old concrete cowboy, and I been scootertrash all my days.

18 - DIRT ROADS AND SIGNS

A few months ago, I returned to the area in which I had grown up. So had the area. Plaza malls where we used to take our cycles and do impromptu motocross races. Trendy little suburban pre-fab communities where we used to drag race. Expanding ugly subdivisions with no soul in places where I broke arms and legs and collarbones. Paved roads where I remember pushing my ride home on dirt.

Maybe that part where they paved the roads has been progress. One time three or four of us met up with Fast Eddie at a place in New Mexico somehow. I think it might have been on our way out to California. Hell, it might have been on the ride back. All I remember is having to ride a couple miles of local surface, unpaved, bad, rough road to get to the meeting place at the campground, seems like it was around Santa Fe someplace, in about a hundred and twenty degree heat. We all climbed down off our bikes and pulled off our boots and belts and emptied our pockets and headed for the nearby lake beside which Eddie had astutely established world headquarters. He encouraged us, told us it would be refreshing as we dove off a short cliff into the deep crystal blue water.

The lake water was about thirty-four degrees. As I recall this one, we walked on water all the way back to shore. And then we tried to warm up by chasing Fast Eddie around. Spoke to one another in soprano voices through chattering teeth for awhile.

Dirt roads are a bitch. In Florida, most dirt roads are mostly sand. I live on such a road. Karl The Kraut nearly cries every time I show up with a crust of sand on my scooter. Can't be avoided, can only be washed off.

But dirt roads are a mess to ride on, too. When I first moved down here to Florida, I lived over on the east side of the state, in my truck, on the beach, north of Daytona, for most of the Winter months. Met some riders over there.

One of them, a boy called Doc, made and marketed a hell of a nice rain fender called an Elephant Ear. And he lived about two miles down a road made of the local sugar sand. First couple times down that road, I damn near lost it several times. His advice was to put it in second and third gear, keep my feet on the pegs, and stay on it easy. Seemed to work pretty good.

By the way, that living on the beach thing, that just flat out rusted everything I owned, truck, cycle, cooking utensils, and my cigarette lighter. I got to eat a lot of fresh caught fish, and I saw some magnificent sunrises. And every scooter coming south to Daytona rode by my campsite that year, but the rust became genuinely problematic.

Had an old highway blood brother move out to east Kansas years ago. He told a story about riding the dirt road into his house one springtime in the rain. Said the scooter just sort of settled into the local muck and mire, all the way to both axles. Told me he stepped off it where it had stuck itself and walked the last couple hundred yards to his house. Three days later, when they dug the bike out, it was still imbedded upright.

One summer, coming east, I got to see a flash flood out in the desert around Morongo Valley, California. One of them things, like tornados and hurricanes and blizzards and such, where nature lets you know who's in charge. One of those things that you're really glad you got to see, but you ain't real sure you ever want to try to live through again. I was briefly in swift water up to my footpegs that time.

As a kid, I lived mostly on dirt roads, so I rode many a mile on them. Come to think of it, I have lived most of my adult life on dirt roads, too. It was easier as a kid, and easier with a 250 Bultaco than an 800 BMW.

I devoted a few pages of that first book to stupid highway signs along the way. Got a couple new ones. Saw one up in the northeast corner of Alabama, said FIRE WORKS. Actually it had one word on top of the other, and at first I thought it was a noun and a verb. I rode along thinking, Well, yeah, fire works pretty good, but only if you are trying to get warm or cook something. Took me a couple miles to figure it out and feel stupid. Had much the same thing happen up north with one of those FROST HEAVES signs.

Speaking of stupid, back sometime in the early seventies, I found myself in New England. Somewhere along the line, one of my front brake discs had burred up a little. Up north, between Boston and Portland, it became troublesome, and I began to seek a machine shop to mill the burrs down.

Coming around a curve I saw a huge sign on a building that said GRINDERS. Oh yeah, it turned out to be a place selling sandwiches, which elsewhere would be called Hoagies, Heros, Subs, or Po' Boys. Then I got even stupider when, after I had figured out my lexical error, the amused folks there asked me if I would like a TONIC. Told them thanks, but I felt just fine. And I had just earlier made an ass of myself down in Boston relative to the damn bubbler.

Some of those western WIND MAY GUST signs still make me chuckle. And I encountered another one of those confusing one word made into two, one on top of the other, signs awhile back. Said EARTH SLIDES.

Had a woman up behind me awhile back who thought the BURN HEADLIGHTS IN RAIN signs up in North Carolina were pretty funny. Lately I have seen a whole bunch of religious billboards signed by GOD. Seems presumptuous to me. Saw one awhile back that I kind of approved of. It said PRAY HARD.

One time, in Michigan, coming off the far north end of the Mackinac Bridge into the upper peninsula, I saw a sign that damn near caused me to fall over laughing. There was the giant, state government inspired and erected welcome sign. It read, SAY YES TO MICHIGAN! Had one of them silly round yellow smiley faces on it. Honest. Made me kind of want to choke a little. I damn near got disgusted off my ride before I saw the second sign. This one was smaller, and real professional looking, even though obviously hand-made. It said, SAY YUP TO DA U.P., EH?

I encountered one some time ago that said LIVE BAIT. It was a real nice sign up on a marquee in front of a bar. But it was a real long way from anything remotely like fishable water, and I had the time to be curious, so I stopped to check. Turned out to be the name of the house band.

And I believe I am going to be around for the demise of the possessive apostrophe, on signs and otherwise. Misspellings are bad enough, but screwing up an apostrophe makes for some pretty weird announcements, especially involving food: Lunch's. I suspect it was a Lithuanian place. Eat's. I'm pretty sure that one was pure English. On the other hand, Burger's was surely a German restaurant. And, even though I thought I was there, I don't know when the 1960's were.

Had a dirt road-goofy sign combination, I think this was in Montana, took me more than a couple miles to figure out. I encountered the sign that said PAVEMENT BREAK and slowed down and got ready to loosen some teeth. Usually such signs, and some of them tell you ROUGH BREAK, indicate that they are about to suddenly drop you a couple fast feet down to a dirt surface for awhile. The area between breaks is often only a few yards long. Usually you get the same kind of steep ledge coming back out of the break. A lot of places will put a flagman out there to slow you down, but sometimes, especially in the West, they don't.

Well, the break part of this one in Montana was pretty easy, only a couple inches or so down to dirt. But the break lasted about forty miles. Forty miles of the rocks, dirt, mud, gravel, sheep shit, holes, puddles, boulders, and beer cans that made up the local soil. And there was no place to stop and rest or reconsider. Two narrow lanes of dirt road, no centerline, cliff up one side of the road, steep canyon off the other.

I somehow wound up on a dirt road out in Oklahoma one time. There wasn't much wind, but the dust was terrible. You could see a car coming from miles away, but you couldn't see the next one for the dust. I wound up pulling a bandanna up over my face and impersonating stagecoach robbers.

A big bunch of us wound up at a fish camp way up in northern California once upon a time a long time ago. Had a real good week or two out there in the woods. Caught fish, too. But the road in was so bad, and there was twelve miles of it, that those of us who had come in on motorcycles had all agreed that we were parked until it was time to leave forever. Whole road was made of loose rocks about the size of baseballs and grapefruits. Real rough, jagged rocks. Real loose. Road was about a narrow lane wide. Big tall trees lined both sides, thereby making it a lot like riding in the dark, or in a really tall tunnel.

And damned if all three vehicles involved didn't break down out there by the river, and some of us had to ride back up and down that rocky road on our scooters in order to return to civilization and search of car batteries and distributor caps and radiator hoses. And beer.

Such rides become work. These only lasted a few miles, but I've had whole days, like fighting the disintegrating interstate surface and the killer traffic, or battling the Wyoming wind and Nebraska dust. And I've had rides when it rained damn near from coast to coast, or trying to survive the killer Colorado floods, or the menace of malicious tumbleweeds, or the sand on the shoreline highway, or the cold, when it all turns into a damn job.

And, as my Grandfather, the Marxist, once told me—If work was a good idea, the rich would keep it all for themselves.

19 - CAMPING, OR NOT, PROMISED RANTS, THE WAFFLE HOUSE, AND LAMENTS

Sometime ago, I became engaged in conversation with an avid camper. When he discovered that anymore it was my tendency to seek indoor shelter at a cheap motel, he got real disappointed. Wanted me to set up camp in the woods and forage for food in my camos I guess. He was the kind of guy who would have found fault at the way I piled the kindling up to make a fire and then tried to administer a lesson I didn't need. So I was grateful to have avoided that conversation. I was also glad that I hadn't been required to tie a knot.

But I've done that, camping I mean. Back years ago, when three or four of us rode together a lot, we spent some time and effort camping. And, just for openers, it's easier if you got several people, several bikes, so you can spread the gear out amongst them. A couple guys carry tents, another one the kitchen stuff, and so forth. It's also easier if you intend to stay in one place for several days, like at a fish camp up on Ash Creek.

And even then, I don't recall a tent that didn't either leak or condense up so bad it might just as well leak. Trying to dry out a sleeping bag and everything else can be a problem out on the road in motion the next day. Trying to get your broke down old body moving around after a damp night on the cold hard ground is even more difficult. And making and breaking camp in a rainstorm is right up there with working for people in suits. And, as we learned in the high mountains of northern California the summer after Mount Saint Helens blew up, it's damn near impossible when there is an inch of snow on everything.

And then there was always the problem of bugs. One time up in the Canadian Maritimes, they damn near ate Lizabeth up. It got so bad that for awhile I thought the insects had organized. She joked that Canadian bugs hardly ever got any Chinese food. But them damn things made a mess of some of that trip for her. Made a mess of more than one camping-riding trip I been on.

Food can go either way. I met a guy down in The Keys and rode with him some years ago. This boy could make better food with a coconut husk fire and a chickenwire grill and a big coffee can than you can find in most restaurants. He did things to fresh snapper that made the fish still in the water try to surrender. Used some Key limes and sour oranges. We trapped a couple little rabbits one day, and if I could duplicate what he did with them, I could open a franchise and get real rich. Corporal Tiger's Lower Keys Swamp Rabbit.

And one time, up in the Nittany Mountains of Pennsylvania, I somehow got hooked up with a boy who carried a whole damn kitchen, packed it in one saddlebag. Tight pack. He somehow got a two burner propane stove and three or four different pans and that many different kinds of knives and spoons and ladles and spatulas and such. Might have had him a whisk and a colander and a damn cheese grater in there. There must have been thirty assorted packets of various herbs and spices, and a half dozen little bottles of different sauces all jammed in that one saddlebag. He had a strainer and two or three other implements I was unfamiliar with in that damn saddlebag.

It was a trick. The son of a bitch was a vegetarian, and it took all the equipment and spices to make the brown rice with hot home-made ketchup almost edible.

After that, I pretty much came to the conclusion that you can either take a ride or you can go camping. But it's real hard to do both. I mean unless you are some kind of commando outdoor survivalist freak, it takes quite awhile to find a campsite. And that is never much fun if it is already dark. Then it takes another real long time to get unloaded and set up. And that is even less fun in the dark. We set up way too many camps by the lights of our headlights. And then, come morning, it takes even longer to decamp and get loaded. And in between, it's damn difficult to carry groceries, especially eggs, or very much water on a cycle.

The alternative is the commercial campground. This way you get most of the same inconveniences, only you are jammed up against some fool with a Winnebago. Chances are he has taken his hearing aids out and is watching TV. But the drone and rattle from his air-conditioner serves to drown out some of the noise from the screaming children on the other side.

And anymore, these campgrounds are likely to charge you twenty bucks for a place to put up a tent for the night. And I have never spent a real comfortable night on the ground, even when it cost me money. And anymore shelter and a shower and a bed and a light to read by for another few bucks seems like a pretty good deal to me.

Had a couple people comment that I had spent a lot of time and ink writing about The Blue Ridge Parkway and The Natchez Trace in that last book. Well, yeah, I've spent a lot of time and miles on those two roads. Both The Ridge and The Trace are devoid of intersections and stop lights and signs. Both are real limited access. And both are real graceful roads.

When I told the story of The Killer Federal Foliage Incident up on The Blue Ridge to a friend of mine, he commented that prior to that, he had always considered pine trees to be among the more benign species of coniferous vegetation. And other than that federal tree smacking me, and the time an old pardner of mine went off a curve at the Peaks of Otter, I have always had a real good time up on The Blue Ridge. Based on some of the experiences I've had coming up on to and down off from The Ridge, it is one of the easier roads in that area to ride. And it's surely the most scenic.

Spent some time and miles out along The Outer Banks, too. That's a pretty good trick; there are only about seventy or so miles of road. And it's all pretty flat and straight, being at sea level and running along the beach as it does. But, like The Ridge and The Trace, The Outer Banks are full of interesting history and geography, and you can stop and take a lesson every few miles.

I listened to a man tell a story about shooting twenty-four geese one day. The tale involved a huge flock of geese. When I asked him why he quit at twenty-four, he told me he only had one box of shells with him. Evidently he missed one. This was thirty or so years ago, back before The Outer Banks became popular among people with money. Back when this man who was telling the story later drove up and down the islands, giving a goose away to people he owed, or people he knew would bring him some fish or game in reciprocation. Lot of good fishing there along the Outer Banks, too.

Actually I guess you can fish along both The Trace and The Blue Ridge as well. But I'm sure it would cost a lot of money for freshwater licenses. You can wade in the Atlantic or fish from shore for free.

And I spent a whole lot of time and ink in that first book telling about old wrecks, getting it all sideways in the rain, and the dying riders' lament. Living in Florida as I do, I get to read about, and see on the TV news and occasionally in person, some of the worst scooter wrecks in the whole history of the event.

Long ago I came upon the aftermath of a real bad one in the early evening as I was riding home from work. There was a wad of traffic stacked up both directions. There were emergency vehicles, and cop vehicles, and a wrecker, all parked with all their lights flashing.

An ambulance, with the flasher lights off and siren silent, pulled out of the mess and passed me as I came to a stop. Never a good sign when they turn the lights and siren off. Traffic was stopped, permanently it looked like.

When I came to a stop, I saw the twisted remnants of a motorcycle on the roadside, a Kawasaki road bike. So I pulled off the road and parked, shut my bike off, and got off it and walked toward the remains of the wreck. I saw a big tarp covering something near the downed bike. Blood was leaking out from under the tarp.

I recognized one of the cops, a former student of mine. When I asked, he told me a rider had broadsided a horse. Just stone center punched the animal as it bolted into the road. The cop said it looked like the biker was doing around sixty. Said there wasn't any skid marks at all.

I didn't know the rider or the horse either one. Both were dead. That brought back memories of livestock and wildlife in the road that I had managed to miss. Made me think about some of them I didn't miss, too.

As I walked back to my bike, I noticed the gouges and scrapes in the blacktop where the scooter had gone down. Brought me back to— How the hell am I still around?

But I am. Some who know me well think I am too ornery to die. Others have determined it will take magic to kill me. And a few believe I am already dead.

Once in awhile at work, one of the students will call me "Doc." I hate being called Doc. Wind up telling the kid that if I was going to be one of them damn Dwarves, I would be Groucho or Ornery or Grumpy. Awhile back, they hung a sign on my office door at work. Sign said—Luddite Curmudgeon In Residence.

Here's why. Some years ago I was up North, visiting one of my nieces. And she made me go watch a soccer game her daughters were involved in. I think mostly she wanted to embarrass her girls with Old Uncle Weirdo's arrival at their game, just like I used to do to her.

Anyway, first of all, soccer is a third world game. It can be played in almost any flat area, barefoot with a goat's head. In soccer, everyone gets to participate, and no one ever plays poorly. Nothing ever happens, and when it almost does, it is anticlimactic. It's a third world game.

But that ain't the point. Point is I got involved in a heated discussion with one of the soccer dads. When I asked him what the hell they were going to do with the several hundred or so trophies there on a nearby table, he smiled at me, used all his teeth, and told me they were to be given to the players.

I said, "All of them?" And he replied, "Of course. They're all winners." I pointed out that the score was 37 to 2, and one of the teams was getting their asses kicked, and that keeping score thing, that was done so you could determine winners and losers. And that touched off the personal self-esteem argument.

That's just one of the problems with team sports. Too many variables, too many referees and judges and umpires, too many lines across the field, too many damn rules and mercurial and mechanical interpretations thereof. As my Grandfather, the gambler, often explained—It ain't a nice clean game where you can count your money and tell who won.

Convenience. People who ain't no good at it riding up and down the interstate highways on giant road bikes. Children less athletic than some rock formations getting trophies for their spastic efforts. Children with fewer academic skills than the aforementioned geologic arrangements receiving all manner of scholastic rewards. No wonder they are whiners. None of them has ever been disciplined, much less punished for failure.

Awhile back I promised to bitch about restaurants. But before I get into that, I need to write a little bit in praise of Waffle Houses. The Waffle House staff never frowns at scootertrash. The waitress at the Waffle House will call you "Darlin'" whether she knows you or not. The Waffle House is always open, even on Thanksgiving and Christmas Day. The Waffle House is always cool in the summer and warm in the winter. In bad weather, you can set and drink coffee at the Waffle House and wait for it to clear.

The Waffle House is always pretty clean, and the coffee and food are always pretty good, if over-priced anymore. I think Waffle Houses are pretty much indigenous to the southeast, and that's a shame. And most of them are on interstate interchanges, and that's another shame. On the other hand, they usually have tiny parking lots, so the eighteen wheelers have to go to the Giant Huge Discount Flyin' Dixie Starvin' J Extra Boy down the line to park easy.

Madonna Kay Tammy Michelle and them other girls up to the nearby Waffle House over by the interstate exit feed me two or three times a week. And they got them a copy of my *Longrider* book and passed it around among themselves. They were some upset that there was no mention of the Waffle House in it. So I promised them I would do this.

Now, on to bitching about other restaurants. Scootertrash just ain't real welcome some places. It's better anymore than it used to was in them bygone days of yore, but there are still some places just don't want your patronage. Most of the time they let you know that right out front, but sometimes they wait until you get sat down before being insulted by your attempt to spend some money in their eatery.

I wound up in a pretty weird place one time coming down off The Blue Ridge, southbound. I think I was still in North Carolina someplace, out there on one of them two-lane roads. Seems like it was in the early eighties sometime. Must have been in the Fall. I recall the apples were ripe and really tasty. Anyway, I saw a sign for a place to eat, I don't recollect its name. There was nothing fancy or pretentious about the name or the sign either one. The place was pretty much on the outskirts of the middle of no-where. I chose it on the basis of it was up on a short cliff with a magnificent view of the valley below and another bunch of mountains off to the west.

Parking lot was empty, and as I walked up the steps and into the place, I realized it, too, was empty. It was a pretty basic looking building. I feared it was closed, but the door opened when I pushed on it, so I went on in.

Well, I got about two steps in, and then I noticed the linen napery and crystal and wine lists and candles and such. And it confused me. Just didn't seem like there would be enough local yuppies to support such an endeavor.

While I stood there and shuffled, a woman with an accent I couldn't identify walked up and smiled and greeted me. I named her: Olga Ekatrina Martina Oksana. She got me sat down near a window and asked what would I like to drink. I said a cup of coffee would be real nice, and she frowned at me like Europeans do when you ask for coffee before the meal is over.

She came back a few long minutes later, shaking her head and carrying a cup of coffee and a menu. I had been admiring the view. Some of the leaves, higher up on the mountains across the valley were changing colors. She opened the menu in front of me, sat the coffee down and began to leave. I glanced at the menu, starting at the right side like my Grandfather, the gourmand, taught me to, and hollered at her to come back.

I hastily explained that I wasn't really up to Veal Oscar or Chicken Cordon Bleu or The Pot Pourri O' Festive Shellfish, it only being three o'clock in the afternoon and all. Told her I'd be just fine with a cup of coffee as I scanned the menu to find the price of my beverage. She took the menu from me before I could find and figure out the expense of the coffee, smiled again, and asked what I would like to eat. Trying real hard to get out of it with some grace, I told her it was OK, that I was just looking to get a hamburger or something.

And with more grace than I will ever master, she said certainly and went back to the kitchen. I alternately admired the scenery and felt like an idiot. Figured I had set myself up for a ten dollar hamburger and a three dollar cup of coffee. But it was a real good cup of coffee. And there was a pair of hawks looking for a meal in the valley below me. I watched the mist move around on the mountain tops across the valley.

Turned out to be the singularly best hamburger I have ever eaten. And I have consumed my share of burgers. This one was so good that I just flat ignored the little plate of carrots and pickles and such. I began raving about it two bites into it, and my sweet hostess brought the chef, Vladimir Boris Theobald Gandolph, out to hear my praises. She had to translate. Told him it was the best hamburger I had had in the last ten thousand miles. And it made him very happy. I doubt he got to make many burgers. Hell it might have been a creative opportunity. And the bill was four dollars and change, including the coffee and a complimentary little piece of chocolate for dessert while I dawdled over another cup of real good coffee and continued to esteem the scenic panorama.

Heeding the frequent admonitions of my Grandfather, the sport, to—Don't be a cheap fuck, Boy—I left a ten dollar bill and went back out on my way.

Mostly, they don't feed you that well. Sometimes they see you getting down off your ride, and they begin trying to figure ways to get you seated far in the rear, where you won't be seen by the regular customers. Once in awhile they will have a hostess posted there at the door who will smile and shake her head to let you know better before you get all the way inside. Even more occasionally they'll have a menu displayed on the front window or door, and you can figure it out for yourself. And sometimes they try to poison you.

But the worst places I can think of to eat are the fast chain-food establishments. And I ain't even talking about the food. Once in a while I can manage a take-out, but anymore the Captain Happy Hungry Colonel Wendy Taco Chicken Whopper McBurger O'Pizza places have become noisy havens for young people to behave badly. Sometimes the employees. And I also believe they have all become anti-smoking facilities, and, as a rule, I'll not contribute money to such places or endeavors.

I also have a pretty firm rule about not eating anyplace where they fill my tray with food from steam tables. Similarly I will not wait in a line for food, even if they're going to set me at a table and bring it to me once they get me sat down. Army taught me both those things. And I dislike shouting into a speaker and trying to stuff my food into a saddlebag. So, with all these biases, I am pretty limited in my places to eat, whether I'm on a cycle or not.

There are other prejudices involved. If there is a local place, a non-chain place, I will try to eat there rather than the nearby franchise. Sort of like I will go to the friendly, local, family owned downtown hardware store before I will darken the parking lot of a Scotty's. I don't know who owns Scotty's or Denny's or Jerry's or Village Inn or IHOP or Home Depot, but I got a hunch it's somebody like PepsiCo, and they don't need no more money.

And, just after not wanting to fill my tray from a steam table, I really don't want my food handed to me in plastic containers over a counter by someone with a paper hat, a two digit I.Q., and a bad attitude. Anymore I expect that eliminates about half the food places in America.

Just recent, I have somehow gotten into places that have a whole bunch of televisions up on all the walls. Got the goddamn things all tuned to different channels on high volume. Even though it's loud and obnoxious, it isn't enough to drown out the egocentric, inconsiderate, and ill-mannered children.

And I ain't even got up to the part about restaurants with

playgrounds and computer games yet.

Had a good thing happen along The Blue Ridge one time years ago. There were four or five of us on that ride. We were northbound and had stopped in, I think it was Boone, for the evening. By the time everyone got a shower and so forth, it was getting pretty late, at least for food in Boone thirty years ago.

But we walked across the road the motel was on toward one of those franchise tough steak places, I believe it had "sizzler" or maybe "corral" in its name. And damned if they didn't shut the door in our faces. Yeah, it was late and time for them to close, but they seemed to over-enjoy it.

We walked next door, to what looked like a pretty classy place. Again, there I was amidst linen table cloths and crystal. But these folks acted like they were delighted to see us. So we sucked it up and sat down. They had one little girl stood near the table with a pitcher of water in case any of us took a drink. Unlike the neighboring franchise, this place had a liquor license, so she wasn't real busy. Another guy changed ash trays out every time we butted a cigarette.

The meal was delicious, as I recall this one, we all had steaks. We chose them individually from a cart they rolled out for us. And we weren't invited to make our own salads at the bar. The staff was friendly and competent, the atmosphere and ambience quite delightful. And it didn't cost all that much.

In fact, I was so surprised at the price that I walked back over to the next door closed up sizzler place after supper. They had a menu on their door. If my math was right, it cost us each about three dollars more, plus drinks and generous tip, to have a good meal. Turns out, as usual, my Grampaw was right.

Over the miles and along the way, I have managed to eat some real good food. And I'm not an especially food-oriented person. I doubt I would bother to eat if it wasn't required. But I've gotten fed some fine victuals. And it's hardly ever on purpose. I just sort of stumble across such places, on back roads, in rural areas.

Most of this good food has happened at such places as the VFW Saturday cookouts, and the weekend fish fries at the local church, and the Regional Egg Festival omelet brunch. And the Wednesday and Saturday all you can eat supper at the Grange Hall, and the rib eye sandwiches the 4-H kids cook in the parking lot at the V-Jay's store, and the clambake the Moose Lodge provides for the public during summers, and the bar-b-que the Daughters of the Confederacy do in the summer, and the Boy Scout Friday Night Buffalo Burger festivity, and the Regional Chicken Cook-Off during the county fair.

As long as I'm not really bitching about restaurants like I promised, I will now briefly address the issue of waitresses. I alluded to a lot of waitresses in that first book like this. Mentioned most of them by name, reverently. Waitresses are lots different than other service people. There is something both primal and intimate about a woman feeding you, about having a woman give you food. At least that's the way it has always seemed to me. If she is good at it, and smiles at you, it's even more personal. It immediately establishes a familiarity that is fallacious and short-lived.

There was a time when I would have analyzed that about half to damn death, worried at it trying to figure out what it meant, and so what. Anymore I've just got to where I'm able to break myself from falling in love with waitresses.

Maybe that's the positive aspect of McNearFood. Ain't no such thing as a waitress. And the little girl poking the pictures of food on the computerized cash register, because she can neither count nor make change, is some younger than the oil they're cooking the French fries in.

Awhile back I ran into an old guy riding an old BMW just like mine. Well, they began as the same bikes back in 1983. This guy had a whole bunch of extras, including weird wing-looking air foils of some kind on the sides of his fairing. Anyway, one of the things he had was electric handle grip warmers.

As I had already been required to admire the compass and the oil pressure gauge and the clock and the gas gauge and the night light and the altimeter, I said something about the handle grip warmers might be a good idea up north, but they seemed some superfluous down here in the sub-tropics. He smiled and pointed to my hands, and told me the handle grip warmers were the best therapy he knew of. I'm looking for some.

Turned out he had ridden The Blue Ridge and Highway 1 down into the Keys and The Outer Banks and down through Big Bend and some other roads I knew of back in them bygone days of yore like I did. We grieved the loss of such places. Then we lamented on the fact that most Mexican roads are made of adobe and that it's cold in

Canada. We commiserated with one another about getting old and going lame.

Both The Blue Ridge and The Natchez Trace are Federal Roads of some kind. Neither really go anywhere. And I think heavy truck traffic is forbidden on both. And, while repair work, and tree trimming, is necessary on them, there is no construction or development going on. There are very few commercial facilities on either of them, no fast food, damn little gas. When they are empty, they are truly wonderful, beautiful roads and graceful roads. When there is no traffic to foul up your trip, both are spectacular rides.

And they have still managed to ruin both of them, just like they've ruined the road into the Keys, and the one along Big Bend, and the ones along the both coasts of Florida and the one coast of California, and the one around the Gulf of Mexico, and the one along the shore of Lake Michigan, and the ones through every single national park in the country. The crux of the problem is, of course, overpopulation.

Anymore, you got to look for such roads, or get lucky and stumble on one. But there was a time back thirty years ago when four of us discovered The Blue Ridge the first time, in the early 1970s, and we thought we'd gone to heaven. The Ridge, like The Trace, is a real elegant road.

A couple years later, alone, I came off the bottom end of The Ridge and rode east toward the coast. I can still recall the first time I rode up over the bridge there at Oregon Inlet and then down along The Outer Banks. And I still remember my first look at the lighthouse there at Cape Hatteras.

Of course we knew these places existed. We'd all done our research and read about them. The Trace, well I knew some about it from history classes, but if it hadn't been for Captain Zero's persistence and tenacity, I sure never would have ridden it. Big Bend was a mission the first time. Next time I was trying to show it to a woman. Time after that, there were For Sale signs everywhere. It had been discovered, and now it was being developed just like The Gulf Coast highway and The Outer Banks and The Keys and the east shore of the Chesapeake and most of the California coast road and the Million Dollar Highway and just damn near every other place worth riding.

One of my worst recurring nightmares involves getting gridlocked in a national park, where I have had to pay money to be.

20 - BAD DRIVERS, GOOD RIVERS,
A CHRISTMAS STORY,
AND EVEN MORE WOMEN

Need to discuss a public menace here for a minute. Bad drivers do more damage in this country than drugs, handguns, and greedy rich people. Living where I do, in a land overpopulated by tourists, teenagers, and elderly retired people, I get to see a whole lot of poor driving.

I consider this a national shame of the same proportions as the condition of the roads, professional athletics (especially at the college level), the public deportment of most children, and state operated lotteries. And there is no excuse for bad drivers. I mean, in the somewhat timeless words of Rodney King, "Can't we all just get along together?"

Apparently not. Part of driving well is skill, and part of it is just regular consideration and manners. Bad drivers pay little attention to what they are doing, and even less to the consequences of their inept and inconsiderate actions. Seems like to me that if the public schools put as much time and effort into driver training as they do into political correctness brainwashing, the roads would be a safer place. But bad drivers continue to imperil all of us through their inattention and inconsideration.

It's sort of like people at the check-out line at the grocery store who act surprised when informed they're going to have to pay money for their food. And, upon being told this, they suddenly but slowly begin to search for their wallet or checkbook. They even have the same sort of semi-stunned look on their faces as bad drivers do when confronted with a repercussion. And it's all just basic cause and effect.

To avoid the shopping stupid, and their children, I buy my groceries at midnight. But I have to ride amongst the bad drivers. There are several things I am able to do for my personal safety. Like I really try to stay off my cycle on Friday nights and Sunday mornings. The freshly paid and the recently enraptured make for poor motorists, their attention being on things other than driving. Similarly, I have learned that the first of the month is when most people cash their social security and welfare checks and then drive around spending the money, looking for a motorcycle to run over. It is also my tendency to avoid cities generally, and local and seasonal festivals specifically.

And, recently, I have come to understand that riding during the lunch hour anywhere near even a small town can be about as dangerous as a holiday shopping thrash. Lunch, the most important meal of the corporate day. At least it seems to be for young professionals and folks who are employed as clerks, but are called associates.

These people who work in neckties and pantyhose and drive minivans and miniature SUVs seem to go at lunch harder than even hungry people need to. I know there is a limited time allotted for the midday meal most places. But, anymore, anywhere there is a conglomerate of plaza malls and offices and stores and people in suits and make-up, the time from about noon to one o'clock or so is terrorizing. And, anymore, there is such a conglomerate nearly everywhere.

The lunch crowd will pull out in front of you as if you were invisible. They will come across four lanes of traffic to make a sharp turn into the take-out line. The lunch people drive twenty over the speed limit and then jam on their brakes so they can broadside into the trendy little Ethiopian restaurant. And then they'll all turn around and do it an hour later hurrying back to work.

And then they'll all do it some more a few hours later when they go home. Rush hour, a biker's nightmare. Anymore, I try to ride far around places where and when such a phenomenon is inevitable. You know, cities and interstate highways. If that's impossible, I try to schedule my own stops to coincide with these morning and evening highway fiascos.

When the bad driver does something stupid: stopping for a green light, slowing down for no apparent reason, leaving a turn signal on in perpetuity, unnecessary lane changes and straddles, don't ever assume he's done doing dumb stuff. Trust them to do what you've seen them do. Beware of drivers who have taken up permanent residence in the passing lane. You just never know when they're going to figure it out and come sideways.

Over the years and along the way I have noticed a developing trend that makes it pretty perilous to ride far or much around most holidays, too. This is especially true during The Modern Christmas Season, which anymore begins around Labor Day sometime, continues through Hallowe'en and, then, completely ignoring Veterans Day, goes on through

Thanksgiving and to Christmas itself and then on beyond New Year's some. Then someone with a government job determines the success of the holiday by figuring out how much money was spent, or at least charged.

Anyway, beware of plaza malls generally, and shoppers driving around with credit cards in their hands during this period. Also beware of people driving around in their Hallowe'en outfit or in their Thanksgiving costume or their Christmas get-up, in heavily decorated cars, or sleighs.

One of the other ways I have developed for staying alive is to observe the drivers' mirrors, see where they've got them pointed. Bad drivers frequently have their side and internal mirrors all pointed at themselves. Honest. Check it out. Do it at a safe distance.

After that, if there is a passenger, oftentimes the bad driver is facing sideways in order to talk to him. If there are multiple passengers, the bad driver may turn around to speak to those in the rear. Eye-contact with everything but the traffic. Conversation is important to bad drivers, both in person and on cell telephones. Gestures loom significant as well, oftentimes with both hands. Beware of all Cadillac drivers, and mind the full moon real careful.

Chances are that a car with more than one bumper sticker is going to contain a poor driver. If that one bumper sticker is an announcement of a religious conviction or a declaration that the driver's kid was Student of the Hour at some school, multiply by about six. Similarly, if it's a singular political bumper sticker backing a guy who lost several years ago, multiply by six. I've also noticed a corollary between the amount of crap hanging from the rearview mirror and the driving capabilities of the operator of the car. Same thing with people who pile an entire ecosystem of cute stuffed animals in their back window.

And if you encounter an SUV or one of those mock-jeep vehicles that is real clean, be careful, especially if it says 4x4 on it someplace. Likewise beware of vehicles with oversized tires or pictures of someone pissing on something in the back window.

Awhile back I came upon a lone rider. It was in the Ozark Mountains in the west of Missouri. Rode behind him awhile. Long enough to become curious about what it said on the back of his t-shirt. I finally got close enough to see that it read—If you can read this, the bitch fell off. And while I thought it was pretty funny, I got away from him.

If it's an out-of-state plate, you can assume the driver is lost or disoriented or angry or confused and is going to drive badly in hopes of making some of that better. Beware of Winnebagos in general, but especially those towing a smaller vehicle behind their giant huge motor home. And, my experience has been that most guys hauling a boat, especially those doing it with a small car with one tiny side mirror, as a group, are inept. Likewise, avoid cars with bicycles or golf clubs strapped on top of them. And if the car appears to be inhabited by Q-tips, it's old people. Watch out.

And, just so no one thinks I am picking on the senile elderly, there is reason to beware of young people behind the wheel as well. They've had little experience, and most of them just ain't no good at it yet. My Grandfather, the developmental psychologist, once opined—They're too new to it to know what they don't know. Also, if you encounter a thirty year old beat up pickup truck spewing smoke and leaking assorted fluids, assume the guy just don't care, and give way.

Cell phone users are among the worst drivers. They may be among the worst telephone users as well. But this one doesn't bother me much because they are all going to develop cauliflower ears and stiff necks and catch brain cancer and die.

Similarly, I have found it prudent to keep an eye on people who are disciplining their kids at fifty miles an hour or in heavy traffic. And anytime you can hear someone's radio from a hundred yards off, you can pretty much assume that he's not among the best drivers out there and try to avoid closer proximity. If he's singing along, or bouncing about in the seat waving his arms to the rhythm, you are assured that he just isn't giving full attention to the task at hand, and you might just as well pull over and set a spell.

Drunks are pretty easy to spot whether they're in a car or otherwise. One time, a long, long time ago, down in The Keys, I encountered The Immaculate Drunk. Used to be some of the Middle Keys had unpopulated areas. Yeah, I know that's hard to believe, but thirty years ago it was true. And you could ride back on a single lane sand and shell road a mile or two and find such a place in the mangroves to camp for the night. You had to bring your own water and everything else. About all there was, was some firewood and fish and mosquitoes.

Sometimes you would encounter other campers, hippies mostly. Sometimes the other campers would be pretty permanent. Back in the late nineteen sixties, I bet there were a thousand people living in their trucks and cars and vans and tents like this between Tavernier and Marathon.

Four or five of us were bound down to Key West one year. Friends of mine had a sailboat parked near Mel Fisher's salvage boats. Mel was destined to find the sunken treasure of the *Señora Nueve Atocha* and get real rich. As I recall, he solicited us for money for his project, and we passed. Years later, one of my sailboat friends commented on that. She said, "Tiger, you dumb bastard."

Anyway, on this trip down to Key West, it got dark and late someplace south of Islamorada. So we stopped at a little grocery store and got some provisions. Then we headed off into the scrub on a dusty shell road. I believe it was off to the east, on the Atlantic side of the islands, away from sundown. We picked the windward side in order to avoid mosquitoes and no-see-ems.

And we found a community of folks living there on the shore among the mangroves and palms. There must have been twenty or thirty people there. Predominantly young people, many of them in psychedelic VW micro busses and vans and cars with northern license plates, hippies mostly.

We found a place to circle and park our scooters and make a little camp beside the faded and abandoned shell of an ancient junked out and plundered Ford van that was up on blocks there in the sand. It was literally gutted, no engine, no transmission, no wheels. Also no seats, no dashboard, no steering wheel. The windows and many of the doors were gone as well.

Many of the friendly permanent inhabitants wandered over to welcome us. Some of them brought refreshments, shared their food and beverages and smoke and music. Hippies. We sat around the fire with these nice folks until quite late. Finally everyone sought a sleeping bag, and we retired for the evening.

A few hours before dawn we were awakened by one of the permanent residents returning to the campground on foot. He was drunk, and he weaved from one side of the narrow road to the other as he sang his way home. Somehow he managed to navigate between our cycles and climb into the junked out old van. He made a whole lot of noise in there for awhile. Then he announced in a disappointed and loud voice, "Motherfuckin' battery went dead!"

Good damn thing, too. But over the years I have come upon people this drunk whose batteries were just fine. They usually smile at you as they drift into your lane.

Oftentimes they have a beer or a Big Gulp in their lap. Which brings up the topic of people eating and drinking as they drive. Like playing with their cell phone, and trying to bust internal organs with their radio, playing with video games, and putting on their make-up, it ain't a good idea.

If you notice that the driver ahead of you slows down for on-coming traffic, you probably ought to try to get away from him somehow. And if the guy in front of you is one of those who feels compelled to speed up and race with folks trying to pass him, caution may be your best move.

Another tangential observation I have recently made regarding modern young people has to do with their reactions and responses. Contemporary youth, and again I am generalizing like crazy, do not react to the sound of an internal combustion engine the way my generation did. Used to be a kid could identify the vehicle make or the kind of motorcycle by the sound it made. Hell, those dogs of mine I keep talking about, they can identify a motorcycle from a half mile off, and a BMW from a quarter mile.

But today's kids don't react at all. I think they are tuned in to computer games and noises, telephones, beepers, dysrhythmic music, and screaming. But they can't tell a Harley from a Yugo. But they all seem to have strong opinions, and few things trouble me as much as a child with an opinion. Note I have refrained from using terms like shavers, whelps, and whippersnappers.

Rivers, as I have mentioned, are fine things to ride beside. But I don't think I have said anything about them being fine places to stop beside as well. Frequently you'll find a picnic area, or a boat ramp, or a place where local folks park and fish near a bridge over a river or a public dock on a lake. And these places make a real nice spot to pull off and set awhile, smoke a cigarette, eat an apple, make a pot of coffee, drink a cup of coffee. Flowing water is pretty soothing, even if you don't get in it.

As often as not, in the morning on the road, I will stop and get some kind of take-out food or some donuts and find me a river for a breakfast picnic. I'll fire up my little propane stove and make some coffee there by the riverside. I try to time this to coincide with any potential local commuter traffic mess.

And, like commercial endeavors, commuter traffic messes have proliferated greatly in the past few years. And, like the Mart-Mart Stores and fake nail parlors, these traffic jams happen in some real unlikely places. It's like running across them quaint little bed and breakfast places out there between oblivion and nowhere.

One time I was out in the early morning fog some west of where I live just drifting along on a two-lane. I don't know why. But I was nearly run over by a big Lincoln, three Mercedes, and a damn Jaguar before the sudden gridlock brought us all to a fogged-in halt.

Commuting doctors. They'd bought acreage and built big houses fifty miles north of Tampa. And they had to drive down to the city every day to find enough sick people to pay for it all. And, as for the issue of doctors' driving, if it came right down to it, I believe I'd sooner have a truck driver operate on me.

My pardner, Captain Zero, and me, in addition to our regular epistles, we correspond by means of cassette tapes. He turned me on to it about thirty years ago. It took him awhile, as I was fearful and suspicious of such modern technology, even then. I feared the damn tape recorder would somehow capture my soul.

Over the years the Captain has sent me tapes from his cable car out there in San Francisco, and the Himalayan Mountains of Nepal, and the western shore of Ireland, and the New Delhi bus station, and the sandy beaches of Hawaii, and the streets of downtown Bangkok, and from the bowels of Tehran, and the shoreline of the Trinity River.

And I have sent him tapes from the road, often from the banks of various rivers. I recall telling him about the road and the ride from the bottom of Looking Glass Falls way up there above it all in the mountains by the French Broad River, and a little boat dock on the Tombigbee River, and from a sandbar out in the Pecos near where they killed Billy Bonney, and from under a bridge over the Columbia River, and a rest area along the Suwannee, and from the top of a boulder beside the South Fork of the Payette, and from the shores of the Rio Grande and the Vermillion, the Mississippi and the Pearl, the Missouri and the Congaree, the Machias and the Ohio. These places, these boat ramps and canoe launches and shorelines and bridges are usually pretty vacant and peaceful, unless it's a weekend with good weather. I recall a time I followed the signs for a canoe launch for about five miles down dirt roads to a place along the White River in eastern Arkansas. I sat there for over an hour, and there was a trout in the air about every four seconds. I didn't have a rod and reel with me, but I did catch some grasshoppers and feed them to the fish.

And I remember sitting beside the Rainy near International Falls watching Canada geese teach their young to swim, and beside the Snake where I watched a half dozen pair of loons bob around in the swift current. And along the Banana River one time I got to watch dolphins chase mullet up on shore. And I have watched bald eagles catch fish from the shore of Reelfoot Lake, and Osprey fish the waters of the Gulf of Mexico. And I once saw white pelicans on the Salmon River. And in the Everglades one time I watched as an alligator came up and ate the last two baby coots in the line behind the mother. Was stone cold.

One morning I was sitting on a dock by a boat launch on the Withlacoochee River eating a donut, and two otters came up out of the water at my feet. I shrieked and knocked my helmet in the water and pelted them with my breakfast before I figured out what they were. Did much the same thing with Oreo cookies and a manatee on the Homosassa River one time.

And there was a time, back a long time ago, I had a woman with me, and as we crossed the Nottawasaga River on our way to Penetanguishene, she commented on the emptiness of it all. I told her most of the miles are lonesome, but then that's the nature of motion. I said to her that you own the road, and you rule the ride, and the sun and the moon are on your side.

And I recall another time, another woman, it was up along the Au Sable, and she wanted to know about the road. I explained that there's two ways of goin' and there's no way of knowin' which one it is you should choose. You can use it up runnin' hard in the fast lane, or you can shut it down and just let it rust in the rain. And sometimes, both ways, you lose.

In addition to stupid, I get just poetic as hell around pretty women, and along rivers. Hillbilly haiku.

You can tell a whole lot about a woman from the way she sets behind you on a scooter. First thing you can tell is whether she trusts you or not. Second thing you can learn is how well she is able to follow simple directions. After that you can figure out all kinds of things like how she handles solitude and silence, her athleticism, her feelings about being outdoors, and how good she might be in bed. Some girls just get sort of spastic on a cycle. They jerk and twitch and try to help you ride it, even though you have just specifically asked them not to.

Sometimes you catch a girl trying to peek around you and look in your mirrors. No, they ain't concerned about what might be behind you. They're trying to see how they look in a helmet. And sometimes you get a woman snuggles up close to you, and you get to thinking how good that would feel if you were face to face. In my case, this one is usually followed by ascertaining that the girl is either scared some or that she's smart enough to have figured out that the closer to you she sets, the better you can handle the machine. Sometimes they're just trying to keep my hair out of their eyes.

Some women look up and out. They see the wildlife and the flowers. Other women bury their faces in your leather, look down at the concrete. You might just as well be riding them through a city. And you can tell how perceptive a woman is when you stop and talk about the road and the ride, about the motion and the freedom and the distance. Some of them hear the Roadsongs.

Some of them misunderstand it all and think it's about being someplace. Some of them don't understand that you're just too damn old to grow up. A few of them understand all them things. Occasionally you'll wind up with a woman who is just scared of it.

Once in awhile you will encounter a girl who thinks you're trying to kill yourself. And then you have to try to explain the thin difference between suicide and self-defense.

Had a girl tell me once that most men love a woman the way I love the road. She said she figured that the settin' still times like I was doing with her were just intervals among the episodes.

Speaking of episodes, I should recount my Christmas Story here someplace. I should preface it by saying that I hate to shop. I am basically, in spite of my Grandfather's admonitions, a cheap person. I dislike spending money, even when it's on stuff like food and gas. So sport shopping is not even on my short list of things to do with my time and money. But each Christmas, I buy myself a gift.

One year I needed socks, so I headed down to Tampa to the Army-Navy Surplus place to get some. The only thing the army ever issued me that fit or made much sense was those double sole olive drab boot socks, and this place sells them for a buck or a buck and a half a pair. The Army-Navy Store is in one of them urban neighborhoods with resident crack addicts and militant winos, so they let you park your scooter damn near in the store. Got a little boy named Constantine who watches it for you there.

The place is run by a real nice, friendly, foreign family, I think they are Greek. And this year they saw me coming. And they somehow knew, or sensed at a more primal level, that I was carrying a hundred and twenty-three dollars cash money. And they wanted that money a lot more than I did, it being Christmas Eve and all.

Their leader, Aunt Evangelia, abandoned her position at the cash register to meet me at the door. She turned me over to Uncle Nicholas who began commenting on my old leather jacket while I was sorting through the sock bin. Then Aunt Melina joined him. They noticed the repairs and patches on my old jacket, most of them hand done, some with dental floss. They noted the age and deterioration of the leather, the frayed cuffs and faded back. They enlisted Aunt Evangelia, who peered my direction earnestly. She apparently didn't ever move far from that cash register. But somehow, even at eight or ten foot off, she saw that my jacket's zipper was also broken.

I bought my first leather in about nineteen sixty, I believe from Sears and Roebuck. I remember it cost me twenty-six dollars, including the wolf fur snap-on collar. I was still wearing it in '68 when I got drafted. Then I handed it over to my first ex-wife and got myself a new leather with some of my discharge money in 1970. It cost about a hundred and fifty dollars, no wolf fur, from the local Harley shop. That jacket was the one this group at the Army-Navy Surplus place was criticizing. They kept it up long enough to make me think maybe twenty-five years was a long time to have a leather.

So I told them I didn't have enough money for a new leather jacket, but if they had a vest, I might be able to afford that. The words hadn't left my mouth before the entire family went into action. I had seen a twinkle come into their eyes at my mention of a vest. Aunt Constantia had my old jacket off me faster than a hooker on overtime. She tossed it to a little boy, Ari, behind the counter. Then she measured me quickly and passed me on to one of the pretty teenage nieces, Carla I think, who hustled me into the stock room in the back where Uncle Theodore took over. Damn stock room was huge, filled with hundreds of leathers. It was so packed with leather goods that I really couldn't see much, but it sure smelled good.

Uncle Theodore, with the help of his son, Christos, showed me several jackets. I tried on a few, and damned if one didn't fit really good. Good looking garment, had an inside gun pocket and all. About then, another of the pretty teenage nieces, Allisandra I think, showed up with a nice leather vest. Had four pockets, two with zippers. It fit, too. I continued to protest that I was just there to get me some Christmas socks, and I really couldn't afford these things. But they weren't listening any better than their kin had up in the front of the store.

Now the vest was made in Pakistan from Bangladeshi materials (it did not specify species), and the jacket didn't even pretend to have a label in it, but they both looked good, and they both fit. They made me wear both articles back up front to the counter with the cash register by the door. The pretty teenage nieces took my arms and walked me back. My old leather looked even worse dilapidated beside the new apparel.

When I found myself at the counter with a leather jacket and vest and ten pair of socks, I tried once again to explain that I didn't have the money to buy all these things. Aunt Evangelia got her pencil out, moistened the point with her tongue and began writing on a paper sack. She paused and stared at me hard as if looking into my soul. Then she announced my total was a hundred and twenty-three dollars. She smiled as she took all my money, punched the cash register, and put the money in her pocket.

Stunned at her accuracy, I also feared that my new foreign leather products would dissolve in the first rain I tried to ride in, maybe in the first heavy fog, hell, maybe in the light of day. I stumbled back out the door to my scooter. Uncle Theodore walked me out. When he saw I had a BMW, he began telling about how the only rich kid in his village in the old country had had a BMW. Just like the one Steve McQueen jumped the fence with in "The Great Escape." He became nostalgic, and I listened to some of his Old Country stories while I put my new Christmas gifts in a saddlebag. I bunjied the new leather jacket down and wondered if the bunji cords would cut through it.

As I started to get on my bike, Uncle Theodore fixed me with the same piercing look as Aunt Evangelia had earlier. Then he asked me how much gas did I have. I glanced at my odometer and realized I didn't have enough gas to get home. He shook his head and smiled and took two very old dollars out of his wallet and gave them to me.

The snaps on the vest have rusted some, but both garments have held up well. None of the zippers has broken, neither vest nor jacket disintegrated in the first rain they got into. Merry Christmas, and God Bless us one and all.

21 - HIGHWAY HISTORY LESSONS, FOOD, AND PHOTOGRAPHS

Back in the nineteen seventies, I rode several thousand-mile days. I was young, and there was far less traffic. And there was still cheap gas and good two-lane highways, graceful elegant roads, some of them. And besides that, the cops were fewer and somewhat less predatory, and there was just a whole lot less between here and where you were going to.

My first BMW had the standard 6.3 gallon tank, and it got a real steady fifty miles to the gallon, sometimes more. And I used to ride it five hours from Flint, Michigan to across the Ohio River to Covington, Kentucky without getting off it. Then I'd get a tank of that cheap Kentucky gas and a carton of cigarettes. And then I continued on, usually southbound.

Anymore, I'm lucky to get forty-five miles to the gallon, and I'm unlikely to ride more than a couple hours without stopping. I'd prefer to attribute that to having more appreciation for the scenery, but I suspect it has more to do with arthritis and prostate glands. However, one time, probably thirty years ago, I took that first BMW from below Key Largo up the road north to Flint in just over nineteen hours, most of it at night. It's about fifteen hundred miles. I-75 wasn't finished yet. Stopped five or six times. Longest stop lasted fifteen minutes.

That remark about Covington reminded me of a time I crossed the river and made the turn east out of there and went upriver along the Ohio on Highway 8. There was an old pickup truck with a young couple in it on that road with me. We took turns running lead. Somewhere around Marysville it began raining. I waved at the folks in the truck and bailed off into an abandoned gas station with an overhang.

A few minutes later, I was still getting my rain gear out, the truck came back. Guy rolled his window down and told me the forecast he had just heard on his radio was for seriously increasing rain on through the night. And did I want to follow them the ten miles or so to their house to have supper and spend the night dry.

I should have prefaced these stories by explaining that this was back in the early 1970s, and people used to do such things. It rained well into the night. But I had some real good chicken dumplings and spent a comfortable night on a sofa that time.

Another time, four college girls in a VW Bug convertible, after they had gone to great lengths to explain their offer was neither romantic nor sexual, only friendly, invited me and another boy to stay the night at their place in Lexington. Got to park our scooters in a garage that time.

And I set out most of two days of rain way too hard to try to ride through in a barn outside of Vincennes, Indiana one time. The couple apologized that there just wasn't room in the house; they had about a dozen kids it looked like. I took two meals at their table, but the children were always in motion and impossible to count. But the barn was clean and dry and warm, and I made pretty good friends with a milk cow and two cats. As I recall, I changed my oil the second day there.

Awhile back I was extolling the virtues of historic and geographic lessons along the road. Need to expand on that some here. There aren't many historic roads like the Natchez Trace. There is a lesson every few miles on that road. Kind of like there is a beautiful place to pull over and admire the view every few miles on The Blue Ridge. There is a lot of history along The Blue Ridge, too. But, mostly out there on the obscure two-lane roads, this country is full of places with little signs telling you some pretty neat things about the history and geography of that area.

For example, the DeSoto Trail runs very near my house, much of it along what is now U.S. 301. There are many educational signs along the Trail. If nothing else, it gives you some perspective. Them Spaniards were hacking their way through the state damn near five hundred years ago. And they somehow kept accurate records of it.

The Lewis and Clark Expedition kept real good records, too. And I have stopped and read roadside signs about their journey from Missouri to Washington there on the north shore of the Columbia River where they spent a winter before heading back east. Hell of an excursion, both ways. And one of them, seems like it was Lewis, later got offed, under suspicious circumstances, at a place on The Natchez Trace. Sign right there tells you about it.

One of my favorites is a little area outside Salina, Kansas. It is referred to as the Coronado Hills. There is the obligatory sign and history lesson along the road. Turns out this is the very place where old Coronado, in search of the Seven Cities of Gold, finally got to, looked around, and just gave up. Turned around and followed the stakes that he had prudently driven into the plains back to the Gulf of Mexico. You stand there on that spot for about a short minute, and you understand his decision.

Much of the Great Plains is full of these kinds of history lessons. And some west of Pratt, Kansas there is the world's largest hand-dug well. And in south Nebraska and also way up in the north of Kansas is a couple Pony Express Stations been turned into museums. Talk about longriders and iron butts. And in the north central part of the state, you encounter the geographic center of the contiguous forty-eight states. Yeah, stuck in the middle again. Out there with Toto and Dorothy and them. Seems like they got a Toto museum out there someplace, too.

Most of these little roadside signs are real educational, especially if you like history. Sometimes you encounter a monument telling you that a couple hundred years back, the pioneer white people all got slaughtered by the local Indians in that spot. Once in awhile, it went the other way. Sometimes you get to read about the Mormon Trail and how the first ones through planted crops for the next wave of immigrants to harvest.

The West is full of these places and signs. Like the Donner Pass and Tombstone and Abilene and Deadwood and trapper and trader and mining museums and Spanish missions and such.

New England is overly full of historic places and signs, but other than the ones about the Salem Witch Trials and all, most of them are pretty boring. Not much in the way of New England blood-baths or cattle drives or gunfights or cannibalism. Some of the whaling history is pretty neat.

The Outer Banks, being the site of the first English colonial effort in America, are similarly full of history. A place called Rodanthe on the Outer Banks of North Carolina is the easternmost spot in the forty-eight states, or so I've heard. And I've been told International Falls, Minnesota is the farthest North. Key West is, of course, the southernmost point, even though they will argue that with you down around Brownsville. And there is a place south of Eureka, California that I have been given to understand is the most western in the country. I been to all these places, all of them on two-lane roads. Maybe I ought to start me a club.

And some other spots, like the Craters of the Moon Monument, and some of the places at the west end of Lake Ouachita, and the

Petrified Forest, and Big Bend and the Painted Desert, you get both a geology and a history lesson. Weird places, all of them. And way less crowded than Old Faithful or Mount Rushmore. Cheaper, too.

In that previous book of this nature, I wrote about some battlefields, primarily Civil War vintage, that I've been to. Many of them are haunted. There is a place near where I live that is the site of the last Seminole Indian massacre. It's haunted, too.

And the memorial they put up there where Geronimo surrendered down in the Pendregosa Mountains down by Douglas, Arizona, that's one of them mystic, holy places where you drop it a gear and ride by slowly. Kind of like you do up by Clear Lake, Iowa.

Occasionally you get really lucky in one of these historic places. Years ago, when I first moved down to Florida, I rode over to the Crystal River Indian Burial Mounds over on the Gulf Coast. Cost a quarter. And the guy in charge of the place was alone and bored, and he took me on a personal tour. Very historic. Turns out to be one of the longest continually inhabited places on earth. The pre-Columbian Indians there had trade routes that stretched up into the northern Great Lakes.

Had the same thing happen up north of here at the Dade Battlefield State Memorial. Me and my pardner Ron rode up there one time. Brevet Major Francis Langhorn Dade got himself and his entire command massacred there. And Ranger Steve had nothing else to do, so he walked us around the grounds and gave us a brief history lesson.

Hell, he even loaded and shot off a replica of the cap and ball rifles the army had back then. We learned that there were far more wounded than dead during the Seminole Wars, mostly because of the small bore weapons. I guess many of the injured died as a result of their wounds though. That may account for the ghosts.

That mention of the massacre put me in mind of another woman who didn't understand. She told me I was just one more outbound dead man with a death wish in his eye. She said I looked like I had seen too much for one man to look at, and that I had come by it honest. And she also declared the same thing about that thousand yard stare. She said this all to me on the occasion of my leaving, soon after her observation that she didn't think I was a two-way rider.

A long time ago I began thinking about trying to take a picture of the shadow beside my scooter, in motion. Never got around to even trying it. Awhile back a girl got up behind of me and took about a dozen pictures like I told her about.

Speaking of pictures, postcards are pictures. One time in a real heavy fog in West Virginia, up along the New River there at Hawk's Nest, I stopped at a roadside restaurant mostly to get out of the fog. It was one of those thick, swirling vapors that you couldn't see much or far in. And what you could see was often a trick because of the moving, whirling fog.

You couldn't see much of the road or the roadside either one. Someone was going to get hurt out there on the concealed curves of that fogged over mountain highway, and I just didn't feel like getting wounded that morning. Sometimes a graceful road becomes a dangerous one.

I been in bad fog before. I was once on out there in California when the tule fog came upon us. It was so damn thick we just couldn't even hear anything. There was about an eighty car pile up south of us that morning, and they shut the highway down before anyone else died. And I recall a thick, wet fog on an empty two-lane road up north of Poplar Bluff one morning. The water kept building on my windshield and then coming over the top and into my face when I hit a bump.

And one time, up along the Skyline Drive, the only thing I was able to see for about forty miles was my pardner's tail light, from about four foot away, at about thirty miles an hour. And it was a bad, dense ground fog, this was out in west Texas or maybe east New Mexico, that completely covered up everything below about your knees. We had to set that one out a few hours as none of us had any idea where the road was.

So I set there in West Virginia at the restaurant on a bluff over the New River, which I couldn't see because of the fog, and drank coffee awhile and smoked cigarettes and talked to the two waitresses and one other local customer for a long time.

Eventually, I began to feel some guilty and bought a few postcards. They had a rack of them by the cash register, and I grabbed a half dozen. I sat and wrote notes to friends and watched the fog swirl around outside. Finally, I turned one of the cards over to see the picture.

Then I jumped back up and bought some more. There were only about ten or twelve selections, but I got one of each. Beautiful pictures of local scenic wonders, mostly rivers and mountains. A couple were of animals, a bear and some deer I think. Might have been a hawk, too.

Over the years, I bet I've bought and sent near five thousand post cards. These were easily the prettiest pictures I'd ever seen. I mean these looked way too good to be commercial. As I was marveling at the photos, the younger of the two waitresses, Rhonda Robynne Rita Rose, brought me some more coffee. As she poured it for me she smiled at the postcards and said, "Ain't them pretty though?"

I agreed, and then she told me that the boy who took the pictures and made the postcards was kin to the other waitress, Hannah Dreama Geneva Mariah. And she told me that he would be by that very morning to fill his rack up. Honest. Ain't often that such an opportunity presents itself, and I have learned to take advantage when one does.

Just about the time the fog finally cleared good, he showed up. The man was much younger than I had presumed. Rhonda Rose introduced us, and I began raining praise all over the guy's photographic skills. Bought him a coffee and me some more postcards. He turned out to be a hell of a nice guy.

He told me about landscape photography and wildlife photography and developing his own shots. And about not being able to make a real living at it and having to take pictures of kids and dogs at the Mart-Mart Store to buy groceries. Then he finished his coffee, loaded his rack with new cards, and asked if I would like to follow him, go with him to a place where he was going to take some new postcard pictures.

Several hours later, up around Judy Gap, I was holding on to a rope the guy was hanging from trying to get a picture. We had to wait for the light. I learned enough about picture taking that day to determine I will never be any good at it. I added photography to the list of things I will never be any good at. I'm up to volume eight.

Florida is a fine place to live most of the time. One of the reasons I live here is so that I can ride my cycle year around. It gets too hot and humid for some people, but my feeling is that the human body is over seventy percent water. And water freezes at thirty-two degrees. I think that skin has pores in it to perspire through, not to make little goose bumps around. I'm not good at much, but sweating is one of the things I excel at. So I greatly enjoy the warmth.

But the Fall is an especially wonderful and beautiful time of the year here in central Florida. The state has three basic climate zones. When it's down to freezing up in the Panhandle, it's forty or forty-five at my house and fifty or sixty in Miami.

November days in central Florida run up into the mid-seventies mostly. There is little rain in the Fall. And the hurricanes and fires are usually about done for the year. The only problem on a bike is that there is often more wind than is comfortable to ride in. The best way to get away from that is to find roads that run through tall forests. There are no riotous color changes, but there are some truly beautiful, if subtle, transformations in the foliage and the sky.

The cypress trees turn a soft, pretty gray color. The raintrees blossom with a hundred different shades from pinks to yellows and russets. Some of the longleaf pines, their needles die out and turn a rusty red color along their bottom branches. Pecan trees lose leaves and thin out. Sycamore foliage turns to a pretty russet brown, and then the trees shed leaves the size of sheets of paper on the pavement in front of you.

There are slender, kind of spindly trees that grow tight together along the shores of lakes and rivers. Might be water oaks. Whatever they are, they somehow lose all their leaves, and then the thin branches wave a little in the wind and look like whispy smoke. Various weeds come to seed, and turn whole fields a sort of soft, misty reddish color. Tawny colored rolls of hay are laid out in serpentine lines across verdant fields. Assorted palms and scrub palmetto lose their sheen and turn a duller shade of green.

And the sun comes to the tropical foliage at a more gentle angle. The rivers slow down some. The swamps dry up a little. The air smells drier. Lots of different shades of browns and yellows replace some of the greens in the fields and the woods both. And there are even a few patches of brilliant purples and reds with names like vermilion and crimson and scarlet and fuscia and puce. Some of the fruit is just coming to ripe, providing more yellows and oranges among the green.

Many of the climbing vines turn colors or die out. The former sometimes creates a real pretty cascade effect of crimson or gold down a tree. The latter leaves the woods looking thinner. Most of the wildflowers are about done, but there are a few remaining ones if you look for them. Mostly yellows and whites. A few little red ones.

If you watch the sky, you can see birds migrating, graceful lines of sandhill cranes and curlews and wood storks, tumbling wads of snipe and ducks. There are still butterflies in the air and some flowers in bloom. Honeysuckle and passion flowers and calicarpia and a few leftover white water lilies on the lakes. Various warts and some lilies nearly clog the rivers you ride over.

There are often so many white flowers that it almost looks like snow on the rivers, especially up near the spring boils. Hibiscus, Mexican flame vine, and some poinsettias are coming to bloom and color in the yards. You can take off on your ride in the morning with your leather on, maybe some gloves. By mid-day you want to change the leather out for a light jacket, maybe even just your shirtsleeves. No sweating.

And then, just about at this time of the year, the elderly migratory Yankees come on down and choke up the roads and ruin your ride. There has been so much growth and development in the state the past couple decades that I ought not bitch about the wintering crowd. At least they go away eventually. But anymore you can find a boutique or an antique shop easier than you can find a place to hunt.

Some days, not just in the Fall, you get to running under the Florida sun, out there on a two-lane, and a canopy of trees covers the road. If it's real dense, thick trees, it's almost like riding in a tunnel. If the foliage is a little thinner, as it tends to be in the Fall, it creates a kind of weird strobe light effect as you roll along through the shifting shadows.

One time during the middle 1970s, one of America's darkest periods, The Disco Era, me and three of my old road riding brothers came down off The Blue Ridge to find a motel and supper one evening. Wound up in one of those little valley towns, so deep in the mountains that the sun hardly ever shined there. One way in and no way out. We found a room for the night, and were directed to the only nearby eatery for food.

After supper, one of my pardners went in search of a six pack. He returned to the motel a little while later with the beer. And he was laughing so damn hard he could hardly talk. Made us all get up and put our boots back on and come with him to the place where he'd found the beer. It was a small town, and we quickly walked the two blocks.

Next to the store was the local version of a contemporary nightclub, a disco dance parlor. And they had a sign on the door. It was on a paper plate, lettered in green crayon. And it advised that they had one of them disco dancin' strobe lights in there, and it warned that if you were prone to attacks or subject to fits, you ought not come in, as the light was likely to touch off a seizure. Attendance was minimal.

A small portion of that first book dealt with local dialects. I had a whole bunch of folks tell me how much they enjoyed that part. Wasn't none of them professional literary critics either. So, I am going to address that issue again briefly. I have had recent inspiration.

Turns out I am still trying to get some of my money back for that Killer Federal Foliage Incident. The woman in charge of tort claims for the Department of the Interior talks so damn pretty it just makes you want to move to North Carolina. I've spoken to her a couple times on the phone, and she has left me a couple of those voicemail message things on my phone at work. Damn, but that girl talks pretty.

She is pretty obviously from the mountains, the western portion of the state. That tidewater dialect over there along the Atlantic shore ain't near as pretty. Sounds some like a college Shakespeare production with the actors all trying to sound Elizabethan. And the dialect in the middle, the Piedmont area of the Carolinas and Virginia and some of Georgia, those folks sound like they're trying to talk without opening their mouths. I used to know a woman from either Fayetteville or Florence, she was a Litratyure major.

And you can still tell you're up in the Dakotas or Minnesota when you hear someone say, "Aw Jeez!" And Canadians as a group will still say, "Go oot and walk aboot da hoose, eh." And in parts of Missouri, if you tell someone they talk funny, they'll tell you they "Cain't hep it." Heard a woman in south Arkansas tell about how she "retched out the car winda and wove at her neighbor." And I've talked to some people from New York who think my name is "Toyguh" (as in, "Toyguh, you dumb bastid") and that I live in a place called "Flawader."

I ought not make fun of such things. One time years back, I got hired to do some radio commercials. Took the producer about twenty minutes to learn me how to say "battery" with three syllables. Only thing wrong with that job was that it came around just about Christmas, and I had to ride down into the bowels of Tampa and Clearwater to various sound studios. Damn wintertime tourist snowbird traffic near killed me several times.

As I pointed out in the previous book, regional dialects are declining and leveling in America. It's damn difficult anymore to find a place where the accent is so thick you can't understand the folks there. I miss that. That's the sort of diversity that appeals to me.

But, anymore, America is becoming so damn bland and homogenized and conformist and alike and limited and non-diverse that not only does everyplace look a lot like every place else, but the people all pretty much talk similar, too. And dress alike and act alike and think alike. And they are inconsiderate, intolerant and abusive of anyone who doesn't conform.

You don't believe that, light a cigarette almost anyplace in contemporary America. Hell, better yet, just take one out and play like you're going to light it. Or remark negatively on the kiddie-centric nature of modern society. Or suggest that Motherhood, particularly Working Mothers, and most especially Single Motherhood, is not the equivalent of sainthood. Martyrdom maybe, but not sanctification.

The politically correct people can talk about tolerance and diversity all they want to. But America is quickly becoming about as dissimilar as corn flakes. The basic differences are Coke or Pepsi and which football team folks cheer for. And besides real social and ethnic and local diversity, I also miss the different speech patterns I used to encounter.

The leveling of American dialects has not affected urban ethnic and racial speech varieties. On the rare occasion that I hear a contemporary Youthful Urban African-American variety of English, I have some trouble understanding it. I've discovered much the same is true with various urban Latino dialects. Again, this is a current generation phenomenon. And, it would appear that many white suburban children do not have such a problem, as they spend much time and energy trying to mimic these dialects.

Some vestiges of local dialects remain. When in Oregon, you ought to learn to say Ory-gun, and then if you're going north, you need to emphasize the Sea- in Seattle. Toronto is locally pronounced Torunna. Sort of like the old people in Miami who insist on saying Miamuh.

Besides dialect differences, you wander into some pretty weird food things out there on the road. In southern West Virginia they grow an especially pungent and strong onion-like vegetable called a ramp. Some places even got festivals dedicated to the ramp. In parts of Alabama and Mississippi I have encountered a local product called Chow Chow Sauce. Best I can tell it's some sort of relish or piccalilli kind of thing.

In the middle part of the country, especially Missouri it seems like, they put some kind of pickled peppers in a jar on the tables with the salt and pepper. Most of the time these things are in a little beaker with a top from which the liquid can be shaken. Some places in South Carolina, a plain donut is glazed, and a plain hamburger has mayonnaise on it. Most places in the southeast, a Cold Drink, and that is often one word, refers to a non-alcoholic refreshment. And you never know if you should ask for a soda or a pop. Or a tonic.

Canadians give you vinegar to put on your French fries, and down along the southern border you get a bowl of salsa there with the salt and pepper on the table. In most of south Louisiana they do the same thing with hot sauce. A lot of the places in the North, I've noticed they put ketchup on the table like that.

In the Upper Peninsula of Michigan (say yup to the U.P., eh) and parts of Minnesota they try to sell you a thing called a pasty. Some areas get real serious about it, and try to sell you one about every quarter mile. It's a kind of, usually unidentified, meat pie full of parsnips and rutabagas. And the only useful function I can think of for a parsnip or a rutabaga is muskrat trap bait.

Put me in mind of the pseudo-fish-like substance by-product-helper McNuggets I got fed in Gibraltar while I was over there in Spain, Europe. Turns out you can't eat there. The damn food is English. And like ramps and Chow Chow Sauce, them pasties might make a good souvenir or be a draw for the tourists, but they sure ain't anything to eat.

Florida has all kinds of food festivals. Many of the tourists and winter nomads come specifically to eat. Eating is real important to many tourists. If you don't believe that, go to any amusement attraction in Orlando and count fat people with ice cream cones.

Many of these Florida culinary fairs are seafood inspired, Florida being a peninsula and all. And, for the most part, the seafood is real good. Maybe not up there with the seafood in Calabash, but good. Oftentimes, anymore, thanks to the proliferation of chain food restaurants, these little fairs and festivals may be your only means of really sampling the local cuisine.

Awhile back I ate a portion of alligator at such an occasion. The gator was pen-raised, and the goddamn meat tasted like Purina Alligator Chow. I made this same observation awhile back relative to domestic catfish. Didn't taste at all like catfish are supposed to. Similarly, some time ago, I was fed some domestic quail that tasted just like the Styrofoam it had been packed in.

It's kind of like all those flavored coffees that are so damn popular anymore. If you don't like the way coffee tastes, you ought to get yourself a cup of tea or a beer or something. Coffee is supposed to taste like coffee, not beebleberries or pistachio nuts, and certainly not like vanilla.

Wild game and fish are supposed to taste like wild game and fish. And if your tastes don't run that way, you ought to remain with Kentucky Chicken and Mrs. Paul's fish sticks.

If you like crawfish, you can eat yourself into a stupor in southwest Louisiana if you hit it right. I mean you can just get greasy faced for days on end. I've found Louisiana a fine place to be hungry, even if it ain't crawfish season. And there are some real pretty and colorful talking folks there, too, them.

Sort of like I have never been impressed with the food in New England, except for the lobsters along the coast and the Annual Egg Festival up in Skowhegan, Maine. And I really don't know if Maine considers itself part of New England, but them damn eggs were the size of my fist. The omelets hung over the sides of the plate. Boy I was with said he wanted to meet the griffin that had laid those eggs. But other than that, the food is right up there with the local dialects for fun and notice.

You can hear dialects better and eat better out on the two-lane roads than in cities and along the super-slabs. There, that's reasons number seventeen and eighteen to avoid urban complexes and the interstate system. Contemporary people are more mobile, both vicariously and in reality. They tend more to move to and live in far parts of the country than in days of yore. That's making a mess of regional and local dialects. So is TV and the like. And that's eighty-three reasons to avoid TV.

Some places have, somehow, over the years, developed a particular food fame. Like the fruit cakes in Claxton, Georgia, and the chocolate in Hershey, Pennsylvania, and Charleston she crab soup, and them pasties in the U.P. of Michigan, and San Francisco and Seattle and Chesapeake Bay seafood, and cheese in Wisconsin, and the pralines and beignets in New Orleans, and artichokes in Castroville, and Baltimore crabs, and Miami Cuban sandwiches, and Maine lobsters. And, locally, we have the Kumquat Festival every Winter. And they'll try to sell you orange blossom honey with your Mickey Mouse t-shirt all around the state.

Florida may be the nation's capital of tourist scams generally. Back years ago, when I was living in the North, I used to come down to Florida often. This was back before I-75 was there, and I usually rode down the middle of the state, down U.S. 441 through Ocala. And there was always a big sign beside the road advertising Big Sam, The World's Biggest Horse. The colorful sign included a poor representation of a big horse. One year, apparently the horse died, for the picture now had big horns, and Big Sam was touted as The World's Biggest Bull.

One time I got into the cherry harvest and assorted festivals up in northwest Michigan. Whole huge bunch of different kinds of cherries. Got into a jalapena pepper festivity somewhere in the southwest one time. And, at a county fair in northern Michigan, I once encountered a Spam carving contest.

Some of it has to do with good food. Some of it has to do with marketing. And some of it has to do with absolute desperation.

22 - *MORE LAMENTATIONS, YOUTHFUL MEMORIES, OSTRICHES, AND OREO COOKIES*

Once long ago, in my sordid and rebelious youth, I got real drunk, and rode my motorcycle into a classroom building on the campus of the junior college I was attending while pursuing an unsuccessful major in draft dodging. Seems like this was about 1963 or '64 probably. Took the cycle down to the end of the slippery, fresh waxed hallway and got it on the elevator.

When I rode it off, on the third floor, I just took a fast lap around the slick corridors one time, blowing smoke and making a lot of noise, disturbed the classes in session, got back on the elevator, returned to the ground floor and exited the building. As I reflect on that, I can't even remember if I did it on a dare or just for fun.

I do remember the next morning. I was drinking hungover coffee in the student union when two deans, a department chairman, my academic advisor, and about a half platoon of security goons all came over and joined me. Everyone frowned sternly. My advisor, normally a dear, sweet woman, had been elected their spokesman.

She sat beside me, and took me by my hand, squeezed it hard enough to hurt the whole time. She spoke to me through grit teeth. Told me not to ever do it again. She began in the time-honored tradition of women correcting me, and said, "Tiger, you dumb bastard."

Another time, while I was still in college, young and wild and dedicated to reckless behavior, I decided to show off in front of the girls. Testosterone and stupidity are near as bad as alcohol sometimes. The girls were a large group of nursing students, maybe fifty of them. The showing off involved popping a wheel and riding it that way the length of the campus parking lot in front of them. I turned the damn thing over on top of myself before the very eyes of all those little nursettes. And I have never seen a group of adult people with less sympathy for the stupid. Not one of them even offered me a bandage or an aspirin. No, these girls didn't even look away from the carnage. They laughed. A couple of them picked me up. One of them, Mary Pat

Cecelia Teresa, it was a Catholic nursing school, she stopped laughing long enough to say, "Tiger, you dumb bastard..."

Getting old sucks. I guess it beats most of the alternatives. But it sure is weird. I recall a conversation several of us had on the way back from Woodstock. Among other things, we all of us agreed that Richard Nixon was evil and that we never figured for any of us to ever see forty. Sure didn't. You can't beat long odds forever. So I have been just stone disoriented and bewildered these past fifteen or so years. Here I am, totally unprepared, and being called upon to make adult decisions.

And the other day when I went out and got my mail, I had a form letter from the Socialist Security Administration telling me I was screwed and couldn't retire until I was sixty-six. And there was an invitation from the AARP or some such group soliciting me to join their merry group of gray panthers now that I am eligible. The final piece of mail, and maybe the last straw, was an advertisement for Lowered Expectations or Last Desperate Elderly Chance, some kind of old people computer dating service.

It's not so much the obvious fact or the realization that you ain't a kid no more. It's the eventually having to admit it to yourownself. And then you have to try to behave accordingly. But I have finally got to where I can't ride far hard and fast like I used to could do. And anymore, I just really don't hardly ever feel like getting bad wounded, especially self-inflicted.

What happens is wiry kids turn into stringy old men. The dying riders' lament. And anymore out on the road, within a couple hours my hands get to aching, then my elbows. Sometime after that, my back goes all to hell. Awhile after that, my bad hip hurts. I can't ride all night long like I used to could do. My damn knees just won't straighten out as easy or as soon as they used to, and I got to pee more frequently than in the past.

It ain't just me. I had a pretty funny conversation with my old pardner, Captain Zero, recently. A few years back me and him went through that arms too short to read thing and on into the bifocals and reading glasses together. This time recently we spoke of our declining ability to see well at night. Each of us had just about polished holes in both our windshields and our glasses trying to remedy the problem.

I think I am going slower and easier anyway. Impatience has less of a hold on me than it did in my younger days. And, except in cases of bad manners, blatant stupidity, or outright silliness, I have gotten more tolerant in my old age. I try hard not to criticize what I don't understand, unless I do it in a book.

And there seems to be more and more that I just don't comprehend. I still can't abide a coward or a liar or a cheat, but I really have gotten some mellower with time. People who knew me long ago tell me so anyway.

But I recall a time in the distant past when my Grandfather and I took his car to pick Lizabeth up from work. And she was late. And I got impatient and pissed off. Grampaw, who was happily married to my Grammaw for over sixty years, she was the only woman he ever loved, he explained to me that Lizabeth wasn't doing it on purpose.

And I ranted and bitched that I had intended to do something later on, and now with Lizabeth late, I wouldn't be able to. He offered me a cigarette and told me that I could do it tomorrow. For after all, tomorrow will be much like today.

So anyway, generally speaking, it takes me longer to get there than it used to. Hell, I've got to where it takes me all night to do what I used to do all night. I made a series of errors on my last birthday. My tendency is to pamper and spoil myself on birthdays, much like I do with Christmas. And, as my Grandfather, the quality control expert, also taught me—A man ought to do what a man thinks he's good at.

Must have either been of a weekend or Spring Break, because I didn't have to go to work. Anyway, I jumped up in the pre-dawn darkness and loaded dogs and guns and went afield for a few hours hunting birds. I returned home long enough to brush and feed my dogs, clean the game, and then the gun. For that was the manner in which my Grandfather, the hunter, taught me to do those things. And then I climbed on my motorcycle. Rode it over to the coast and along the Gulf awhile, came back through the forests. Got home about an hour before sundown. Just in time to saddle Nokomis the horse and find a short hill to watch sundown from. I damn near couldn't move at all the next day. Aspirins for breakfast again.

But then tomorrow really will be a lot like today, so there seems to be less reason to hurry than in the past. That's easy for an old man to say. For I've rode my thousand mile days and done my ten thousand mile/twenty-some state runs. I've already got my million miles. I've done passed through.

And that brings me back around to the nature of motorcycle travel. I spent long enough driving a truck to resent imposed schedules and deadlines and destinations and such. Especially on the highway. Spoils the independence and the reverence both. And if you don't take some time along the way, you won't have many highway stories to tell.

There was a long period in my youth, sort of between seventeen and twenty-seven or so, when what I had for transportation was I had a motorcycle. Cars were just too expensive, especially the insurance and gas and upkeep after the costly initial outlay. Scooters were cheaper. Cheaper to buy, cheaper to maintain, cheaper to run and cheaper to license. And a whole lot more fun, if sometimes pretty inconvenient.

And I got lucky because a boy I lived with for awhile when I was in college was the heir apparent to a local giant junkyard. He always had a car. Never had a new one or a pretty one, but he always had a damn car. And later, in the army, I also lived awhile with generous people with vehicles. But what I had was I had a cycle.

Motorcycles are real handy when you are looking for a parking place, but they ain't worth a damn for toting a huge pile of dirty clothes to the laundromat. Even harder carrying it back clean. Pretty difficult to get much of a load of groceries home intact on a bike, too. And a sheet of plywood is impossible. I found that one out the hard way.

Motorcycles are wonderful things on bright, clear, warm summer days and nights. But it's hard to be anything but miserable in a cold hard rain. Even harder when the cold hard rain is coming down on you in the dark. I recall coming out of classes in the evening to find my cycle buried in snow. In the North, in the endless dark of Winter, I often became a permanent pedestrian for weeks at a time. I rode a lot in sub-zero weather, and I can't remember ever enjoying it much.

And then there was the problem of transporting women. As I recall, I did a whole lot of double dating back then, at least in the Winter months. It was hard enough to get a girl on a motorcycle in the Summer. Now that I review that, I wasn't all that popular with the fairer sex, even as a young man, so maybe this really wasn't a big problem. About the only women who went out with me were trying to piss their parents off.

Years ago, like twenty or more, I noticed, with sadness, that technology was making great strides, inroads into the hinterlands. On this ride, I kept running across official CALL 911 FOR EMERGENCY signs. I mean I found some of these signs so deep in the woods that, back then, I doubt the local people had telephones. Anymore, I imagine they got them a cell phone on the Allis-Chalmers.

Five or so years later, I observed, again with similar sorrow, another burgeoning same sign phenomenon. This time the signs heralded nearby video game parlors. And, again, I was encountering these damn signs in the wilderness between little towns that were far apart. In places where they ought not to have had electricity.

Anymore I've got to where these things don't disturb me. Oh, hell, that ain't true. They still trouble me, but I've about got used to it. Much of the time I have no idea what the sign refers to or is selling. I've run across video movie rental facilities far out in the wasteland, out beyond the Forbidden Zone. And I've come upon quaint little beds and breakfasts in some damn unlikely places. Places where there ain't people or a reason for any to be there.

Incidentally, I've done some research and finally figured out the basic difference between a bed and breakfast and a motel all by myself: fifty dollar breakfast. This nationwide mercenary commercial consumption frenzy is partly the result of overpopulation and partly due to institutionalized greed.

A long time ago I was taken to what I was told was The World's Largest Mart-Mart Store. The enormity of the emporium, the insane variety of stuff for sale, the size of the crowds of savage shoppers, the very nature and magnitude of the abominable greed involved, it all scared me. I feared getting lost in the store, and I worried about finding my motorcycle in the vastness of the parking lot. And I was anxious that the Sportshopping Police would figure out I didn't have a charge card or an intention to buy anything I didn't need and couldn't get in a saddlebag, and that they would carry me off to Shopper Prison.

So I sought sanctuary on a balcony—mezzanine some above the frenzied throng. I was looking over several acres of Commercial Stuff For Sale. Must have been a half acre of various popcorn poppers alone. And I realized, with gladness, that none of it had anything to do with my life. Anymore, there is a store like this at both ends of every little town in the country.

Many years ago, when the fake fingernail craze was in its infancy, before it became an industry and an institution, I rode past a big sign on a business in a little nothing town out beyond the middle of nowhere.

Sign said—JUST NAILS. I wondered how you could maintain such a business. Thought it would probably be better to carry nuts and bolts and screws as well. Maybe even some washers.

A month later, a woman straightened me out on the nature of that concern. She initiated her lesson the same way such explanations almost always begin. She laughed and said, "Tiger, you dumb bastard..." It ain't easy being The Last Longrider sometimes.

And I guess there ain't much point or profit in complaining about getting old. As my learned Grandfather, the intellectual, explained—Bitching, like prayer and worry, won't help none.

One time long ago me and a highway brother come at it from both ends so we could meet in the middle. He rode south and I rode north. And we met up at a rest area up high on a hill on the road that runs between Austin Peay State University and Fort Campbell early the second day. Then we rode west until we couldn't no more. Dropped south from there and took the southern route down through Big Bend to Presidio and then on up to Las Cruces and then over to the coast through Tombstone and Death Valley. Wound up riding up the Pacific coast all the way around the Olympic Peninsula. And then we turned right, toward the dawn, and come back east on a northern route. We eased down into the Great Lakes where he lived. I rode on home alone.

From the beginning of that paragraph to the end was something like twelve thousand miles. Twenty-some states. Two full moons. Second one was blue. We rode through one damn serious storm and two lesser ones. Killer heat in the Dakotas and frigid sleet in the Upper Peninsula of Michigan. The Badlands and the Heartland. Downtown San Francisco and downtown Seattle, downtown Crossett and downtown Choteau, and the hinterlands, the wastelands, and the wilderness.

It was still pretty chilly in north Tennessee when we got it together and got to it. So we dropped down south to get warm and to run a piece of the Natchez Trace, even though it ran the wrong direction. But it gave us a chance to stop at the visitors' center there by Tupelo and spend some time with the sweet lady who ran the place. Over the years, several of us often used that tourist center as a meeting place, especially when we were headed west via a southern route.

And that lovable woman did everything from checking long distance weather reports for us to feeding us. Zero and me discovered this place on The Perfect Ride long ago. She made us sign the guest book that time, so she knew my name. First time after that, when we met there, it was raining. I was the first among us to arrive.

And when I pulled up to a picnic table under some trees for shelter from the rain, she stood in the doorway shouting and waving at me. I figured she was going to yell at me for not parking in the designated parking area. When I rode over to her to plead my case, she told me to put my bike up under the overhang at the side of the building and to come inside and get dry and warm. She shook her head and smiled and said, "Tiger, you dumb bastard..." I reacted to the news of her retirement with mixed emotions.

Then we rode west from there toward The River and down out of the hills. We crossed The River at Refuge, headed steady west to Texarkana through the pine forests and past the paper mills. And then we come sideways across Texas. Took about forever. Rained hard enough to pull over and set it out around San Angelo. That first full moon was out south of there along the Rio Grande.

I bet we crossed thirty or forty rivers, the Red, the Nueces, the Noyo and the Russian and the Mad and the Eel, the Columbia and the Vermillion and the Medicine and the Crazy Woman River. We rode out beside the Skaggit awhile, and some along the Omak. We two rode through Twisp and Okonagan and along beside the Spokane.

Went through Coeur d' Alene and Sand Point and on to Glacier Park. That was where the second moon, the blue one, came to full. Then we rode Highways 200 and 12 on east through Montana. Somehow we wound up at a place called Mule Shoe. After that it was a day of wheat fields and then into the northern forests up there far above the forty-fifth parallel.

Temperatures varied from a hundred and fourteen down around Blythe someplace to thirty-one up north in that sleet storm. We rode through four time zones, twice each. We rode below level, and we rode some up around ten thousand feet. We did ride through deserts and towering sequoia forests, past glaciers and high alpine meadows full of wildflowers. We rode past Joshua trees and seguaro cactus and right through a big giant redwood tree. Cost us a dollar each. And we rode through three or four oil changes, and a rear tire apiece. We did ride along the northern California cliffs above the ocean, and we rode the road along the low shore of Lake Superior.

We had burritos from a roach coach down around Douglas and

fine meals at fine restaurants in San Francisco and Seattle. And we had picnics in the parking lots of convenience stores in the wasteland and woman-cooked, homemade food twice. We had been treated better than kin by some friends of ours. And we had been badly dealt with by a couple strangers.

We had seen roadrunners and seagulls and eagles and magpies and swallows and hummingbirds. We saw wild turkeys and pheasants and sage grouse and prairie chickens and a dozen different kinds of ducks. We had seen sundogs dance in the western sky, and we'd seen rainbows in the east. We had ridden along beside low rivers and over snow-capped mountain peaks.

And we had seen prairie dogs and antelope and big horn sheep scamper up the high steep slopes. We saw white tails and mule deer and buffalo. We had seen javalina and moose and marmots and seals. We'd seen rattlesnakes and gila monsters. We saw coyotes and badgers and elk. We'd seen wild horses and some tame ones, too.

Like rivers, we ran through a lot of mountains on this ride. I recall the Talladegas and the Van Horn and Davis Mountains, the Chisos and the Pyramids and del Nortes, the Maricopas and the Gilas and the Sangre de Cristos, the Sierra Nevada and the Coastal Range and the Northern Cascades. We rode over the Rockies and the Bighorns and the Big Snowy and the Little Belt Mountains, the Black Hills and the Porcupines. And coming back home down out of the big lakes by myself, I drifted over east and got into some of the Smokies.

That was where I encountered the ostriches. I was blowing along real easy down a two lane, someplace around Mineral Bluff, or maybe it was Sweet Water, on a two lane. It was a narrow, sort of easy serpentine road, and I wasn't going but about forty-five or fifty. When I saw the pickup truck in my mirrors, I noticed it was hauling a stock trailer.

When I saw his turn signal come on, I realized he was going to pass me, and I drifted to the right a little to help him. It was a pretty narrow and curvaceous road, and I wanted him past me more than he did. As the truck pulled even with me, the old boy riding shotgun waved and nodded at me. I smiled and waved back.

I was sort of focused on the pickup, trying to stay in the driver's mirrors for him as the truck got ahead of me. And I wasn't paying good attention. The stock trailer got even with me, and about a half dozen ostriches poked their heads out between the slats and looked me over keenly and attentively. As ostriches have especially long necks, they looked me over closely, from about six inches away.

For a minute, it looked like some kind of weird Medusa or monster of the hydra or something like that. Ostriches have real expressive eyes it turns out, real unlike any other bird I have ever looked in the eye. I damn near bailed off the road. It was the sight of the passenger in the truck laughing, I could see him watching me in his mirror, that saved me.

I pulled off next chance there was, to compose myself some. Had a cup of coffee, smoked a cigarette. Got out a map to investigate and research things. It took awhile, but I finally found the obscure road I was on. I studied the map awhile, and that road essentially went nowhere. My conclusion was that them boys just loaded up some ostriches every once in awhile, and then drove them around to fuck with people. Didn't look like there was much else in the way of entertainment around there.

Before and since then, I've seen a lot of strange species in livestock trailers. I've seen rabbits and buffalo and llamas and pygmy goats and big dogs and children. It was them long necks and near proximity that got to me with the ostriches. And their eyes. Seems like there was another, a third moon come to full a day or so later as I was getting back home.

There was a whole bunch of really neat things happened as a result of that first Longrider book getting published. I hope the same thing goes down around this one. My favorite part of all was that my dad somehow got a copy of it to some friends of his, a couple he had gone to school with. Well, and again, this addresses that niche market fallacy, they loved it. They have sons who used to ride motorcycles, and they wound up buying a half dozen books and that many tapes. And in the meantime, we wrote several letters back and forth, and I made a couple new friends.

That Spring semester, toward the end of my Expository Writing class one day, the classroom door opened, and a cute, elderly woman I had never seen before stood there looking at me, looking me over. Then she turned to the tall gentleman behind her and said, "Yeah, it's him." Then they both walked into the classroom.

I quickly dismissed the class and greeted my visitors with, "Who the hell are you? And do I know you?" As I am a constant source of mirth on campus as well as on the highway, most of the students lingered on their way out. The sweet woman giggled, handed me a gift-wrapped box of Oreo cookies, and introduced herself and her companion.

Yup, my dad's old classmates, my new friends. Broke the kids up. I only had a couple hours between classes, but I had a fine time with those folks. We went back to my office, drank a cup of coffee. Had some Oreos.

This dear old woman, who I had just met, sat me down and looked at me somewhat sternly, and said to me, "I enjoyed your book very much, but all I could think of was how worried your daddy must have been for all these years." As she was a mother, she had been carrying that one around since reading the book. And she felt obliged to get it out of her system and into mine.

And you know, I don't think I had ever thought about it like that before. So we called my dad from my office. Asked him if he had ever been bad worried about me being out there on a scooter. He said he always figured everything I got after about the age of thirteen was somewhere between a bonus and a miracle. This is the son of my Grandfather, the faith-healer, we're talking about here, so I listened to him careful. He reflected on how he had been on a first-name basis with everyone on all three shifts in the emergency room at the hospital when I was a kid. I pointed out that, as often as not, I was being stitched up or getting a cast put on for a non-motorcycle related incident. He laughed, and then he spoke of the time I had called him after my near fatal fall on Red Mountain, my legendary Downfall In Durango. Said that one had worried him some.

Hell, I had waited a few weeks, until I was healed up enough to ride again, before I called him to tell him about it. I was lucky that time, and I was riding with a couple good friends when I dropped it there in Colorado. These boys rode with me out to San Francisco, but then each of them had to leave out different before I was healed up good. And then I eventually got gone back east alone, still among the riding wounded. I'd done about ten yards on my face that time, and people kept looking at me like I was a damn leper.

As I remember this, I called my father from a phone booth on the banks of the Powder River. It was the only structure for many miles. There was no water in the river bed, and the fine grit was mostly blowing up my nose as my dad and I talked on the phone. So I said something to him about the damn dust. And he, being the son of my Grandfather, the etymologist, pointed out that was why they had named it the Powder River.

That sweet woman who brought me the Oreo cookies into my classroom, she was the first one to do that, to give me Oreos after reading my book. But a few others have since. Had a girl step off an airplane, Oreos in hand, awhile back. I handed her a helmet as she handed me the cookies. Hell, my mom even sent me some Oreo cookies for Christmas. And any time you got a pretty woman giving you food, you're in good shape.

Oreos will hold up in a saddlebag, won't disintegrate into a bagful of crumbs or melt into a unattractive lump o' cookie. And Oreo cookies will last for about ever. You got to keep them in an airtight baggie. Otherwise they will go stale on you and soak up moisture like a sponge. Also turns out prairie dogs, marmots, black bears, and wild ponies are real fond of Oreo cookies, too. And, in a pinch, you can chum fish and repel manatees with them.

Between that first book and that epic motorcycle poetry tape, I made several new friends. Most of them remain people I have never met, but now write back and forth to. There is one boy, a BMW rider up in Virginia, he wrote me to ask about doing a review of the tape in some magazine.

We exchanged several letters, and he wound up turning me on to Whitehorse Press up in New Hampshire. And they wound up selling a whole bunch of books and tapes both for me. And me and them folks up there at Whitehorse have maintained a pretty neat epistolary relationship. Boy up there rides a Kawasaki.

And there is an old one-eyed trike rider from Boston who writes back and forth to me. He just sent me several omega stickers. And there is a woman up in Pennsylvania someplace who sends me an occasional letter or card. She and her old man have gotten into my stuff about as right and thorough as a writer or a rider either one could ask for. Thanks, you all.

23 - LESSONS ALONG THE WAY, ODD JOBS, AND DIRECTIONS

Once upon a time, before I had learned better, I loaned a guy I knew the money to buy a bike. It would be wrong to speak ill of the dead, and I finally got my money back anyway. Boy killed himself on that very same scooter ten or so years after I had helped him buy it. Actually he just busted himself up real bad. The doctors finished him off later on at the hospital.

But he sure put some miles on that machine before he went down. I remember going out to get the bike with him, rode him out there behind me I think. There was another guy with us. Anyway, a price was come to, hands were shaken, papers were signed and notarized, titles and money were exchanged. I figured our next step would be to ride to the nearby Secretary of State office to get him a registration and a license plate. Au contraire.

The guy got into a little package he had carried with him. Office supplies. He got a blank sticky label out and cut it to the size of the sticker in the corner of the plate that indicated the expiration date. Then he got out several magic markers and matched colors, and made himself a lawful looking license plate. Looked as official and legal as anything the state ever issued. I was told that when he went off The Highside with that scooter many years and several states of residence later, he still hadn't bought a license plate. I often wondered why he didn't hand-do counterfeit money.

I recall he damn near wrecked that bike the afternoon he got it. The three of us took off someplace. I remember there was a hard curve to the left, followed by a long curve to the right. It was tempting. So we hit it pretty hard. Me and the other guy who had gone with us to buy the bike went hard left and then easy to the right, with a straightaway in between. The guy who had just bought the bike apparently determined the shortest distance was the most direct line. That route cut through someone's yard. He scattered chickens for a quarter mile.

In the previous chapter, I mentioned taking time along the way.

Boy I rode with thirty years ago taught me some of that. He was an artist. Still is for that matter. When the officers in charge of us in the army found out he was an craftsman, they made him paint a mural on one wall of the mess hall. Told him to do a battle scene with helicopters coming into a hot LZ and so forth.

He did the best caricature of such a scene you can imagine. He even had evil, sinister looking VC hiding in marijuana thickets and little balloons with machine gun noises written in them. It was a magnificent anti-war cartoon. And the damn officers not only didn't get it, but they loved it. Thereby proving what my Grandfather, the veteran, had told me about the army—The Inept Leading The Unwilling To Do The Unnecessary.

Anyway, when this old friend of mine was out on the road, he would pull over and shut it down and then wander off into a field to look at a dew covered cobweb that had somehow gotten his attention. Or he would turn it around and ride back a half mile to see what the shadows on the road looked like coming from the other direction. Or he might get intrigued by an old barn or a bridge, and stop long enough to make a sketch of it. He met a lot of neat people this way, too. Colorful characters and unusual individuals all of them.

One time, on the north shore of Prince Edward Island up near Tignish, we stopped for a couple hours so he could rearrange a huge pile of old abandoned lobster traps and then take a picture of it. Turned out to be a hell of a picture. But this was the same boy who somehow managed to get up on the stage with Big Brother and the Holding Company and Janis Joplin at a festival near Atlanta. He got some fine pictures that time. And he got some good ones at Woodstock, too. And he became quite adept at landing safely when he got thrown off the stage.

He went to Europe after we got discharged, and he bought himself a Triumph over there in England. And then he had toured the Continent with it awhile. You used to could do that, and then bring the bike back to the U.S. as a used machine, and pay far less tax than on a new one. Anyway, he somehow ran into one of the main Triumph engineers who had designed this model, I think it was a 650 Tiger, while he was riding through France.

The man told him everything that was going to go wrong with the bike, and when. Most of it was electrical. That was the first time I ever heard that joke about how the English drink warm beer because of Lucas refrigerators. The engineer gave him some parts for when he was going to need them. Hell of a bike. Hell of a man, too. Like I said, he taught me a lot.

One time, I put what this man had taught me to practical use, and made a U-turn and went back to examine more closely and determine precisely what had I seen. It was a guy with a horse and wagon coming in off the mud flats in the Bay of Fundy at low tide. The wagon was loaded with live, flopping fish the man had picked up from the ground when the tide was out. The wagon had real wide truck tires, and the horse had especially big feet.

Another time I went by what appeared to be two guys fishing a big ditch with a chain and a hook and a winch on their pickup truck. It was a huge ditch, and there was a small lake situated at the far end of it. There was enough water to fish, but it sure didn't look likely. So I swung back around to see what was going on and to check out the catch of the day. Turned out to be a dead cow stuck in the drainage culvert.

Sometimes, when your curiosity overwhelms you, or when you follow the teachings of an old friend, you can get in trouble, get drafted into helping out on the project. I wound up participating in a goat roping event one time because I hung around to see what had I seen. This was years ago, on a two-lane someplace up by where the Hatfields and McCoys had at it, up around the Tug Fork someplace. I came around a curve harder than I should have, and rode a hard slalom around a whole bunch of goats, a pickup truck with a stock trailer, and two young guys with lariats. I was gearing down and braking the whole while.

There was another truck across the road and two more guys and another group of goats down the road a couple hundred yards. Turns out they were kin to the first two boys, uncle and daddy I think. They waved me over to them. So I rode slowly on up to them once I got control of the bike again. I got off my cycle and introduced myself. These old boys, Emmett Earl and Orville Otis, had somehow gotten the scattered herd of goats into an area where the road was fenced on both sides. Now it was up to them young boys to capture the damn things.

Actually, I didn't rope any goats myself. I wound up herding and blocking for the ropers, Monty Merle and Joshua Joe, with my motorcycle. A time or two I acted as the Judas Goat. Mostly I sat back with old Emmett and Orville, drinking what they referred to as One W. Harper until I damn near couldn't get back on my bike when we had gotten all the goats on the trailer.

This was when I discovered that the goats didn't even belong to this family. They were owned by a distant kinswoman named Miss Maudie Mahalia, apparently an elderly widow woman. And these boys were re-capturing them as an act of kindness and moral obligation. They invited me back to the house for supper once they had all the goats on the trailer. But, as they lived several miles off the highway on a dirt road, all of it uphill, and it was already getting on toward dark, I thanked them and passed on the meal.

One other time, when I had been pressed into emergency service waiting and bussing tables at a little place in Utah, I accepted the meal. Turned out the real pregnant waitress, Laura Lee Linda Lou, had decided to have her baby that morning, shortly after her husband had dropped her off at work. And the guy who cleaned off the tables and washed dishes had to take her. Seems like the hospital was in the next county. So the owner and cook, Velda Jean Viola Joyce, kind of ensnared me in an apron and put me to work when I walked in. I worked about three hours before backup arrived. Made around seven dollars in tips and got a real fine pancake and link sausage breakfast.

Over the years and along the way, I have stopped to help many broke down bikers, and an occasional stranded motorist, and a few long haul freight drivers in trouble. But these have always been pretty much voluntary activities.

The time I was conscripted into service at the gas station-garage was anything but. This was a while ago, probably thirty years. This was before over-priced self-service gas, back when you could get your windshield wiped off clean and your oil checked and a tire changed at the same place where you bought your gasoline. Back when the people who ran the places where you got gas were mechanics instead of turban-clad greed mongers. It was up North, over on the east coast someplace, and the people who owned the place were real Italian.

Don Carmen, the patriarch, was the only one there in the real early morning when I pulled in for gas. Ocean fog still hung on the coast. When I ran over the hose by the pumps, a bell rang. Then I heard a voice holler at me to go ahead and please pump my own gas. When I looked around, I saw feet poking out from under a car in the service bay. So I pumped my own gas. Then I walked into the garage and squatted down to tell the man I owed him three and a quarter. I held a five dollar bill in my hand.

He peered at me from the gloom under the car. I could see he was at a crucial stage in putting a transmission back together. I could also see his silver hair and moustache and a classic Roman nose in the glow of the dropcord light. He asked my name and told me his. There was a medium thick accent to his English. Next thing he asked was what kind of bike I was riding, and I told him. Then he said for me to go to the cash register and put three dollars and a quarter in it, make change for myself. He muttered something, most of it in Italian, about his three sons, Vincenzo, Angelo, and Rocco, all being late for work. He asked me to hand him a wrench. And then he went back to work, grumbling, again in Italian, about someone named Anna Maria.

While I was making change for myself, the bell rang indicating a gasoline customer was at the pumps. Don Carmen again hollered at me from his place beneath the car. This time to ask me was I in a big hurry. And I told him no, said I was just passin' through. He asked me to please go pump gas for him. So I did, and when I came back in, waving a twenty, Don Carmen yelled for me to get back into the cash register, ring up the sale and make change and so forth. Next chance I had, I moved my scooter away from the pumps and into the shade by the building. By the time I had pumped gas for about a dozen or so of his customers, he was done with the transmission and moved that car out and another one in. When he came out from under the car and into the light of day, I saw that he was much smaller and older than I had figured. He was a very regal, distinguished looking gentleman, even with filthy hands and grease-stained overalls.

I waited on another couple gas customers, wiped off some windshields, checked some oil while Don Carmen tried to get some bookwork done. He said he knew several bills had to be paid that day, and his sister Anna Maria, the bookkeeper, was also late to work. It was about then that Rocco showed up. Rocco was forty, a carbon copy of his father, only with black hair and moustache. Don Carmen screamed at him in Italian and beat him kind of gently about the head and shoulders briefly, hugged him at length, and then told him to get his ass out there pumping gas and wiping windows.

Somehow Don Carmen also persuaded me to change the oil on the car he had just brought into the service bay. It was Japanese, the first car of Oriental origin I had ever put a wrench on, and I had to ask about a few things. Don Carmen answered me in impatient Italian, then corrected himself and began again, "Tiger, you dumb bastard."

He continued to thrash around on Anna Maria's desk looking for the delinquent bills. Before this morning was done, I had changed the oil on two cars, replaced one headlight, made a pot of coffee, sold two of those pine tree air fresheners, and pumped some more gas while Rocco took an authorized personal comfort break. And I also managed to find Don Carmen's reading glasses and one of the overdue bills he was looking for.

Around eleven-thirty, just as the morning rush of business slowed down, Aunt Anna Maria arrived with Vincenzo and Angelo. It was obvious they were the sons of Don Carmen, the older brothers of Rocco. Aunt Anna Maria was obviously kin, too. Her moustache was a little thinner, but she had that same pretty black hair and the Roman nose.

Before Don Carmen could beat on these boys for their tardiness, Aunt Anna Maria spoke up in their defense. She said it was her fault. Her car wouldn't start, and she had called the boys to come to her rescue. So Don Carmen yelled at them in Italian and smacked them both around a little for not calling him to tell him they would be late.

He pointed to me as a paragon of virtue. This was where he swapped over to English words like Hillbilly Biker Nomad and Just Passin' Through. Yelled at his sons that I had worked twice as hard as either of them, maybe the two of them combined. Then he hugged and kissed them both and sent Angelo out to a nearby deli to get lunch. I headed to the bathroom to wash up.

It was about then that a young black guy, Jim, showed up and began sweeping up the office. Don Carmen rushed over and shouted at the man and beat on him a little bit for being late. When he was done, he hugged the guy and kissed him on both cheeks. I don't think this boy was a relative, but Don Carmen was an equal opportunity boss. He hollered at this man in Italian, too.

The sandwiches were delicious, several kinds of salami and cheeses, a salad, and little pastries for dessert. Real good espresso coffee afterward. Don Carmen put Anna Maria to work looking for the outstanding bills, Angelo was ordered under the car in the garage, and Rocco was positioned under the hood. Vincenzo pumped gas. Jim mopped out the bathroom.

And Don Carmen and I relaxed over a fine meal and a bottle of excellent homemade Chianti wine. He told me some stories about the Old Country. I told him some about the passin' through. When our lunch was finished, he offered me a good cigar, looked hard at his watch a minute, and then handed me three ten-dollar bills.

I'd been there, working pretty steady, for about four and a half hours. Damn good pick-up wages for the time. I took two of the bills but handed one back to him. Told him he had bought lunch. He laughed and accepted the ten back but insisted I take a five instead.

I put the cigar in my pocket, shook his hand, said my thank yous, and started off on my way. Don Carmen grabbed me, squeezed me harder than a small old man should have been able to, kissed me on both cheeks, told me I was always welcome at his business or at his home, and thanked me for my help. I paused at the doorway and turned and asked Don Carmen for some words of advice. Told him it had been good work and better wages, tasty food and excellent wine and a fine cigar. And a little Italian wisdom would be the perfect end to this episode.

He looked pensive, cocked his head to the side briefly. Then he removed the cigar from his mouth and said to me, "You come into this world alone, and later on you leave this world alone. And in between, your family don't show up to work on time."

I, on the other hand, always show up to work on time. That time me and Captain Zero put together The Perfect Ride up out of New Orleans, we had gotten to work on time for the previous several days. Zero knows a lawyer, The Duke, who ran summertime scams to supplement his excessive attorney income. He would find out where certain national conventions were going to be, and then he would provide an expensive babysitting/sightseeing/chaperone service for the children of the conventioneers.

Local attractions, zoos, parks, and like that would be visited. Meals would be eaten, theme parks attended, games and parties arranged, massive picnics put together, restaurants invaded and laid waste to, and fun had. The Duke would put together the whole deal. Then he would hire guys like me and Zero to fix things when the master plan went all to hell, and to do the grunt work. It was usually a three or four or five day job. Twenty hour days. But the pay was generous, and we got room and board and parking. And I got to see some things and places I doubt

I would have otherwise.

These deals sometimes involved a thousand children, about five to eighteen years old. The logistics were complex and monumental. Busses would have to shuffle the kids from the hotels to the theme attraction to the zoo to the park to the movie, catering services would have to arrive on location on time, bathrooms had to be located, kids would get sick or hurt or forget their medicine and have to be taken to a parent or a hospital, souvenirs were gleaned, children had to be frequently counted, schedules had to be adjusted and readjusted.

I recall one time in Orlando, it was magic. I am pretty sure they passed a local statute after one of these kid conventions, the Duke The Lawyer Ordinance. Henceforth it became illegal in Orlando to feed nine hundred children lunch from styrofoam containers at curbside, downwind of diesel buses, in temperatures over ninety. Jesus wept.

That time in Orlando, there was a whole group of kids from way up north, Minnesota and Canada. The convention had cleverly been planned for July. And it was between ninety-five and a hundred all five days of the convention. Poor damn northern kids had never seen such a thing. And I have never seen that many pale, blonde, heat stunned, sunburned young people in one place. And I also have no idea how the guys in the mouse suits and whale costumes and such manage in the heat.

The Duke used to start the festivities by marching me up on a stage in front of the several hundred children involved. Then he would point to me and say to them in a loud voice that if they missed a bus, or tarried too long at an attraction, or got lost, or screwed up in any way, "This man will come looking for you. And he will find you." Scared the crap out of the kids. But I never lost one.

Most evenings, after the kids had been returned to the care of their parents, we would have a personnel meeting. Some of those staff gatherings got near as funny as some faculty meetings I been to. One time, one of them got pretty ugly. I thought for a minute The Duke was going to have a rebellion or a strike or a riot or something on his hands. But he cleverly, using convoluted logic, mercurial lawyerly rhetoric, and smoke and mirrors, converted his entire staff from being angry at him to turning our fury against the convention's board of directors. And then The Duke joined us in our outrage.

This time in New Orleans, I rolled on into the giant parking structure that was attached to the giant hotel where we were headquartered, and quickly made friends with the parking garage attendants. The Duke, he said he would pay for my parking while I was working for him. And the guys working the parking lot let me put my scooter where someone was always watching it. Good thing, too, because I was so damn busy that I didn't hardly even see my bike for the next four days.

That lawyer found out two quick things about me. First day, the supply delivery system broke down, and we were out of ice at a crucial time, mid-day in New Orleans in August when The Duke was trying to get away with Kool Aid instead of soda pop. And I ran back into the kitchen at the hotel and talked to the Rastafarian staff a minute. Came back with a hundred pounds of ice. That impressed my employer. Not only the foraging part, but the dealing with scary looking, funny talking minority people, too.

Later on, The Duke and I were driving a load of picnic food to a distant location, and I got briefly lost out there on the streets of New Orleans in the rental car. I looked around and up and told The Duke I figured we were going north, and we needed to get turned around and head back toward The River. This knowledge of geography and solar navigation impressed him more than the Rastas wishing me peace and respect as I left with their ice. Up to then, I ain't sure The Duke knew there was a river in New Orleans. I became his personal driver.

In Jackson Park one day, one of the convention kids made an observation. He was a really sharp little boy, about ten. And he had me and Zero's number the minute he saw us. So we made him our assistant.

This day the kid stopped us at a park bench where a particularly rough and raggedy looking wino had nodded off into blissful slumber. Then the little boy looked at the both of us hard and said, as he pointed to the sleeping wino, "You see that? You two guys are just one short step away." He held his thumb and forefinger a hair's breadth apart to make his point as he smiled up at us.

I recall one other time I got me an assistant. This was a different one of them conventions. And one of the kids got caught shoplifting at a theme park. It took me a very short time to convince the Nazi security squad holding the lad that if they would just give him to me, it would be far worse than any punishment they could devise, arrange, or make up. He was my assistant for the next three days.

I taught that boy in the same manner my Grandfather, the

criminologist, taught me, that you ought not ever steal anything you can't eat or drive.

This time in New Orleans, we took the children off to Lake Ponchartrain Amusement Park one night. Keeping track of several hundred kids in such a place is a lot like herding cats. And it happened to be the same night that a group of retarded children had been taken there on an outing. And, as luck always has it, some of them found me. Their leader and spokesman, he approached me and politely asked if I had seen Booger Red. The chorus chimed in behind him, did I know where Booger Red was. They all said please and thank you. I sent them down to the other end of the park where I figured Captain Zero to be. I knew they would find him, too.

In New Orleans this time, we took the kids to some restaurant on the last night there. I don't recall which one it was, but it was set up for such things. They even cleared out the chairs and tables so the kids could have a dance after supper. After four days of riding herd on this group of juvenile mankind, I was knee-walking tired. And I had copped my usual lean into a dark corner, about half asleep really, watching the young people cavort and the waitresses work at a high trot.

One of the several hard hustling waitresses, Michelle Monique Marcella Mavis, paused to look me over as she one-armed a tray of food past. She smiled and told me I looked bad wasted. I nodded toward the mob of frolicking dancing children. She asked if I was one of the chaperones, and I told her for the last four days. She took great pity on me, called me You Poor Man, and pushed me into the kitchen and put enough cocaine up my nose for me to join the children in their dancing.

The Duke always fed us pretty good, paid us off in cash money, and took his staff out to breakfast the morning after the work was over. This time in New Orleans we got taken to Brennan's for one of the finest meals I can remember eating. It was the perfect beginning to The Perfect Ride, upon which the Captain discovered The Natchez Trace. Always good when you can leave town in the company of a good friend, with a fine meal behind you, and cash money in your pocket.

You ever notice how much different men and women give you directions? I've made a study of this. Over the years I have spent a whole lot of time at phonebooths out on the highway in foreign places trying to get instructions to a friend's place. Sometimes I am trying to write the directions on a matchbook with a crayon in a rainstorm. And I have spent lots more time between the phonebooth and the destination confused, disoriented, lost and trying to figure it out.

Women will tell you—Turn left, toward the Mega Publix Kroger Kash n' Cub Save Food store, and then keep going until you see the Mart-Mart store on the right, and then go past that a little until you get to the King Wendy McBurger and the Family Clinic, and then turn right between them, there is a light there, and go until you get to a plaza mall with two pet stores and a Dollar General and a travel agency, turn kind of left just before you get to that, the store there has the cheapest milk in town, and then go four or five blocks, well maybe it's more like ten, until you get to the second light where the Hess Station is, and go left there, and we are the third house on the right not counting the one on the corner, the one with the flowers.

And guys will tell you - go west a couple miles until you get to highway 44, turn south and go five and a half miles to highway 31 which is also called Johnson Bridge, turn west again there and go nine or so miles to highway 614, turn south, go six blocks and turn east on Stone, ours is the green house with the black Chevy pickup and the Springer Spaniel.

The best way to get directions to where you need to get to is to find you a local mailman. Over the years I have been saved by as many route delivery guys as savior waitresses. Usually they will tell you the best way to get to where you want to go. Only time that didn't work out easy was in Alameda, California one time when the mailman was Chinese and hardly spoke English. But we smiled and nodded at one another a lot, and I got a pretty accutate and detailed map with some lovely pictographs on it.

24 - DREAMS, SCHEMES, HOPES, FANCY FANTASIES, AND ENDINGS

This might just somehow indicate that I am getting better at endings. Just about five months from the day of The Killer Federal Foliage Incident, the feds offered to pay for the damages to my ride. They referred to it as a tree "striking" the front end of my scooter. No, they ain't going to pay for the woman's plane ticket back north or any of that. But, if I sign a release promising to never remember, think about, or ever again refer to the incident, they said they'd pay for my parts and repairs. And now I don't know which is the bigger wonder— that I lived through the tree dropping on me or that the feds are going to partially pay off with almost reasonable speed.

But besides that, I been going back over this, proofreading and fixing, and fine tuning and like that. Trying to make sure I didn't repeat my senile self, either in here or from the prior book. Reviewing slowly at some length. Got to wondering if, by some goofy quirk of fate, some of the folks I mentioned from back down along the way might read this and recognize themselves. And how neat that would be.

Wouldn't it be wonderful if that nice lady who used to run the Tupelo Visitors Center on The Natchez Trace is still around to see this, and does. I expect old Don Carmen has gone off to an Italian final reward by now. But them boys of his might still be around to read that little tribute to their daddy. And it would be good if some of the folks between the coasts saw this and laughed as they remembered me passin' through there looking for 20W50 oil. Or old Arky.

I would like to hope that the pregnant waitress I filled in for out there in Utah named her baby after me, Tiffany Teresa Tammy Tiger. But I would settle for her just seeing this. And it is my fervent desire for some of them women along the way to read about themselves here. I wish for young Martha to have got gone from the Northern convenience store. And I hope she finally got to see warm sandy beaches with palm trees, and get sunburned.

And I am confident that pretty Amanda the waitress, the one who knew all about me, escaped from that little town on the far side of The Big River. Wouldn't it be fine if both them girls read this and recollected me passin' through there. It would be even better if they somehow remembered me fondly. I don't know what I hope for about that pretty girl in the sporty car down by The River in Louisiana. But I doubt she remembers me at all.

Long as I'm doing all this hoping and wishing, I might just as well hope that I wake up tomorrow morning young and pretty, with the lottery numbers. And a beautiful companion. And breakfast. I doubt any of that will come to pass, but maybe some more pretty women will bring me Oreo cookies.

I knew another woman once, she lived out there in them short hills beyond that second river. She always called me Cowboy. Girl agreed that I wasn't much to look at, but she said my company she always did enjoy. Hope she gets to read this, too.

It would make me feel real good to know that Beau Davis and Joel Lee Sherman got to read about their help and Southern hospitality, and that some of the bikers and others along the way find out how much I appreciated their help. Karl The Kraut Mechanic will surely see this book. I expect it will get passed around and critiqued there at Karl The Kraut's After Hours Scootershop and Social Club. But wouldn't it be a wonderful thing if the children or maybe the grandchildren of Charlie Syms and Coach Robinson and Doc Baum got to read about their forebears.

I sure hope that pretty woman in the Smokey the Bear hat at the Booker T. Washington National Memorial is married and breeding beautiful girlchildren for the next generation of longriders to appreciate. And I hope that boy who took them pretty post card pictures finds out that I have fond memories of the time I spent with him. It would be a shame if the hospitality industry didn't pass this around, at least among some of their alien contingent.

Be pretty funny if some of the Asian tourists who took my picture thinking they were photographing Willie Nelson saw this. Or if the Cuban kids who didn't kill me that night in Miami read it. Or the crew of the *Christian Raddich*.

I would very much like to think that somehow at least some of the various law enforcement personnel mentioned get to read about themselves. I especially hope that about some of the good ones like Ranger Cody and that Alabama trooper who mistook me for someone else.

And it would make my day if someone in the p.r. division of BMW finally caught on and furnished me some support and backing. But I suspect the Oreo cookie people will provide me sponsorship and assistance first.

It would be a cryin' damn shame if them polite children at Lake Ponchartrain didn't find Booger Red and learn that I recall them fondly. And it would be good for some of the folks in Dwyer and Torrington to discover that I made it through that windstorm. I think it would be a real kick to find out that some of the kind waitresses along the way read this and wondered.

And it would be nice to know that some of them teenage Ninja bikers read this, and that they are packing their loads low and horizontal like I showed them. Be even better to discover that old Zack is still around and somehow found mention of himself in here. And I sure hope the sound system guys in Nashville and some of the former nursing students in Michigan get to read this. Them girls would be real surprised to find out I'm still around. Hell, them boys might be, too.

And wouldn't it be cool if Willie Nelson and Sam Elliott got hold of a copy of this. Be pretty neat if someone read that part about the perfect job and hired me to do it. Or if I got made the posterboy/spokesmodel for the Waffle House. Or the poet laureate for the Interstate Highway System. Or the clown prince.

I am positive that those cheerful folks up in Opelika remember me. If I recall that one right, that was a regional convention they were attending. So I suspect jocular rumors of me were spread from Savannah to Little Rock. Be nice if some of them got to read this. And there are a couple grown men who were my assistant children at those Duke Conventions years back. Be a hell of a thing if they both read this. One could be assured that neither Zero nor I have taken that one short step. The other could review some of The Wisdom of my Grandfather.

There was a woman one time out some south of San Antonio. She said to me that I ride like hell through the wind and the rain. And only the highway below me knows my name. I would like to hope she sees this and finds out she was right.

And there was another girl, this one was in Wyoming. She called me a loner savant. And she claimed the mountains inquired about me in the solitude of winter. She told me they asked where it was I've been. She said the rivers asked after me when they iced over. Contended they wanted to know was I coming back again. Be good if she read this and found some answers in it.

Both these girls understood why I ride alone. And they both of them allowed as how The Redoubt might be where I come back to park my ride, but the highway is my home.

I doubt that any Mennonites will read this, so the guy who handed me his tiny infant won't know he's well remembered. But maybe some of them boys working on the logging crew there in the Southern forest will find out about this and know how grateful I am to them. Or maybe Aunt Evangelia will find out about this book and tell her family. And I have a dream that some of the women I have made mention of will maybe gather their children around them and read them a chapter or two.

If things work out beyond everyone's wildest fantasy, and this somehow becomes a widely read best-seller, someone is going to read it and tattle on me. And then there is somebody in Poison Springs going to want me to replace a few yard gnomes. And if the people at the gas station who sold me the diesel fuel read this, I hope they step forward and confess. I don't know if they have many book stores in Hell, but I hope Satan somehow finds out I wrote of him with respect.

I hope the motorcycle festival goers and rally attendees and folks who trailer their bikes, and the retired elderly, and some others, took no offense. Never really meant to piss nobody off. Well, maybe the P.C. people. But, it is similarly my hope that several individuals and groups do take some offense and that they mend their evil ways. Nothing wrong with constructive criticism. Same deal with the reviewers and literary critics. How often do such folks get to read a review of their review. Some of them taught me some things. And I'm damn grateful. I'm obliged to all the women who taught me so much along the way, too.

Speaking of that, I recall one last woman here. She was from someplace in northern California, up along the coast somewhere. And she told me I was an old soldier of misfortune. Said I had ridden too long alone in the Broken Promise Land. Told me I had seen too much for one man to look at. Hope she reads this and understands that she was about half right.

It is my fondest fantasy that somehow a copy of this winds up in the hands of someone someplace, who gets to wondering, and then takes it down to the local cafe and says, "Melba May Mabel Joy, do you recall one summer about twenty-five or thirty years ago...?"

And I am confident the ghostriders and my other ancestors will all know about this book, and the other one, and that epic motorcycle poetry tape, too. For the very last thing my Grandfather, the shaman, taught me was about today being a good day to die. He smiled and said to me, "Hell, Boy, I'm just dyin'. I ain't goin' to quit lovin' you."

Tiger Edmonds does hold a doctorate, though he doesn't tell many people that. He also teaches at St. Leo College in Florida. He has written some pretty fine poetic ballads and has a CD of them done to the accompaniment of a guitar and banjo. His horse's name is Nokomis.